ART WORK

aRt WORK

INVISIBLE LABOUR AND THE LEGACY OF YUGOSLAV SOCIALISM

KATJA PRAZNIK

UNIVERSITY OF TORONTO PRESS
Toronto Buffalo London

© University of Toronto Press 2021
Toronto Buffalo London
utorontopress.com
Printed in the U.S.A.

ISBN 978-1-4875-0841-8 (cloth)
ISBN 978-1-4875-3819-4 (EPUB)
ISBN 978-1-4875-3818-7 (PDF)

Library and Archives Canada Cataloguing in Publication

Title: Art work : invisible labour and the legacy of Yugoslav
socialism / Katja Praznik
Names: Praznik, Katja, 1978– author.
Description: Includes bibliographical references and index.
Identifiers: Canadiana (print) 20210146621 | Canadiana (ebook)
20210146699 | ISBN 9781487508418 (cloth) | ISBN 9781487538187 (PDF) |
ISBN 9781487538194 (EPUB)
Subjects: LCSH: Art, Yugoslav – 20th century. | LCSH: Art –
Economic aspects – Yugoslavia. | LCSH: Unpaid labor – Yugoslavia. |
LCSH: Socialism and art – Yugoslavia. | LCSH: Yugoslavia – Cultural policy.
Classification: LCC N7248.P73 2021 | DDC 709.49709/04 – dc23

Title page and chapter opener ornament from Pixel-Shot/Shutterstock.com.

University of Toronto Press acknowledges the financial assistance to its publishing
program of the Canada Council for the Arts and the Ontario Arts Council,
an agency of the Government of Ontario.

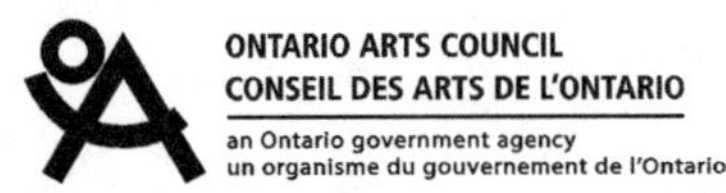

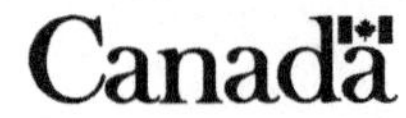

Contents

List of Illustrations   vii

Acknowledgments   ix

Introduction: The Paradoxical Visibility of
Yugoslav Art Workers, or Should Artists Strike?   3

1 The Autonomy of Art and the Emancipation of Artistic Labour   17

2 A Feminist Approach to the Disavowed Economy of Art   35

3 The Making of Yugoslav Art Workers: Artistic Labour and
the Socialist Institution of Art   47

4 The Mystification of Artistic Labour under Socialism   71

5 Art Workers and the Hidden Class Conflict of Late Socialism   101

6 The Contradictions of 1980s Alternative Art   117

Conclusion: Post-Yugoslav Dispossession and the
Contradictions of Artistic Labour after Socialism   141

Notes   151

Bibliography   185

Index   203

Illustrations

0.1   Jaka Babnik, *Pygmalion*, a pile of non-winning lottery tickets,
           exhibition view, Jakopič Gallery, Ljubljana, 2019   4
4.1–4.5   Goran Đorđević, International Strike of Artists, postcard with a
           response to the call for an artists' strike, Belgrade, 1979   80
4.6   Page three of the magazine *Prvi broj* (1980)   95
4.7   "An Indicator of the Relationship between the Income of an
           Independent Visual Artist and Their Actual Personal Income as well
           as the Personal Income of a Worker in the Field of Culture," a chart
           on page six of the magazine *Prvi broj* (1980)   97
5.1   Dušan Mandić, "*Kaj je alternativa?* (What Is the Alternative?)" poster
           for a symposium at Disko FV, Ljubljana, 1983   107

Acknowledgments

For reading and rereading drafts of this book and for their incisive and insightful comments that helped sharpen my argument, I thank Eda Čufer, Carine M. Mardorossian, Luka Arsenjuk, and my anonymous peer reviewers. I am grateful to Goran Đorđević, Dalibor Martinis, Dušan Mandić and Jaka Babnik for granting me the permission to reprint the documents of their work.

Research presented in this book received institutional support by University at Buffalo in different phases: through a research grant from the Baldy Center for Law and Social Policy, and a fellowship from the Humanities Institute. The publication of this book is supported by the College of Arts and Sciences Julian Park Fund.

Equally important was the support of colleagues at University at Buffalo. I am especially thankful to Kevin Leary, Cristanne Miller, and the late Roy Roussel – the champions of University at Buffalo's Arts Management Program, as well as to Amy Graves Monroe, Jasmina Tumbas, Marion Werner, Jaume Franquesa, and Mateo Taussig-Rubbo. Beyond the realm of University at Buffalo I thank Serhan Ada, Tony Busch, and Sabina Potočki.

At University of Toronto Press, Stephen Shapiro has been the most kind and supportive editor with astute and encouraging comments on the manuscript.

For early mentorship and support I am indebted to Rastko Močnik, Lev Kreft, Mitja Velikonja, and Vesna Čopič.

I thank my mother Mara Praznik for her continuing patience and support despite the ocean between us. Finally, I dedicate this book to my father Avgust Praznik, who demystified unpaid labour in the arts and academia through his persistent threats of buying me a beggar's hat. His life was in my view an exemplification of Yugoslavia's promise to working-class people and continues to inspire me even though he is no longer with us.

Earlier versions of this work previously appeared as "Artists as Workers," *Social Text* 38, no. 144 (2020): 83–115; "Autonomy or Disavowal of Socioeconomic Context," *Historical Materialism* 26, no. 1 (2018): 103–35; and "Ideological

Subversion vs. Cultural Policy of Late Socialism: The Case of the Scipion Nasice Sisters Theatre (SNST) in *NSK from* Kapital *to Capital: Neue Slowenische Kunst – an Event of the Final Decade of Yugoslavia*, Badovinac et al. (eds.), Ljubljana/Cambridge: Moderna Galerija/MIT Press, 2015.

All translations from Slovenian, Serbo-Croatian-Bosnian, and Macedonian sources are my own unless otherwise noted.

ART WORK

The Paradoxical Visibility of Yugoslav Art Workers, or Should Artists Strike?

In the spring of 2019 a photographer invited me to write an essay for an edited volume accompanying his exhibition in Ljubljana, Slovenia. The exhibition had been commissioned by a public art institution and was thematically focused on a social critique of various objects to which people ascribe magical or symbolic functions. I began my research by interviewing the author about his working conditions. At the time of our conversation he had been working on the exhibition for at least six months and the opening was still four months away. As I learned the unsurprising facts, a sense of indignation ensued. While the author was payed an honorarium the sum was pitiful – three hundred euros. This figure felt even more egregious when I asked the gallery director what the overall budget for the exhibition was. It was 30,000 euros. The gallery prides itself on offering good working conditions for artists, explained the director, especially because the budget covered the material or production cost, in this case the cost of large still-life photographs. While I curbed my impatience and did not ask what exactly they would hang on the walls of the gallery otherwise, I spared no ink when it came to emphasizing that the actual labour of the artist involved in the exhibition was (de)valued at 1 per cent of the entire exhibition budget.[1] As the gallery director, a public servant to boot, took great offence, she rushed to console the freelance artist with the familiar adage: you are not doing it for the money. Scholars have defined this particular form of exploitation by relating cultural work to the idea of sacrifice, emphasizing that artists are trained in "sacrificial labor," whereby the enjoyment involved in this type of work and the potential for future reward justify a discount in earnings.[2] Here, one should recall Marx's sardonic remark: "Nobody – not even the practitioner of *Zukunftsmusik* – can live on the products of the future […]; just as on the first day of his appearance on the world's stage, man must still consume every day before and after he produces."[3]

The protagonists of this book are art workers. The term may appear as an oxymoron because art in the West is predominantly considered as non-work. Unless discussed in the context of arts and crafts, most Western traditions undermine the

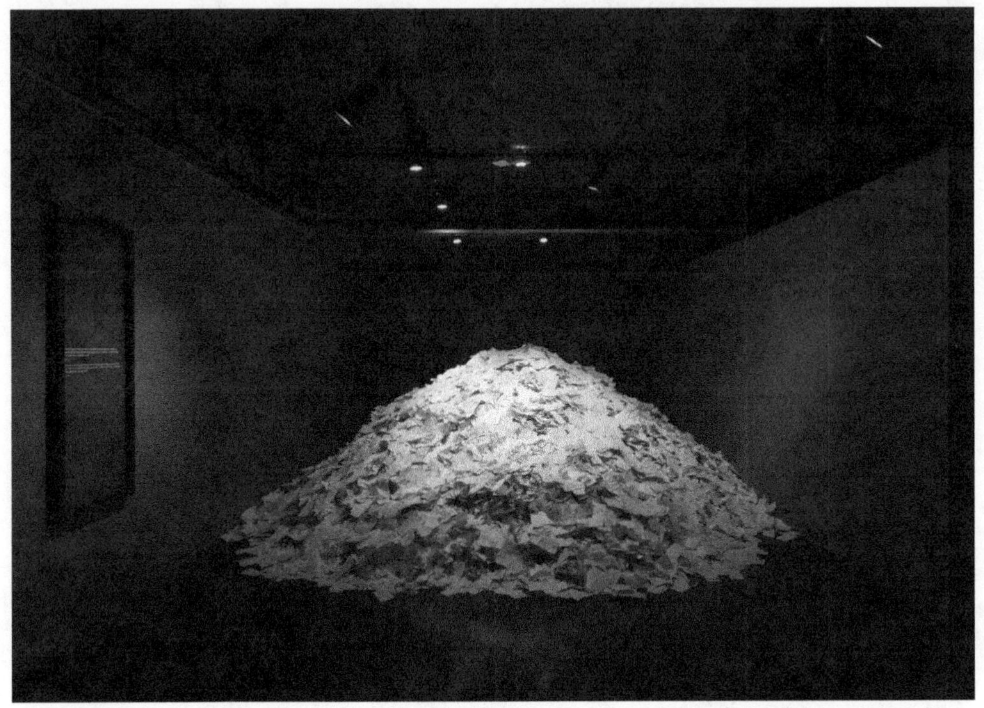

0.1. Jaka Babnik, *Pygmalion*, a pile of non-winning lottery tickets, exhibition view, Jakopič Gallery, Ljubljana, 2019. Photo by Jaka Babnik. Courtesy of Jaka Babnik.

labour in the name of a creativity they divorce from the actual painstaking work involved in creating art. The labour of art is neither seen nor defined as work let alone appropriately remunerated. I term this condition the paradox of art.

Commonly perceived as an ingenious act of creation unaffected by monetary concerns, the invisible labour of artists, this unsightly cog running the wheels of the art world, is one of the most formidable contradictions of Western art. At once idealized as the opposite of work and used as a blueprint for contemporary capitalist work ethics, the lofty status of artists and the rampant economic exploitation of their labour is at the core of the paradox of art. The contradiction powering this enduring paradox lies in the perceived exceptionality and elevated status of artist's labour, and the uncertain, poorly compensated, and socially unprotected working conditions of artists and creative workers. While scholars and international reports candidly ascertain that the largest subsidy to the arts comes in the form of unpaid or underpaid artistic labour,[4] the question remains about what perpetuates the paradoxical status of artistic labour, glorified intellectually yet undervalued economically.

The artifice of this Potemkin village, as this book argues, lies in the historical disavowal of art as a form of labour. Informed by the Marxist-feminist critique of housework as invisible labour, my argument draws on an analogy between domestic work and artistic labour to uncover the mutual mechanisms of normalization and economic disavowal of these types of labour and the structural exploitation inscribed in them. Unlike the ways in which feminized domestic labour tends to be culturally disparaged, artistic labour is perceived as an act of creation and maintains a status of exceptionality; however, the indifference to labour involved in art makes it vulnerable to economic exploitation. The mystification of artistic labour – that is its historical attachment to the idea that artistic practice is not work but creativity emanating from artistic genius – is central to the paradox of art. Since artistic genius is racialized and gendered as a white male, the majority of artists, especially women, people of colour and of non-European descent are situated in a systemic setback of double oppression. In conjunction with the historical origins of art as a realm of freedom and autonomy that emerged in eighteenth-century Europe, the mystification of artistic labour makes it possible to divorce its productive activities from other kinds of labour and enables a particular form of exploitation.

Taking the viewpoints of cultural policy and politics and explicating how they affect the relationship of art with labour, this book illustrates the historicized nature of the contradiction at the heart of art work. This has implications for the contemporary moment since it challenges art's continued obfuscation of labour. In its dismantling of the welfare state mechanism, neoliberal rationality laid bare the problems of the mystification of artistic labour inscribed into the Western conceptualization and institutionalization of art practices. The discrepancy between artistic labour and subsistence, which underpins the current neoliberal instrumentalization of discourses about creativity and autonomy became more pronounced after the fall of socialist political systems.

Dissecting the paradox of art and undoing its false oppositionality, I use the case of socialist Yugoslavia as the stepping stone for my analysis and a test case for my theoretical intervention about art. The experiences of art workers and the history of labour regulation in the arts in socialist Yugoslavia (1945–91) and its aftermath, helps elucidate the contradiction at the heart of artistic production and the origins of the mystification of *art as labour* to showcase the endemic and economically difficult problem of the remuneration of artistic labour. The Yugoslav case can be treated as the proverbial canary in a coal mine because it points to some of the more general insidious processes under way globally – most notably the impact of the rising neoliberal socio-economic and political processes taking place across the globe starting in the late 1970s and still taking place today. The ubiquitous understanding of art as non-work reinforces an amnesia about times and places where art was seen as work in the best sense of the word.

The Yugoslav example affords an excellent case study to uncover the interconnected aesthetic and economic mechanisms at work in understanding the mystification and subsequent exploitation of artistic labour. As this book demonstrates, Yugoslav socialism's recuperation of the Western bourgeois aesthetic and philosophical traditions produced a mystification of art as a realm of freedom. Especially after the 1960s, Yugoslav artists were increasingly seen, and also saw themselves, not as workers but as creators, which enabled their exploitability and precarious working conditions. There were a couple of rare exceptions that I explore in this book. For example, the actions of Goran Đorđević who took issue with misleading conceptions of artistic genius, and initiatives by the working community of artists RZU Podroom (or, *Radna zajednica umjetnika* Podroom) that addressed invisible and unpaid labour of artists. These examples notwithstanding, even socialist Yugoslav culture was at the time not ready to deal with the problem of mystification of artistic labour, which makes the case of Yugoslav art workers an important lesson about the history of art and labour both in a socialist country and in the West. I point out the specificities of the Yugoslav socialist model of culture, but I also show the historical trajectory of how policies toward art and artistic labour changed by the end of the 1980s. That is when neoliberal tendencies prevailed including in a socialist country and in the aftermath of Yugoslavia's breakup.

While the political economy of Yugoslav socialism, also known as Yugoslav selfmanagement, was based on full employment including for artists, protests against the exploitation of artistic labour had grown in intensity by the end of the 1970s. This apparent contradiction, the existence of the exploitation of artistic labour in a country that was governed by progressive socialist labour policies and considered itself as part of the socialist vanguard, is the fulcrum of my analysis. Furthermore, I use the case of socialist Yugoslavia and compare it to the origins of the historical institutionalization of art in the West to reveal the persistence of the mystification of artistic labour and its detrimental consequences in divergent political systems.

The Yugoslav case is therefore a great foil for understanding where and how the paradox of artistic labour happens more generally because it was both an alternative political economy and an extension of the dominant Western model; it ironically showed the prevalence and universal encroachment of the Western model's exploitative ethos and the mechanisms that govern its perennial existence and its flourishing across the world. There is a lesson to be learned by looking at the socialist experience and its cultural politics for the equity of labour standards in the arts today. On the one hand the tension between art as work and art as a creation of artistic genius during the last two decades of Yugoslav socialism pivoted toward a reinforcement of artists' exceptionality rather than toward an emphasis on their rights as workers. On the other hand, it engendered a process of concealment, which made artistic labour increasingly invisible. Understanding the transformation of artistic labour in socialist

Yugoslavia helps elucidate how a severance of artistic labour from workers' rights made artistic labour expedient in the current neoliberal paradigm.

Drawing on the experiences and history of art workers and labour regulation in the socialist Yugoslavia and employing a Marxist-feminist lens, this book suggests that an understanding of artistic labour as work provides a tool for the demystification of artistic labour's exceptionality; in so doing, it offers a strategic point in the struggle for equity in the context of institutionalized art production under contemporary neoliberal capitalism. I offer a historicized labour-focused critique of art and ideologies still operating in the contemporary art world that is shaped by the experience and the legacy of Yugoslav socialism but also makes parallels between the former socialist East and capitalist West, showing similar results.

The bourgeois aesthetic and its philosophical traditions historically instituted a misleading and deceptive representation of artists' labour, which is not only extremely resistant but also central to the existence of unpaid artistic labour. The changes in art and artistic labour that occurred in Yugoslav socialism show this trend quite clearly. While Yugoslav socialism treated art as labour, its challenge to the Western ideas of art, autonomy, and artistic genius turned out to be inadequate. Once the labour polices fell apart due to economic and geopolitical pressures, the older Western concepts of art and autonomy were recuperated and art was turned into invisible labour. The Yugoslav cultural politics of the postwar era allow us to reflect on the inherent conflict between art as labour and art as a commodity precisely because the country embodied a hybrid sociopolitical mode with two seemingly opposing forms coexisting: a socialist self-management and a version of a market economy. Consequently, art that arose in its sociopolitical context represented an idiosyncratic system of cultural production.

Yugoslavia's cultural ideology, which initially followed a Marxist critique of Western bourgeois aesthetics and its ties to the commodity fetishism typical for market capitalism, was combined with a strong antifascist stance. The Yugoslav understanding of art and culture stemmed from these basic oppositions within which art and culture had a prominent role in building socialism and were not limited to a privileged position only available to a particular social stratum. They were considered a social right that needed to be accessible to the widest segment of the population. Socialist cultural policies supported cultural production not only by professional artists but also by people in general – hence, Yugoslavia's widespread and well-developed amateur artistic and cultural production. As a result of art and culture's roles in building socialism, the Yugoslav government supported professional artists and protected their labour and economic rights.

This was in strong opposition to the capitalist West, where older forms of capitalist economy and its newer, twentieth-century iterations in the form of neoliberalism, had created a consistent mode of perception of artistic labour as severed from the realm of subsistence. Historically speaking, once artistic labour was separated from everyday life in the late eighteenth century, its disconnection directly contributed to the exploitation of artistic labour. The Yugoslav counterproposal to this was embodied in the idea of an art worker that not only implied a link between art and work but also a possibility of subsistence while doing artistic work.

The term "art worker," or "cultural worker" (*kulturni delavec/radnik*), was a prominent feature of postwar socialist discourse, pertaining to individuals working in the field of culture. The notion's legacy, as intended by Yugoslav art workers, is deeply connected to socialist ideas, the labour movement, and the ethos of the historical avant-garde movements, especially those that appeared in the 1920s in Russia.[5] Its background also relates to Marx's ideas about work as a defining element of human life and as a conscious, free, and creative activity, that is, to the idea that all human labour possesses creative character.[6] Furthermore, the idea of an art worker stems from a typical socialist understanding of art as an accessible social good, created by artists whose labour is valued on the same level as that of factory workers, for example. The prioritized concept of the "art worker" and "artistic labour" in socialist cultural policies stands in stark contrast to the dominant concept of the "artwork" or "the work of art," which represents a key focus of bourgeois aesthetics, that is, the understanding of art as a product and an objectification of an artistic genius that is affordable only to the privileged classes, although individuals of any class might produce artworks if they are endowed with the exceptional faculty of creativity. How ideas about art workers took hold in Yugoslavia may also be traced back to one of the foremost revolutionary moments, the Paris Commune, which had strong echoes in Yugoslav socialist policies. During the time of the Paris Commune, artists articulated a demand that was consequential for the relations between art and labour: art should cease to be privatized in the hands of the aristocratic wealthy classes.[7] Instead, art needed to become a general social good accessible to everyone. As the global labour movement and socialist revolutions gained momentum in various parts of the world, the term art worker rose to prominence, particularly in the early twentieth century.[8] Regardless of disputes about what it actually implies, the term art worker points to artists' attempts to embrace a labour identity on par with that of factory or other workers.[9] In socialist Yugoslavia, the term art worker or cultural worker denoted a direct connection to the socialist revolution and a relationship between art and work, attesting to the importance of both cultural labour and of working people building socialist prosperity after the Second World War.

Nevertheless, during the 1960s and 1970s, forms of unpaid artistic labour, exploitation, and the precarious socio-economic circumstances of art workers paradoxically re-emerged in the Yugoslav system. The number of freelance self-employed artists was constantly growing. As documented by one researcher, their economic and social conditions were not equal to that of peers that worked in art and cultural institutions. In particular, the issues contributing to their precarious working conditions were related to modest social security, high premiums for retirement funds and very low pensions, difficulties in earning an income and instability of income, unfavourable terms for securing a loan or mortgage, lack of housing and work space, dependence on self-reliance, and unequal status in comparison to cultural workers in art institutions.[10] In socialist Yugoslavia, one of the earliest articulations of the paradox of unpaid labour was epitomized by a question posed by Belgrade-based conceptual artist Raša Todosijević in 1975: "Who makes a profit on art, and who gains from it honestly?"[11] His long satirical answer listed an expansive array of individuals who make up the art world and offer services that are part of producing an artwork. On the long list of contenders, however, we search in vain for an artist.[12] Four years later, in 1979, another Belgrade-based conceptual artist Goran Đorđević posed an even more radical question to both Yugoslav and international artists: "Would you take part in an international strike of artists?"[13] An artists' strike, maintained Đorđević, would be "a protest against [the] art system's unbroken repression of the artist and the alienation from the results of his practice."[14] Two and a half months after the deadline for Đorđević's challenge, forty predominantly noncommittal responses manifested that an artists' strike was a utopian wish. Other now celebrated Yugoslav artists, among them Sanja Iveković, and her colleague artist Dalibor Martinis, amplified these issues in remarking that Yugoslav society considered "artistic labour socially useful," but it "regularly remunerate[d] labour of everyone (curators, translators, reviewer, guards, cleaners etc.) involved in the realization of an exhibition except the artist."[15] To combat these exploitative conditions, Iveković and Martinis drafted an artist contract, but it gained little support and was never commonly used by Yugoslav artists. Moreover, in 1980 the 21st General Conference of UNESCO was held in Belgrade. Among resolutions, the assembly of delegates issued a *Recommendation Concerning the Status of Artists* (the *Recommendation*).[16] They established the "need to improve the social security, labor and tax conditions" of art workers, as well as the right of artists to benefit from "the legal, social and economic advantages pertaining to the status of workers."[17] The *Recommendation* has become a frequent reference for initiatives that strive to improve the remuneration of artists and guarantee social welfare for artistic labour.[18] Additionally, the spirit of the *Recommendation* appeared to correspond to precepts of self-management established in socialist Yugoslavia, self-proclaimed as the country of the working people.

Central to Yugoslavia's political economy was the commitment to workers' welfare grounded in full employment, free education, and healthcare. Artists' protests against the exploitation of their labour, however, tarnished perceptions of Yugoslav self-management's success. The analysis of Yugoslav artistic and cultural production, and its relationship to artists in particular, shows that similar trajectories of exploitation of artistic labour have occurred in Yugoslavia and in the West. The history of Yugoslav socialist culture and related policies serves as a litmus test, then, which reveals that the mystification of artistic labour and its exploitation goes deeper than the differences in the political economy per se; it shows itself both in capitalist and socialist regimes, and turns artistic labour into a convenient avenue for the production of alienation and inequality. The example of Yugoslavia points to an issue with artistic work as a form of labour that is not framed by economic contexts alone but by deeper structural problems in the conception of art itself.

The attitude toward art as labour in combination with progressive labour policies and social protections for artistic labour introduced in the first half of Yugoslavia's existence proved fruitful. However, due to the implementation of market ideologies the Yugoslav political economy reproduced the general contradiction between notions of free emancipated work and the structural effects of commodified, exploited labour. Socialism's mystification of art as a realm of freedom and its attachment to the understanding of creative work as an autonomous practice, made it easier to divorce these productive activities from other kinds of labour. Together with the shifts in economic policies, which introduced market elements in Yugoslav socialism, the mystification of artistic labour turned cultural workers and artists into a sort of experimental vanguard for the neoliberal reforms that began in the 1970s.

While Yugoslavia was committed to the idea of full employment and general welfare for all its citizens, the Cold War geopolitical pressures on the country's self-management and the politics of nonalignment effectively sabotaged the political potentials of labour's emancipation within socialism. This book traces the effect of these important shifts in economic policies that introduced self-management and market elements in Yugoslav political economy during the 1960s and 1970s. Slovenia and Croatia, the two richest and economically most prosperous socialist republics, as well as Macedonia, implemented new specific laws on cultural labour at the end of 1970s and in the early 1980s. While there were no specific laws for artistic or cultural labour in Serbia, Montenegro, and Bosnia and Herzegovina, decrees or contracts existed that protected art workers to a certain extent and included them in the welfare provision. The discrepancies among the republics and ways of artistic labour regulation were due both to the uneven development of the country and to the process of federalization, which allowed each constituent republic to implement its own cultural policy measures. These new policies of the late 1970s and early 1980s restructured the material conditions of art workers from a model based on welfare, social security, and labour rights guaranteed in the early socialist period, to a freelance and self-employed labour model, increasing the number of freelance and self-employed art workers and turning them into self-sufficient socialist entrepreneurs during the 1980s. The shifts and the new laws were the portents of the ensuing neoliberal turn that, in the final decade of Yugoslav socialism, created a large, precarious, and unemployed labour force. The case of artistic labour's transformation in Yugoslavia, where socialism maintained and glorified the unique status of artist, demonstrates that artists were among the first to be turned into self-employed and freelance labourers, with much lower incomes and access to less or no social security.

Concurrent with the demise of labour-centred identity in the arts at the dawn of the post-socialist era during the 1990s, the employment of unpaid or poorly paid creative labour became a prominent trend in the Western neoliberal political economy. In the decades since the above-mentioned 1980 UNESCO *Recommendation* calling for the improvement of artists' socio-economic status, working conditions have not improved for artists or people working in the arts; in fact, they continue to deteriorate.[19] Follow-up reports by UNESCO and other organizations across the world provide evidence that artists' earnings, even in countries once considered welfare states, are insufficient for subsistence.[20] The social security, workers' rights, and legal frameworks regulating artistic labour in various countries are in most cases substandard. They contribute to the precarious social, economic, and legal status of art workers.[21] Furthermore, artists and scholars contend that the artist has become a model worker in the new service economy.[22] For instance, they point out that many companies in a service economy count on what Tiziana Terranova conceptualizes as "free labor" or what Erin Duffy labels "aspirational labor."[23] Artistic labour as a self-fulfilling activity unconcerned with subsistence has greatly affected the process of labour transformation in the past three decades. Andrew Ross sums it up best:

> [T]he traditional profile of the artist as unattached and adaptable to circumstances is surely now coming into its own as the ideal definition of the postindustrial knowledge worker: comfortable in an ever-changing environment that demands creative shifts in communication with different kinds of clients and partners; attitudinally geared toward production that requires long, and often unsocial, hours; and accustomed, in the sundry exercise of their mental labor, to a contingent, rather than a fixed, routine of self-application.[24]

In a word, creativity became a perfect petri dish to grow a culture of unpaid labour to spur staggering economic growth.[25] The gains, however, are neither in favor of artists nor the majority of workers in the new service or creative economy. How expedient is it, then, to understand art as a form of disalienated work that results from the self-fulfilling pursuit of creative individuals? The challenge for the present moment, therefore, is to rethink the separation of art from subsistence, as well as the kind of class politics and inequality it reproduces.

Discussing art as a form of labour and considering the material conditions of artistic labour from an interdisciplinary perspective informed by art history, aesthetics, cultural policy, sociology, labour theory of value, Marxist feminism, and political economy, my study poses a challenge to art historical discussions of labour in the arts. While I discuss issues that are important for art history, I examine them from the viewpoints of cultural policy and politics to explicate how they affect the relationship of art with labour. The ways in which the Western concept of art obscures art as labour has largely remained unchallenged, particularly in the context of art history, despite the increase in literature on precarious labour in the arts and studies of art, autonomy, and labour over the past two decades, predominantly emerging in North American and British academia. Since even critical studies about art, autonomy, and labour commonly consider art as non-labour and take it as a given rather than as an ideological category that needs scrutiny, my aim is to help readers understand how art's institutional history in the West obscures the status of art as labour; how art got institutionalized through this obscuring of the question of labour; and how the mystification of artistic labour is reproduced in various political systems and ideologies.

The point of this book is not to depict the Yugoslav system as a flawed political project, but rather, to reveal its contradictory nature, deeply interconnected with Yugoslavia's geopolitical position but also with the neoliberal economy.[26] While the book discusses the history of Yugoslav socialist culture it uses Yugoslavia as a model to elucidate the contradiction at the heart of artistic production. It is informed by scholarship that unveiled Yugoslavia's complicated position between the Eastern and the Western Blocs and how the country was forced to subvert its political economy, implementing policies that went contrary to its original political intent.[27] The changes in political economy affected the ideas of self-management and emancipation of labour not only due to internal political conflicts but more importantly to external pressures of the increasingly globalized Western capitalist system. During its entire existence, the country played an intricate diplomatic game, in which it had to signal an inclination to join either side of the Cold War divide yet persisted in establishing its own version of socialism based on social ownership, full employment, and generous welfare provision. This tension prevented the government from fully realizing its political objective to establish a transformed society based on labour's emancipation and consequently to change the relationship to artistic labour that had its potential in embracing artists as workers.

Drawing on art history, sociology, political economy, East European studies, and studies of the avant-garde, I break down the history of artistic labour under Yugoslav socialism. Foregrounding the role of art workers in socialist Yugoslavia and the economic and material reforms that affected artists' working conditions, the book bridges the political economy with the study of art during

Yugoslav socialism. My study advances uninvestigated aspects of artistic and cultural work in Yugoslavia, thereby filling a gap in recent scholarship on Yugoslav art, which does not address questions of the material conditions for artistic labour under socialism. Moreover, studies of artistic labour under socialism are rare in the context of East European and Slavic studies, especially in the English language. One rare case is Christina Kiaer's scholarship, which despite its art historical disciplinary affiliation touches on issues of art and labour, due to her focus on the concept of commodity in Russian constructivism and productivism, in which one can find a historically explicit effort to establish a Marxist aesthetics in theory and practice focused on matters of labour and production.[28] While I consider socialist Yugoslavia as a site of shared culture and politics, the limitations of my study and the uneven geographical range of my examples is based on the limited material available to archival research of cultural policy regulation and legislation on art and labour in the countries previously making up Yugoslavia. Moreover, the interventions by artists and groups I discuss are the few rare cases of Yugoslav artists who have addressed the structural contradictions of art as labour, and the implication of Western intellectual traditions about the autonomy of art on artistic labour. While scholars have analysed political aspects of postwar Yugoslav art and discussed these artists and groups in terms of political ideologies, they seldom examined the actual labour regulations that governed the lives of artists. They neither considered the economic and material conditions for artistic labour, nor questioned the Western category of art as it affects the invisibility of artistic labour.[29]

Central to my analysis are therefore not artworks that thematize labour and their political and symbolic implications and meanings, but rather the legislative systems and conceptual attitudes of artists, policy makers, and intellectuals toward art as labour and the category (or institution) of art itself. The analysis proceeds from a Marxist point of view not only to demonstrate the usefulness of a Marxian critique as the quintessential theoretical framework for dealing with the question of labour under capitalism, but also to foreground the discussion on art *as* labour. By interlacing materialist sociology and theory of art the book intervenes into the scholarship on art and labour by questioning the Western category of art and its philosophical underpinnings that establish it as a form of creation rather than work.

This is why an unapologetic analysis of art as a historical social system and the ways in which it reproduces inequality by obscuring labour on the account of autonomy is necessary. More broadly, however, this study's engagement with the legacy of Yugoslav socialism complicates the ostensibly emancipatory understanding of artistic labour, artistic autonomy, and creativity. It expands the discussions of post-Fordist neoliberal rationality and the ways in which it "liberated" the worker. While scholars argue that artists have become the model workers in the era of neoliberal capitalism, I contend that this transformation is internally vested in an unexamined instrumentalization of aesthetic autonomy, which continues to divorce art and/as labour. My aim is not to debase the practice of art, quite the contrary; my goal is to open a new avenue of discussion about artistic labour that stops looking at artistic labour as an exceptional practice because it provides excuses for exploitation. Creative work, I argue, is devalued precisely because of its exceptionality that allows its invisibility as a form of labour.

Chapter 1, "The Autonomy of Art and the Emancipation of Artistic Labour," is a theoretical exposé on the paradox of art embodied in the denial of art as a form of labour. It explains the paradox of art by historicizing it and linking it to the widespread Western understanding of the autonomy of art while it also highlights an important critique of autonomy by the early twentieth-century avant-garde art movements. The chapter provides a critique of the ideal of autonomous art as a symptom of a larger structural and ideological problem related to artistic labour as a form of exploitation that emerged during the ascent of capitalist mode of production. Despite the history of attacks on and examinations of ideological aspects of autonomous art, the problem of exploitation of artistic labour prevails and contributes to rendering artistic labour invisible.

Chapter 2, "A Feminist Approach to the Disavowed Economy of Art" extends the critique of art's autonomy as a gendered notion and theorizes the specific invisibility of artistic labour. Employing a perspective informed by labour theory of value and feminist epistemology the chapter juxtaposes artistic and domestic labour. While I discuss the parallels between domestic and artistic labour's unwaged condition and the ways it contributes to the exploitation, I also examine important distinctions between the two types of labour that help explain the paradoxical nature of artistic labour's invisibility.

After providing theoretical and historical context the following four chapters focus on the case study of socialist Yugoslavia and the country's intervention into the problem of art as labour. They present socialist Yugoslavia as a historical test case to expose the ideological developments surrounding the invisibility of artistic labour and the dissolution of artists as workers.

In chapter 3, "The Making of Yugoslav Art Workers: Artistic Labour and the Socialist Institution of Art," I provide an analysis of the three seminal stages of cultural policy pertaining to artistic labour in socialist Yugoslavia that took place from 1945 to 1991. I discuss the institutional environment for the arts in Yugoslavia and outline policies that regulated artistic labour. During the first two stages, Yugoslav cultural policy originally designed welfare protections for art workers based on workers' rights. However, a tension emerged between Western philosophical traditions and the radical stances by the proponents of the historical avant-garde that demanded a new social role for art in postwar Yugoslavia. This tension turned into a conflict that played itself out during the third stage. The trajectory of the three stages points to a contradiction present within the socialist institution of art where ideas of autonomy coexisted with ideals of art as labour. I argue that the Yugoslav case was historically emblematic because it attempted to build socialist prosperity on an alternative version of socialist self-management, which became the official political system after the split between Yugoslavia and the USSR in 1948. At the heart of self-management was a humanist ideal of labour's emancipation informed by early writings of Marx and the theory of alienation. The central goal of self-management was the emancipation of labour and the worker but these ideas were undermined by Western influences that impacted not only the Yugoslav understanding and institutionalization of art but also the country's political economy.

Chapter 4, "The Mystification of Artistic Labour under Socialism," shows that there was a discrepancy between the labour policies of self-management and the neo-Marxist critically engaged art practices known as the alternative art practices (as they were dubbed by art critics and art historians). I examine Zagorka Golubović's analysis of the social role of art under socialism as well as rare but important critical interventions by artists who addressed the problem of art as invisible labour and its exploitation. The first example is Goran Đorđević's critique of creativity and quasi status of artists as a subject; the second example is a proposal for an artist's contract developed by Dalibor Martinis and Sanja Iveković in the context of Podroom, a working community of artists. The chapter reveals how hegemonic Western philosophical traditions about art and labour were also deeply ingrained in Yugoslav socialist culture, and how they contributed to the undermining of socialist cultural policy concerning artistic labour.

Chapter 5, "Art Workers and the Hidden Class Conflict of Late Socialism," and chapter 6, "The Contradictions of 1980s Alternative Art," focus on the last decade of Yugoslav socialism and explain the complex process that disenfranchised Yugoslav art workers by turning them into socialist art entrepreneurs. I re-examine the political agenda of the alternative cultural and social movements of the 1980s and the problematic ways in which they wanted to reform Yugoslav self-management through a critique of self-management's ideology and repressive state apparatuses. The discussion is centred on artists' attitudes towards the socialist institution of art, their attempts to come up with new production models for art, and on the cultural policy changes in labour regulation of artistic work. I show how the internal dynamic merged with the West's pressures on Yugoslav economy and what the effects on the mandate of the socialist welfare state and on the country's final and violent collapse in 1991 were.

In my conclusion I reflect on the process of dispossession of artists' labour rights and the rise of inequality among art workers after the destruction of socialist Yugoslavia and the neoliberal attack on the welfare state. Neoliberal ideology, which divorced art from labour, used the essentialized notions of creativity to do so, but Western ideals of creativity and autonomy proved to be its valuable assistants. I discuss the return of invisible labour in the post-Yugoslav era and point out the detrimental effects of the removal of state protection for the economic rights of art workers.

Chapter One

The Autonomy of Art and
the Emancipation of Artistic Labour

The pervasive cultural exclusion of labour from our understanding of art can easily be tested by checking any English language dictionary definition of a work of art; the paradox of art I outlined in the introduction is patently reproduced there. Dictionaries tell us that a work of art is an object – a piece of creative work in the arts, something that is made in a skilful way, or a product that gives aesthetic pleasure – but they make no reference to the labour of art, nor to the person undertaking the activity that results in the work of art. The obfuscation of labour occurs at the level of the basic definitions of art that we all take for granted and that hide more than they reveal. There is a glaring absence of a unified or agreed-upon definition of artistic labour. The fields of art history and aesthetics tend to understand such labour as a creative, non-utilitarian human activity, even the opposite of work, that is, as a form of self-fulfilling and expressive labour in and of itself.[1] By contrast, the social sciences define artistic labour as an occupation or a profession for which one may be paid, even though the payment, they sometimes may point out, is miserable.[2] These definitions may integrate and demystify, or isolate and mystify artistic labour from the rest of the society, but they don't discuss artistic labour as a particular form of exploitation. That artistic labour is poorly remunerated is normalized. As cultural-policy scholar Kate Oakley explains, "Talking about artistic production as *work* still produces resistance or discomfort in some quarters."[3]

While acknowledging this definitional ambivalence, I will, however, hereafter limit my discussion of artistic labour to the labour that takes place within the context of institutionalized art in the West even though many artistic practices take place outside of the Western institution of art.[4] Art is an institution because art and artistic labour are not transhistorical universal phenomena. The hegemonic Western idea and practice known as art emerged as a relatively autonomous social sphere in a historically specific process of institutionalization of aesthetic practices in European bourgeois societies in the late eighteenth century.[5] In other words, the formation of aesthetic practices that are grouped together under the term or notion of art, alongside the discourse on beauty, the aesthetic gaze,[6] and the emergence of various art organizations, were concurrent with the rise of bourgeois society and the dominance of the capitalist mode of production. Among others, these practices include the following types of labour: production and subsequent installation, publication, performance, or realization of an artwork; artistic collaboration; research; securing and administrating funding; copyright permissions; legal and tax administration; public presentation and promotion; and many other tasks. These tasks are usually unaccounted for or invisible. Yet, in the institution of art, the "work" of art holds a central position, and autonomy defines its functional mode.

In this chapter, I explore the ways in which the paradox of art (as a labour that is not recognized as such) is linked to and partially reproduced by a particular and widespread understanding of the autonomy of art that stands in opposition to the ideal of artistic labour. Indeed, the institutionalization of art practices in the West is profoundly bound up with ideas of autonomy and the rise of capitalism, which are in turn directly related to the invisible status of artistic labour. My argument is theoretical but also historical. It starts in the eighteenth century when art and aesthetic discourse was established in Western philosophy and then follows the changing ideas of autonomy and avant-garde through the nineteenth century to finally arrive at the twentieth century and the avant-garde challenge to the idea of art and autonomy. I argue that the erasure of work from art, or the institutionalization of art as a form of invisible labour, is the flip side of establishing the autonomy of art as a depoliticized bourgeois category that disavows the economy and neutralizes the class dimension of art production. I do so by invoking the pivotal yet obfuscated dimensions of the early twentieth-century avant-garde art movements' attack on the autonomy of art.

Scholars, critics, and artists discussing art and aesthetics ostensibly agree on the definition of the notion of art's autonomy, yet its meaning is highly ambiguous and even contradictory. The autonomy of art pertains to artists and their independence from political pressures on the one hand, but at the same time, it is also used to refer to the independence of the works of art (from the market, economy, or social utility) on the other. What is more, the autonomy of the artist versus the autonomy of the work of art appear to be in conflict. The autonomy of art as understood by eighteenth-century philosophers positions works of art beyond economic commerce, and, at least in theory, it disavows their having a price. However, the mythical pricelessness of works of art since the rise of capitalism paradoxically also translates into artists not getting paid. In this discussion, then, the autonomy of art is considered as a symptom of a larger structural problem related to artistic labour as a form of exploitation that emerged as a hallmark of autonomous art in the West and its imbrication with capitalism and class politics.

The dispossession derived from the concealment of artistic labour lies at the heart of art as an institutionalized practice in the West and parallels the rise of capitalism, which ironically puts a now invisible exploitation of labour at the centre of the economic sphere. While this process developed over two centuries ago, it is by no means a straightforward process. Through it, art as a (social) institution, alongside its related forms of labour, was constructed in opposition to the dehumanizing aspects of labour in the factory system, as well as labour's primacy in the economic sphere. However, for subjects whose only property is their capacity to labour this is a predicament; it is a non-issue for the members of the propertied bourgeois class. In sum, the separation of art from the exigencies of the capitalist economy and from labour was a class project and as such deeply contradictory.

I am not the first to criticize the autonomy of art. The avant-garde art movements of the early twentieth century were the first to contest its dynamics; influential critics like Peter Bürger have theorized the important ways in which the historical avant-garde movements exposed the ideological blindness behind the autonomy of art. In fact, one of Bürger's central aims has been to explicate autonomy as "the normative instrumentality" of art, or as the central ideological category of art in bourgeois society.[7] Despite the importance of his intervention, which theorized art as a social institution that affects the reception of works of art and provides critique of autonomy in its ideological dimensions, his work has been mostly ignored or misunderstood and criticized in the North American scholarship on art. My critique of autonomy is indebted to his findings and his sharp Marxian methodology even if I point to some of its shortcomings. While I draw on Bürger's argument in relation to the invisibility of artistic labour, I also show the ways in which it cannot help but inadvertently reproduce another form of autonomy, one as problematic as the one he was so right to criticize. In focusing on the content of what he identified as a bourgeois form, he not only failed to address the issue of labour's exploitation but contributed to rendering it even more invisible than it already was.

My critical reconsidering of the autonomy of art does not imply or defend an inevitable relationship between art and money. Nor does it refute the idea that art is or is not an autonomous practice per se. In many respects my argument draws on these debates but does not fall in line with the existing disciplinary critiques.[8] I offer neither a survey of debates on autonomy of art nor of concerns pertaining to the early twentieth-century avant-garde movements in socialist Eastern Europe, but an analysis of selected intersections between the concerns of interwar or, in Bürger's words, historical avant-garde movements, the critique of autonomy of art, and their relation to issues of artistic labour and class politics. In other words, while I rehearse points of familiar debates, I offer a new way of bringing together a critique of art's autonomy with a discussion of the early twentieth-century avant-garde movements that is informed by class politics. These movements' critique of autonomy and attack on the bourgeois idea of art simply did not go far enough.

Let's briefly revisit the definition of the avant-garde in relation to the ways in which the autonomy of the arts is linked to the obscuring of artistic labour. The very history of the avant-garde explains why the autonomization of art occurred in the first place. In general parlance, the term avant-garde is used as a noun or as an adjective that refers to phenomena in the realm of culture that press the boundaries of accepted norms, or stylistic and formal concerns, and are considered advanced. This is an apolitical understanding of the avant-garde. The term was originally used in the military, and began to be associated with radical socialist politics that promoted political reforms in nineteenth-century France. It was applied by a Saint-Simonian socialist to the context of art to refer to art as a catalyst for social change, which was attached to a concrete political project of utopian socialism.[9] To be avant-gardist in this sense "means not, or at least not primarily, the claim to be in advance of contemporary art …, but rather the claim to be at the peak of social progress" that aims for "the realization of Saint-Simonian utopia."[10] An artist is an avant-gardist not as a creator of works of art but rather as a revolutionary who actively builds and works toward social change. That makes the project of the avant-gardists parallel and related to the anti-capitalist socialist struggles. The concept of the avant-garde is not consistent and remains disputed in the fields of aesthetics, art history, and literary studies.[11]

My understanding of the avant-garde is closer to the one developed by Peter Bürger, one in which the critique of the autonomy of art is the centrepiece.[12] Bürger, who is the primary theorist of the avant-garde as a break with the bourgeois notion of art and its autonomy, importantly underscored that "inasmuch as avant-garde artists go beyond the sphere of art, they stand in a relation of tension to the principle of aesthetic autonomy."[13] I should note that this point implies an awareness that art is a social institution that is related to a historical understanding of class politics and the origins and norms of Western art (that is, who is an artist, what constitutes a work of art, and finally what the function of aesthetic autonomy is). Going beyond the sphere of art means an end to a historically specific institutionalization of art in the West and its productive apparatus created by the bourgeois class. In other words, the aim is "[t]o deprive the bourgeoisie not of its art but of its concept of art" – and, I should add, of its apparatus and relations of production that are based on an invisible artistic labour.[14] The end of art of course does not mean the end of art practice as such but an end or at least a radical transformation of the exploitative relations of production that characterize art as a bourgeois institution. In sum, it implies self-reflexivity in the field and a possibility of (self)critique.

One of the central tenets of the historical avant-garde movements was precisely to question the very autonomy of art (regardless of how divergent the political positions of various artistic movements may have been) and to "call the institution of art into question."[15] More so, these movements implicitly mounted a critique of the class character of art by exposing and questioning art's social function and the purpose of producing works of art. But not all art movements of the early twentieth century that are considered by art history and literary criticism as avant-garde were equally radical, which contributes to the divergence in the understanding and definitions of the avant-garde. For example, Bürger emphasized that to the extent that "the historical avant-garde movements respond to the developmental stage of autonomous art epitomized by aestheticism, they are part of modernism; in so far as they call the institution of art into question, they constitute a break with modernism."[16] Avant-garde as the break with modernism means a break with the bourgeois conception of art and its productive apparatus. This important distinction that is ignored in most scholarship on the avant-garde reveals that scholars predominantly conceive of avant-garde as a stage in the Western canon of art, but are not concerned with the anti-institutional attack that these movements mounted against art as a social institution and against autonomy as its defining ideology. Most scholarship about the avant-garde turns a blind eye to its confrontation with the ideological effects of autonomy on the institutional and productive relations in the arts, that is, they obscure the avant-garde's anti-institutional attack as it relates to the invisibility of labour and the class character of art. This bifurcation in the notions of the avant-garde is parallel to the two aspects of the autonomy of art.

In relation to art and autonomy, it is important to distinguish between two aspects of autonomy, the structural and ideological, which are in tension with one another. First, the structural notion of autonomy refers to the process of the autonomization of social spheres affected by the rise of a capitalist mode of production and the division of labour.[17] This process had two implications. The distinction between toilsome labour and creative work was reconceptualized as the opposition between alienation and self-realization.[18] Moreover, this dynamic established the institutional framework of art as a separate social sphere and artistic practice as a specialized profession that embodies the mythical power of creation and expression of "genius."

In the words of Peter Bürger, "the process by which the social subsystem 'art' evolves into a wholly distinct entity is part and parcel of the developmental logic of bourgeois society. As the division of labor becomes more general, the artist also turns into a specialist."[19] This is true for art of the nineteenth century onward. These developments sharpened the segregation of various types of labour whereby artistic work came to signify the sole embodiment of human creativity.[20] While, until the seventeenth century, various classifications of work coexisted, including distinctions between contemplative (monastic pursuits) and active work, artisanal work as a vocation, and the protestant ideal of hard work as a virtue, the rise of capitalist production during the eighteenth century shifted work discourses from an ethical to an economic domain.[21] "In this way," as Adolfo Sánchez Vásquez asserts, "labor loses its creative character while art becomes a distinct, substantive activity, an impregnable stronghold of the creative capacity of man, and forgets its remote and humble origins."[22] Paradoxically, then, the division of labour along with the separation of the private and public spheres of work during the eighteenth century set in motion a disappearance of certain kinds of work from the history of work and from definitions of labour. By the nineteenth century, the labour performed by the artist appeared to be impervious to the corrosion of alienation, which is specific to other forms of labour under capitalism. It even began to connote creation although the power of creation was habitually ascribed and granted only to white male subjects. This process of autonomization through which the professionalization of artistic labour took place was also deeply gendered. It had paradoxical consequences for the position of women artists as well as for my discussion of the invisibility of artistic labour. (We will return to the gendered nature of autonomy in the next chapter.)

The second, ideological aspect of autonomy relevant to the position of artistic labour is the notion of artistic autonomy that belongs to aesthetic discourses. This one outlines the separation between art and the pragmatics of mundane life but obfuscates the class politics that undergird it. The discourse of aesthetics has had a profound impact on the understanding of artistic labour as a non-utilitarian activity superior to market relations and pecuniary concerns. Among the proponents of this understanding was the eminent eighteenth-century philosopher Immanuel Kant, who, along with several Romantic artists,[23] conceived of fine art as an activity that is free and unsubordinated to the principle of capitalist accumulation and profit-making.[24] That applies to both levels, the aesthetic judgment (audience) and the kind of work that is involved in making art (artists). In Kant's words: "For fine art must be free art in a double sense: it must be free in the sense of not being a mercenary occupation and hence a kind of labour, whose magnitude can be judged, exacted, or paid for according to a determinate standard; but fine art must also be free in the sense that, though the mind is occupying itself, yet it feels satisfied and aroused (independently of any pay) without looking to some other purpose."[25] English translations inadequately represent the word choice and emphasis on art's distinction from wage labour and wage in the German original, in particular the part where Kant is quite literally saying that art should not be wage labour (*Lohngeschäft*) and should be done independently of wage (*Lohne*).[26] Aesthetic discourse thus separates artistic labour from everyday life and existence, which is determined by the pragmatics of wage labour and/or capital accumulation. While Kant's intention may be read as a philosophical defence of art against the valorization of capital and a claim for the universality of aesthetic experience, this stance is in Bürger's words blind to "the particular interest of his class.... What is bourgeois in Kant's argument is precisely the demand that the aesthetic judgement have universal validity. The pathos of the universality is characteristic of the bourgeoisie ..."[27] Furthermore, it also begs the question of which classes can afford to practice art independently of wage. In sum, the historical definition of the autonomy of art positions the art-work beyond the constraints of subsistence and alienated labour; it redefines it as non-work divorced from the economic sphere and obscures its class provenance.

There are several issues with the concept of autonomy and its effect on the invisibility of labour. The major problem with the autonomy of art stems from the scholarly lack of acknowledgment that this idea of art's autonomy is his-torical and not atemporal.[28] Moreover, it is deeply rooted in the ideology of the bourgeois class and the rise of capitalism. Another important issue is that the notion of the autonomy of art conflates various levels: the work of art, the artist, and the entire social subsystem called art. Several levels to which the idea of autonomy of art applies, however, are a consequence of the historical devel-opment of the notion of autonomy. In this process the idea of art's autonomy progressed from the autonomy of artists to the autonomy of art as a social system. In other words, the autonomy of art is an ideological category and shows that "art is institutionalized as ideology in bourgeois society." Exposed so brilliantly by Marcuse and Bürger, this ideology's contradictory structure conceals art's attachment to socially conditioned pragmatics of everyday life under capitalism. The profound separation of art from questions of economy therefore attests to the deeply rooted class nature of the term autonomy (of art).[29]

After initially referring only to the autonomy of the artist regarding rules spe-cific to courtly feudal society, the concept of the autonomy of art was expanded both to the artwork and to the field of art production during the eighteenth century, with ideas of aesthetic experience and artistic genius, and referred to the "status of art within society, its independence relative to moral claims and demands for social utility."[30] This is also where the tension between the ideological and structural levels of autonomy emerge. The autonomy of art enables artworks to become political at the level of content, that is a realm for the theorization of social problems not just the aesthetic experience of beauty. Yet, as Marcuse and Bürger point out, this contradicts the institutional position of art in bourgeois society that presumably releases art from having or fulfill-ing a social function. Finally, the contemplative attitude that autonomy implied made art not unlike a religious experience.[31] Nonetheless, the avant-garde idea of art as a catalyst for social change complicated the particular concept of art's autonomy that had surfaced in Europe during the late eighteenth and early nineteenth century.

The key target of the avant-garde attack was precisely the ideological aspect of the autonomy of art that confers on art a distance from social reality and political action. This tendency to go beyond the sphere of art and to critique the autonomy of art was quintessential for what Bürger terms the historical avant-garde movements that emerged during the early decades of the twentieth century, such as futurism, dadaism, surrealism, constructivism, and bauhaus. The aim of the avant-garde artist was not to produce artworks to advance a new style that would become available for aesthetic contemplation, but to contribute to a social change, which implied a transformation of the social role of art, and an aim to dispel with the idea of the bourgeois institution of art altogether, but not the practice of art as such.

On the institutional level, the historical avant-gardes' rejection of the idea of autonomy was two pronged: it aimed at and attacked key bastions of Western art – the author, artwork, and aesthetic attitude – and thereby the social role of art in bourgeois capitalist society engendered by the autonomy of art. Bürger points out that rejecting the ideology of autonomy implied, not without ambivalence, that an artist renounces their exceptional social position as a genius/creator, and that a work of art (object) can no longer be central but get replaced or employed by an action of social transformation. Art would then no longer be separated from life and the distinction between individual production and individual reception would become obsolete.[32]

An example of how these ideas manifested can be found in Russian constructivism where the artwork as commodity was reconceptualized as a "comradery object" in a world where as one scholar puts it there are no possessions.[33] In other words, these radical stances offered a potential for a reconfiguration of the social function of art beyond capitalism, and also had important implications when we consider the effects of the autonomy of art on the understanding of art as labour: they demystify artistic labour as an act of creation and redefine it as work. However, Bürger underlines, "It is a historical fact that the avant-garde movements did not put an end to the production of works of art, and that the social institution of art proved resistant to the avant-gardist attack."[34]

Bürger's theory explains why historically this attack has failed because the institution of art survived it by integrating self-criticism and self-reflexivity in its realm and reproducing a new version of the autonomy of art. Equally important, this failure was due to a formidable historical constellation of political, economic, and cultural forces that clashed and characterized the first half of the twentieth century. The avant-garde art movements contested the autonomy of art. However, they did so in a very specific historic context that generated its own host of problems related to the social upheavals against capitalism, the class struggle, and the rise of fascism. The critique of autonomy and the anti-institutional attack on art by the avant-garde was diluted precisely due to this historical context and had consequences for the critique and the status of autonomy today.

On the one hand, the avant-garde artists were confronted by larger political movements that were not necessarily aligned with their goals to end the institution of art since art in its ambiguous autonomy proved to be effective as an ostensibly neutral propaganda machine. On the other hand, the avant-garde artists faced the resistance of the institution of art, which welcomed the institutional critique but remained structurally unchanged. The Western institution of art welcomed the idea of the professionalization of the artist and of the political content of art work but maintained the invisibility and exploitation of artistic labour. I outline very briefly some of these issues here because the institutional apparatus of Western art, with the category of autonomy, triggered a contradiction at the heart of Yugoslav socialism, the system that was initially not exploitative in relation to artistic labour but that paradoxically would come to reproduce Western bourgeois aesthetic traditions. (I will return to and illustrate this point in later chapters.) The reason for the schematic historical detour that follows is that these historical developments impacted the theory of avant-garde, including the disputes about it, as well as the critique of art's autonomy. This critique, by and large, completely ignored the early historical avant-gardes' important attack on Western art as a social institution and its potential consequences for artistic labour and its exploitation.

For example, in the USSR, after a brief period of coexistence, the political establishment largely suppressed historical avant-garde art movements and collectives (constructivism, OBERIU[35]) and imposed the doctrine of socialist realism by the mid 1930s.[36] Stalin paradoxically and ironically appropriated the avant-garde idea of total change. It is historically bitter and ironic that one version of the historical avant-gardes' demand for a total social change was realized in a conservative way, making art subservient to the political aims of the party and suppressing avant-garde artists on the left. In the Soviet Union, the "newly imposed academicism," as John Berger calls socialist realism, was a regressive conservative appropriation of avant-garde ideals.[37] In this process, a suppression of the left-oriented avant-garde artistic movements in the USSR took place[38] and thereby marginalized alternative conceptions of how a transition from capitalism to socialism could be achieved. Comparatively speaking, the fate of the historical avant-garde in the USSR represents one side of the conflict between avant-garde art movements and radical politics.

Another version of the appropriation of avant-garde ideals took place in the United States. For instance, revolutionary activity among artists was invigorated there during the Depression and culminated in the New Deal Art Projects, which were congruent with historical avant-garde strategies and their antagonism toward the institution of art, in particular the "hostility toward individual production and reception of art as well as the distribution of art through laissez-faire markets and institutions."[39] Some scholars acknowledge an important resonance between the New Deal artistic projects' desire to eliminate the opposition between producer and recipient and the historical avant-garde movements' similar goals. They demonstrate that this radical avant-garde strategy was empowered by the government or state's labour politics toward artists.[40] Szalay argues that during the time of the New Deal the aspiration to unity between producer and consumer affected a "redistribution of cultural wealth" and provided citizens the means to produce culture. However, while the experience of art was equated to the production of art it "crushingly, would enshrine consumption as a legitimate form of political action."[41] In other words, breaking down the barrier between art and life fostered a bond between culture and consumerism rather than democratized the practice and access to art in the long term.

Avant-garde movements in the East made more progress in terms of transforming the institution of art than in the West due to their revolutionary context. For example, during the interwar times, artists of the historical avant-garde movements[42] on the territory of what was then the Kingdom of Yugoslavia made an alliance with the social revolutionaries that established postwar socialist Yugoslavia and its culture. They were connected to leftist intellectuals though they had a variety of political orientations, from Marxist to anarchist.[43] Sometimes these artists were members of the Communist Party of Yugoslavia (CPY). Artistic avant-garde movements promulgated subversive and critical attitudes toward the nascent bourgeois culture emerging in the Kingdom of Yugoslavia.[44] Stevan Majstorović maintains, "The representatives of all these genres opposed bourgeois academism."[45] Even more, their opposition to the bourgeois culture extended beyond the sphere of aesthetics into the political domain. Once monarchic dictatorship was introduced in 1929 Yugoslavia, the majority of intellectuals and artists of artistic avant-gardes "joined the political left and adopted the communist ideology."[46] In sum, rejecting traditional art and its bourgeois provenance, artists of the historical avant-garde movements made an alliance with the socialist revolutionaries; they actively participated in the antifascist resistance and established postwar socialist Yugoslavia and its culture.

However, in the final analysis, they also faltered in this goal. Specifically, the new visibility of artistic labour that unfolded in postwar socialist Yugoslavia was animated by the tension between a programmatic Marxist commitment to emancipation of human labour on the one hand, and the power of the Western institution of art to devalue artistic labour on the other. This disempowering contradiction was the symptom of the larger structural issue with art and autonomy that is echoed in the contemporary critique of autonomy.

One reason why the anti-institutional questioning of these avant-garde movements was obfuscated or distorted was related to the outcomes of the socialist revolutions of the twentieth century. Discussing the twentieth-century avant-garde movements in socialist Eastern Europe, Rastko Močnik points out that the attempts of the early twentieth-century avant-garde movements to subvert the institution of art were strongly dependent on the presence or absence of the "revolutionary situation" that enabled the subversive confrontations with the bourgeois institution of art. If such a revolutionary situation existed artists were able to articulate alternatives to the existing political economy of art production, which in addition to challenging the central precepts of bourgeois art – the author, artwork, and autonomy – included the organizational aspect.[47] It was "precisely this organizational aspect – the multitude of practices and practical forms – which broke with the inherited romanticist individualistic and neo-romanticist 'group' or 'artistic movement' logic, and introduced on a mass-scale a completely new organizational concept, defined in terms of class."[48] As opposed to other aesthetically radical art movements that preceded them, the methods of the historical avant-gardes became vehicles of social conflict that in Lev Kreft's words attempted to "shatter the means of production of the old art."[49] Understood in these terms, the implications of the historical avant-gardes aiming to break the ivory tower of autonomous art were on a structural level similar to the political goals of the socialist political movements that attempted to subvert capitalist social relations.

In other words, during the early twentieth century, a parallel emerged between the socialist political movements and some of the historical avant-garde art movements, one that would unfortunately not live up to its full potential. The former were grounded in Marx's analysis of capitalism and attempted to emancipate the working classes from an exploitation of human labour; the latter set out to emancipate artistic practice from the depoliticizing implications of the institutional framework of autonomy. While both of these projects can be understood as emancipatory, one striving for the liberation of labour by overturning the logic of capital accumulation, and the other attempting to redefine the productive apparatus of art by attacking the autonomy of the bourgeois institution of art, their relationship to one another was strained. The utopian aims of the historical avant-gardes to destroy the institution of art did not come to fruition in capitalist society.[50] Likewise, they were not realized in the existing socialist societies of the twentieth century. Nonetheless, the incisions made into the edifice of Western art by the historical avant-garde movements remain as relevant as the institutional critique of autonomy they started but which remained unresolved and restrained. While the avant-garde movements enabled a critique of the institution of art this had little effect on the paradox of unpaid labour because a new ideology of autonomy was reproduced.

Entanglements of the avant-garde art movements with radical left and right political parties during the interwar period resulted in a general rejection of these movements and their radical attacks on Western ideas of art. Avant-garde artists were mostly misunderstood by the political parties that saw their work and ideas only in terms of the efficacy their artwork had in terms of propaganda, mass appeal, or cultural diplomacy. In that sense, political parties also did not conceive of art beyond its ideological function. Scholars of the avant-garde who built on Bürger's theory point out that a rejection of the anti-institutional goals of the avant-garde art movements is common to "all dominant ideologies of the twentieth century" because "not one of them forgot to mention, that the methods of the aesthetic left and the avant-garde represent a disintegration of art, nation, class and everything sacred."[51] Finally, these processes resulted in the terminological distortions of the term avant-garde. The conflation of avant-garde with modernism that emerged during the Cold War's cultural and geopolitical conflicts led to the political neutralization of what the avant-garde meant. This in turn resulted in reinforcing the notion of autonomous art.

The end of the Second World War and the fragmentation of the left resulted in an international realignment of power and a transformation of the notion of the avant-garde during the Cold War. The political notion of avant-gardism was suppressed in the West. The institution of art and its central pillars resisted the attack by the avant-garde artist and reinforced the ideas of artistic autonomy at the expense of the labour behind the art. The anti-institutional attitude of the historical avant-garde art movements was largely disqualified and linked to "totalitarian" tendencies and obfuscated in the ideological wars between the liberal West and socialist East. Simultaneously, the term avant-garde as used in the West was equated with a radical formal innovation and conceived as belonging to the tradition of modernism.[52] "The artistic reception west of the Iron Curtain accepted mostly the formal innovations of the avant-garde and excluded the ideological-revolutionary context. In other words, they proclaimed the suprematist Kazimir Malevič as the father of geometrical abstraction"[53] and "fetishized the abstract formalistic experiment."[54] However, for the artists in the East and between the blocs, "Malevič counts as the founder of a comprehensive, total, and totalizing intellectual system [i.e., suprematism]."[55] In the West, the postwar reception of the left-oriented historical avant-garde movements was limited to and emphasized formal aspects at the expense of avant-garde's political concerns that aimed to revolutionize art and its traditional institutional framework defined by autonomy.

The utopian political dimensions of left-oriented historical avant-garde movements that were critical of the bourgeois institution of art were largely omitted or marginalized. The notion of avant-garde in the mainstream cultural discourses was instead conflated with modernism and became a convenient export good to spread the liberal ideology of individualism and freedom during the Cold War.[56] Paradoxically, the capitalist West, and the United States as its leader, appropriated the antibourgeois impulse of the historical avant-garde to foster an immanently (neo)liberal art system.[57]

Notwithstanding the depoliticization of the term avant-garde during the Cold War a resurgence of avant-garde movements and projects under a variety of designations re-emerged with ambiguous effects on the transformation of the institution of art and notions of autonomy. Despite all the influential proclamations of the death of the author, the genius artist kept a stronghold in the context of institutional art. Later, in the 1960s, artists in the West that were inspired by the historical avant-garde movements and were resisting this post-war system ruled by the art market became known as neo-avant-garde (conceptual art, minimalism etc.) and were related to various civil rights movements, intellectual currents of the New Left, and the philosophy of postmodernism.

During the Cold War, the heirs of the interwar avant-garde art movements re-emerged in the East under a variety of designations. While the historical avant-gardes were suppressed or marginalized in Eastern Europe, their ideas remained present among the artists of the so-called nonconformist or unofficial art movements, collectives, and groups, such as conceptualism in Moscow; TOTART in the former USSR; Actual Art, Imaginative Art, and Second Culture in the former Czechoslovakia; and the underground art scene of "second publicity" in Hungary.[58] In the context of socialist Yugoslavia this phenomenon was known as the alternative art practices.

In socialist Yugoslavia, the pursuit of self-managed socialism after 1948 created a new momentum for questioning the institutional design and social function of art that the historical avant-garde movements began. It gave rise to an alternative understanding of the function for art in Yugoslav society and was connected to Marxist and neo-Marxist intellectual circles that critically examined the discrepancy between the theory and practice of self-managed socialism but also criticized both the consumerist art market and apolitical modernist art. The term alternative art practices referred to those art practices in Yugoslavia that challenged the institutional framework of art under socialism.[59] According to Ješa Denegri, what was "alternative" or "different" about the alternative route in Yugoslav socialism was precisely its commitment to "question the existing definition and the status of art in a particular historical moment."[60] They drew on "or indirectly follow[ed] the rare and at that time neglected and forgotten legacy of the historical avant-gardes of the 1920s."[61] Throughout the postwar decades, a variety of art movements exemplified alternative art practices as heirs of the historical avant-garde in Yugoslavia, among them Exat 51, New Tendencies (*nove tendencije*), OHO, Theatre Pekarna, Pupilija Ferkerverk, and New Cinema.[62] Furthermore, alternative art practices were equally critical of Western models of art in general and the art market in particular.[63] As such, they were actively connected to neo-avant-garde groups and sought alliances with similar groups internationally.

A variety of notions used for resurgent avant-garde movements, such as unofficial or nonconformist, or alternative art during the Cold War, signalled an absence of a suitable signifier and suggested an issue with the naming of the postwar neo-Marxist and anti-authoritarian cultural and intellectual practices that existed within the "officially" anti-capitalist leftist political systems of socialist countries. These practices articulated a critique of existing socialism without eschewing its emancipatory potential. In Yugoslavia, alternative art practices are also known under several designations, such as new art practice (*nove umetničke prakse*), 1980s alternative culture (*alternativna kultura osemdestih*), or non-institutional culture (*neinstitucionalna kultura*). In addition to alternative art practices and movements, examples of anti-capitalist leftist practices in Yugoslavia were, among others, the intellectual circles around the journals *Perspektive* and *Praxis*; the Korčula Summer School; Tribina Mladih in Novi Sad; and student cultural centres in Zagreb, Belgrade, and Ljubljana. In the West, an example of such practices was the Situationist International.[64] However, while very few and isolated voices, such as sociologist Zagorka Golubović, a core member of the Praxis group, and conceptual artist Goran Đođrević who I discuss in this book, took up the critique of autonomous art and the difficult problem of artistic labour, socialist Yugoslavia maintained the mystification of art as a realm of freedom and its attachment to the understanding of creative work as an autonomous practice – as if it was a neutral, ahistorical, and classless concept.

In addition to the entanglements with political parties, the attempts of the historical avant-garde movements were also faced with the institutional resistance of the autonomous art sphere to radically transform the relations of production.[65] While some of the most radical avant-garde movements aimed to subvert the idea of art object and its relation to commodification of art, the idea of authorship and the law of property, and the totalizing effects of aesthetic discourses, these three central posts of Western art remained key elements in the institution of art and the strings art had to the market forces.[66]

What is more, the means and methods of the avant-garde's attack on the autonomy of art were integrated into the institutional canon of art and turned into aesthetic procedures, which subverted the anti-institutional aspect of this revolutionary strategy. In Močnik's words, "Avant-garde practices remain cloistered within the autonomous art-sphere, doomed to repeat an ever-recuperated subversion of aesthetics, and to try occasional escapades out of the art-sphere which, with no historical process to articulate to, are repeatedly rejected back towards the sterility of their autonomous domain."[67] The historical avant-garde movements did not destroy the institution of art, or as Bürger put it, they failed, because the autonomy of art as the decisive ideology of Western art is sustained. While views about the avant-garde's defeat or failure are some of the most contested in the scholarship of avant-garde, they do not imply that avant-garde movements were not impactful, or that the institution of art was not internally changed in any way by the avant-garde art movements. The institution was indeed changed, especially in terms of the kinds of work that are produced and the new possibilities of political issues they bring forth within the institution of art. Political protest is now part of and regularly takes place in the institution of art. Since the

Second World War the notion of avant-garde is often related to the idea of newness or of being advanced or progressive politically but is devoid of the anti-institutional dimensions that was emphasized by Bürger, who understood the anti-institutional attack by the historical avant-gardes as "the decisive event in the development of art in bourgeois society."[68]

The significance of the avant-garde movements' attack on the autonomy and the institution of art was indeed obscured. The subverted notion of avant-garde as a stage within a specific intuitional framework of Western art is also linked to the limited horizons of the critique of autonomy. The obfuscation of historical avant-gardes' attack on art as a social institution is also the vanishing point of the critique of autonomy and the ways it affects the issues of unpaid artistic labour today. In vigorous scholarly discussions that have taken place in the past several decades about the failure of the avant-garde, the question that remains neglected is the ideological effects of the autonomy of art on working conditions in the institution of art. The criticism of the autonomy of art re-enacts the problem I am addressing. The reason for invoking these perennial questions and debates here is to address the mystification for which autonomy is instrumental as the functional mode of the institution of art and which also has consequences for relations of production. I am not claiming that unfair working conditions and unpaid labour in the arts are caused by the autonomy of art but that the autonomy of art and labour's invisibility coincide. This invisibility is partially facilitated by the ideology of the autonomy of art because the latter rests on a separation of art from its socio-economic context rather than an acknowledgment of how they are imbricated. The lack of recognition contributes to the mystification of the labour process and the prevalence of unpaid labour.

Avant-garde movements made the institutional relations of art obvious and visible and pointed to the ideological character of the autonomy of art; however, these movements only impacted the possibilities of political engagement within the institution of art, not the actual ideological effects of autonomy relating to the working conditions in the arts. The critique of autonomy by the historical avant-gardes had therefore little impact on the invisibility of artistic labour as a form of exploitation. This of course was not the fault of the avant-garde but hinged on the historical context in which the attack took place, as well as on the postwar disciplinary reception of the avant-garde's anti-institutional attack and political appropriations.

The critique of autonomy by the historical avant-gardes was overlooked not only by the general public but also by a number of influential Marxist scholars of aesthetics.[69] While Adorno elevated avant-garde art, Lukács rejected it as decadent, yet both understood it as "the expression of alienation in late-capitalist society."[70] Bürger conclusively demonstrated that the disputed legitimacy of avant-garde art both in Adorno and Lukács is "confined to the sphere of artistic means and the change in the kind of work it involves" but it is not concerned with avant-garde's anti-institutional aspect that questions the autonomy of art.[71] Lukács and Adorno argue within the framework of the institution that is art, specifically they discuss works of art, and are for that very reason unable to criticize art as an institution with a specific set of labour relations and working conditions. "For them, the autonomy doctrine is the horizon within which they think,"[72] which implies that that they don't consider the producer of the works of art or her labour. A distinction between works of art and the social function of art as a social sphere is missing or is obscured, as is the labour of an artist.

Moreover, Adorno effectively restored and reanimated the importance of the work of art and its autonomy, which took place on account of the invisibility of artists' labour and transformation of relations of production within the institution of art.[73] While in his study on Wagner, Adorno remarked that "a contradiction of all autonomous art is the concealment of the labor that went into it,"[74] he did not analyse this paradox further. Bürger diagnosed the issue with Adorno astutely: "It is precisely the break with art as an institution that Adorno failed to bring out in his study of the avant-garde movements. When this is done, art becomes recognizable both as an institution and as a possible object of criticism."[75] While Adorno elevated the avant-garde artwork as the means through which one can stare into the abyss of capitalist alienation, his oversight on the level of production relations maintained the invisibility of the actual working conditions and unexamined status of genius artist.

Neither Adorno nor Lukács addressed "the attack that the historical avant-garde movements launched against art as an institution"[76] that allows us to question what is obscured by the autonomy of art. These undisputedly important critical theorists have not pushed the limits of the institution of art or its hidden exploitative relations of production, which engender invisible artistic labour.

Bürger's theory of the avant-garde and his insistence that the avant-garde made the institution of art visible precisely by critiquing the autonomy of art has pertinence for our understanding of invisible artistic labour. His lifelong insistence on the failure of the avant-garde to destroy the institution of art remains one key reason for the negative critical reception and disputes with his work by other scholars. However, in the final analysis the failure of the avant-garde posited by Bürger's theory also means a reanimation of the notion of the autonomy of the work of art and art's autonomy in general. Despite his insights about the autonomy of art determining the ideological framework that defines art as a social institution in the West, Bürger did not theorize a relation between the ideological and structural aspects of autonomy of art. His reading was ironically also defined by a focus on the works of art as the principal agents in the institution of art. His theory remained focused on the effects of works of art but not on the people who were producing them, that is, on artistic labour.

The critique of autonomy as ideology that was put forth by the avant-gardes does give us, however, a path to demystify artistic labour. One way to interpret the historical avant-gardes' critique of autonomy and its attack on the Western institution of art then is as a demand for an emancipation of art practice and a transformation of the social conditions for the production of art, which implies labour. By questioning the very autonomy of art, historical avant-garde movements made evident that autonomy is another name for a specific social function of art in bourgeois society that mystifies the relations of production, conceals artistic labour, and depoliticizes class relations. However, by obscuring the focus of the avant-garde's anti-institutional attack, their radical intervention gets diluted. This is so true that even the critique of the autonomy of art becomes part of the problem when it produces and reproduces the oversight of the invisibility of artistic labour as a form of exploitation and inequality in the arts. I am not claiming that artists are not disputing unfair and unsustainable labour conditions but that the link between exploitation of labour and autonomy remains obscured. The perspective on the exploitation of labour is the blind spot even as it allows us to see autonomy of art in its structural aspect. Making the link between autonomy and labour visible gives labour its due place and allows for a discussion of its exploitation.

Attacks on the autonomy of art backfire when they too make labour invisible. Discussing labour issues in the arts and pointing out how they derive from notions of autonomy in the arts is suspicious to those who confuse the critique with hegemonic representations of socialism, Marx, and his labour theory of value. This often leads to the dismissal, as ideologically biased, of a human rights issue that involves exploitation at its core. Marx's understanding of labour rested on a profoundly humanist view. He understood labour as the basic human way people interact with the environment, but his insight about the exploitation of labour under capitalism has been politicized to the point that it is often dismissed, in mainstream discourse and especially in the context of the arts, as overly politicized or as impertinent. Partly, this is due to the fact that, while Marx focused on how human labour gets commodified and becomes the platform for exploitation in capitalist accumulation, feminist scholars in turn exposed his failure to include all unwaged labour that is not understood as an economic category.[77] Still, our aversion to seeing labour in the arts as a profoundly political issue should not detract from the fact that Marx's insight in the commodification, abstraction, and exploitation of labour is primarily a human-centred and humanist contribution, which is relevant to art not merely as a topic of artworks but even more for the actual people working in the arts. It is not that Marxist scholars do not examine art, labour, and commodification or that Marx's ideas do not have resonance when scholars discuss art, but discussing art as labour creates discomfort instead of nods of agreement. It is perceived as a threat to art's idealized autonomy and leads to reluctance toward perceiving art as labour.

This being said, giving the exploitation of artistic labour its due place and highlighting its connection with the ideology of autonomy is not to say that art has no autonomous existence. It is quite possible for artists to get paid and for the autonomy of art to be preserved. It is the historical polarization I have exposed that makes the two incompatible not the act of exposing it.

The autonomy of art is not just an illusion, a chimera dreamt up by agents in the field of art production; rather, it is a structural condition of the existence, organization, and functioning of aesthetic or artistic practices. Although the autonomy of art and the invisibility of artistic labour coincide, this is a historical conjunction rather than an inherent or necessary one. That is to say the ideological dimension of autonomy is not a delusion, it has material consequences and material existence. The autonomy of art may be viewed as an ideological construct since it conceals the material social relations in the arts and the ways in which art is bound to the socio-economic processes. However, there is an additional structural dimension of autonomy that affects labour's invisibility. The tension between the two affects the problematic and absent remuneration of artistic labour and exploitative working conditions. While the institution of art historically secured a relative autonomy and determined the parameters of artistic labour as a specialized profession or occupation, it has also fostered an exploitative system characterized by free, discounted, or unpaid work; irregular employment; wage inequality; and unreliable job and economic security for art workers. The prestige and perceived exceptionality of artistic work tend to eclipse the injustice of the precarious, often unpaid labour that sustains art as an institution. There is a structural issue at work when we discuss autonomy that is visible precisely from the point of view of labour.

Individuals working in the arts appear to find it challenging and limiting to see themselves as workers. The ironic words of Theodor Adorno are fitting: "To make works of art into magical objects means that men worship their own labour because they are unable to recognize it as such."[78] Even when artistic labour is understood as work, particularly in the context of cultural policy, it is still viewed as an exceptional, atypical kind of work based on special talents or artistic genius – in short, what artists do is not labour. What is more, the autonomy of art turns out to be a gendered concept that further corroborates its devaluing as labour. In the following chapter, I use feminism's insights into the invisibility of domestic labour to frame my discussion of art as a form of invisible labour, and emphasize how it bears on the separation of the social spheres and the critique of the autonomy of art.

Chapter Two

A Feminist Approach to the Disavowed Economy of Art

Autonomy has historically been a gendered notion, a defining feature of masculinity as opposed to the relational otherness and dependency that has characterized dominant representations of femininity. It therefore follows that the notion of artistic labour, which as we saw in chapter 1, is rooted in the idea of art's autonomy, would also be a gendered concept. This convergence of labour and gender calls, I argue, for an approach that is informed both by labour theory of value and a feminist epistemology to unpack the implications of autonomy of art. In this chapter, I therefore employ a feminist epistemology about the gendered nature of (women's) work as an element of my labour-focused analysis. This is not to say that I discuss gender as an attribute of the artist's identity (with its inevitable consequences of pay differential or marginalization), but that gender mobilizes art as much as artists, irrespective of a person's gender identity. In Angela Davis's words, "I want us to see feminism not only as addressing issues of gender, but rather as a methodological approach to understanding the intersectionality of struggles and issues."[1] Certainly, when we discuss gender and art, white men have historically and arguably been the norm.[2] While the celebrated question by Linda Nochlin, "Why have there been no great women artists?" still needs to be asked, the answer, however, is not how we will demystify the production process and unearth the structural disavowal of labour in the arts. Or, to be even more precise, the central focus point in my approach is the question of labour, why and how art is not understood as labour, and how feminist epistemology can help us explain this mystification of artistic labour. In other words, I am practicing what Teresa L. Ebert has termed a new Red Feminism, which in her words "is not only concerned with the 'woman question,' it is even more about the 'other' questions that construct the 'woman question': the issues of class and labour constituting the very conditions of knowing – and – changing – the root realities of global capitalism."[3] In sum, if we can claim that the invisibility of labour is what was exposed by Marx's critique of the political economy, it was Marxist feminists who took a deeper look from the women's viewpoint to demonstrate that the double invisibility of women's work is part and parcel of the capitalist exploitation equation. The method of how they exposed that and the conclusion they drew about the character of women's work are relevant to discussion of art as labour and its inevitable exploitation.

Any analysis that exposes the invisible forms of labour will therefore necessarily invoke well-known feminist analyses of the invisibility of women's domestic labour, and the concept of "housewifisation" or "housewifed labor" as the term describing flexible, atypical, devalued and unprotected forms of labour.[4] We owe it to feminism, alongside colonial and postcolonial studies, to have made us aware of the ubiquity of unpaid work to begin with.[5] Although artistic labour is a particular form of invisible labour that cannot be conflated with the forms of domestic labour that have historically preoccupied feminists, there is a lot to be learned by juxtaposing artistic and domestic labour. The specificity, exploitation, and paradoxical character of artistic labour can be teased out and become all the more visible through comparison but also, and maybe even more so, through contrast.

Unpaid or invisible labour is a phrase that has historically evoked women's work and more specifically, domestic household work or the duties associated with mothering.[6] The effects of industrialization and the rise of capitalism in Europe and North America during the late seventeenth and eighteenth century caused the separation of work and home into a public and a private sphere, and turned housework, subsistence or reproductive domestic labour into non-work or socially invisible labour. This is so true that the term "invisible work" requires no qualifier for us to immediately think of the gender gap and women's unequal lot. Feminists not only demonstrated that the invisibility of housework devalues such work, but also that that "devaluation was at the same time a precondition for the appropriation of unpaid work."[7] Because domestic labour was considered a "personal service outside of capital,"[8] it did not require payment.

It was Marxist feminists who, in the 1970s, articulated the most prominent critique of domestic labour, by revealing how its social and economic devaluation derived from the essentializing link to the female character or physique. As feminist activists relied on Marx's findings about the centrality of the exploitation of the wage labourer, they also revealed that the exploitation of the non-waged labourer had been modelled on domestic labour's status as non-work.[9] These feminist activists helped redefine domestic labour or housework as actual work.

It was the transformation of domestic work into an internal need, aspiration, and an attribute of female personality – its essentialization or naturalization – that made unpaid housework invisible as a form of labour and its economic as well as cultural devaluation socially acceptable. Because housework was viewed as a woman's natural calling – it was "transformed into a natural attribute of female physique and personality" and thereby altered into non-work, invisible work.[10] In her seminal text, *Wages against Housework*, written in 1975, Silvia Federici emphasized that "[the] unwaged condition of housework has been the most powerful weapon in reinforcing the common assumption that housework is not work, thus preventing women from struggling against it."[11] Because it is not defined as work women cannot fight against their economic exploitation. However, a demand for wages for housework, Federici argued, needs to be understood as a "political perspective" rather than a "lump of money."[12] As a political perspective, this demand implies a rejection of domestic labour as the expression of female nature and the social role that capitalism intended for women. In other words the lump of money is not going to solve the problem (since getting paid is not the ultimate goal), but drawing attention to the unwaged condition of domestic labour turns the issues of invisible labour into a realm of political struggle against unjust exploitation of labour.

While there is much more to the Marxist feminist critique of domestic labour and the role of the sphere of reproduction articulated by Federici and others, in my analysis I focus on the theoretical and epistemological dimension of their intervention to develop a critique of unpaid labour in the arts.[13] For example, in her essay "The Reproduction of Labor Power in the Global Economy and the Unfinished Feminist Revolution," Federici discusses the ways that feminist analyses of domestic labour from the late twentieth century must be revised to account for new conditions of accumulation in late capitalism (such as the hyper-exploitation of migrant workers, the financialization of the household, the closure of the gap between reproduction and accumulation, and so on).[14] Nevertheless, and for the purposes of my critique of unpaid labour in the arts, the earlier feminist analyses of domestic labour remain important for the critique of artistic labour precisely because they so clearly articulate the internal mechanisms that contribute to the unwaged and invisible condition of domestic labour.

A comparative approach between the invisibility of domestic and artistic labour gives insight into the very mechanisms that drive the economic exploitation of artists' labour to this day. Specifically, there are two theoretical contributions in feminist epistemology that are particularly resonant when we theorize the invisibility of artistic labour. First, the structural component of invisible work that rests on the separation of public and domestic/private sphere (or, if you will, the sphere of production and reproduction) under capitalism whereby the latter is excluded from the economy but is nevertheless a site of both value-creation as well as social and economic exploitation. Second, the essentialization of particular types of work or skills, which leads to their economic and/or social and cultural devaluation. In other words, the first contribution helps us understand that treating art as non-labour under capitalism leads to its invisibility and consequently exploitation. The second one helps us understand what the operating logic behind the invisibility is. I use the parallels between domestic and artistic labour as a fruitful epistemological base to unpack the paradoxes of unpaid artistic labour.

As I pointed out in chapter 1, the autonomy of art in structural terms means that art becomes an autonomous social sphere in which artists are professionals, but their work is paradoxically treated as a private matter that is powered by a psychological or subjective need for the expression of creativity rather than labour. The feminist critique of the division of labour and separation of the public and the private spheres offers a useful lens to unearth the specific form of invisibility that defines artistic labour and its exploitation. Moreover, it also helps reframe work as a political issue and not a private matter.

The postulation of art as an autonomous sphere divorced from the rumble and drudgery of everyday working life and economic pressure falls quite squarely into the private sphere of work, into which women were relegated with the onset of industrialization in Europe and North America; by contrast, the public sphere was the realm of men. What is more, some feminist scholars demonstrated that the ideological underpinning of artistic labour, specifically literary labour, as an exceptional type of work that supposedly surpasses the grind of alienated labour and market relations, had historically and paradoxically appropriated a middle-class Victorian representation of women's domestic labour as nonalienated work and as an expression of a selfless self.[15] The labour of a writer is like the labour of a housewife. In the words of cultural historian Mary Poovey, "Like a good housekeeper, the good writer works invisibly, quietly, without calling attention to his labor."[16] The reliance on the domestic ideal established the appearance of an alternative sphere where rules of competition and market relations don't operate; however this alternative sphere depoliticized the reality of the class dimensions that operate within and affect it. On the one hand the separation of spheres excludes and establishes some forms of labour as not contributing to the economy, on the other hand these separated spheres appear to be untouched or unaffected by the market logic that pertains to other forms and spheres of work. Put differently some forms of labour are not done for the money. However, it is precisely this exclusionary operation that makes the labour invisible and depoliticizes such work. Poovey contends, "The effort necessary to construct and maintain the separate sphere of the home and literary labor reveals itself in its failure: the reappearance elsewhere of what has had to be displaced – the 'stain' of sexuality, the 'blight' of class, the 'degradation' of work."[17] While domestic and artistic labour appear "to provide an alternative to alienation endemic to class society," they in fact reproduce the logic of capitalist society through obscuring class difference and alienated labour. Or, if I phrase it as a question, who can afford the unpaid labour?

Work as a political question and as a structural condition in contemporary societies is often obscured by what Weeks terms "the privatization of work" in the sense that employment is experienced as a "unique relationship" rather than as a "social institution"[18] whereby the workplace figures as "the province of human need and sphere of individual choice rather than a site for the exercise of political power."[19] The ideas related to the privatization of work have traction and are redolent of circumstances in the institution of art due to the strong relationship of artistic labour to ideas of individuality, self-realization, and creativity. The consequences manifest themselves in the depoliticization of labour issues in the arts.

Artistic labour culturally constructed as an expression of genius and creativity is a fitting example of the privatization of work. Navigating between the Scylla and Charybdis of subsistence on the one hand and the expression of an artistic or creative personality on the other, it becomes an ambiguous business that leads us to unpaid labour. In the satirical essay "A Portrait of the Artist as a Worker," Dieter Lesage phrased it well: "You are an artist and that means: you don't do it for the money. That is what some people think. It is a great excuse not to pay you."[20] The expressions of your creativity are your gifts to yourself and humanity and their admiration is your reward. That is what some people think. It is (another) great excuse not to pay the artist while others may profit from her creativity.

While work is not just an economic category, most individuals living under capitalism are "expected to work for wages or be supported by someone who does."[21] Paid work is a structural condition that affects a large part of the world population.[22] Remuneration, a salary, a fee, or a wage, recognizes subjects as workers and as a party of a social contract under capitalism. Of course, contemporary neoliberal capitalism would prefer to convince us otherwise: material conditions are not what matters we are told; rather, we are led to believe that what matters is the freedom to express our personality. Such extreme subjectivism, Sergio Bologna asserts, belongs to the "ideological *dispositifs* which have the purpose of dissolving the notion of 'labor.'"[23] Labour, then, no longer means "human activity exchanged for subsistence, but an activity in which the individual externalizes his own personality, knows himself better, almost a mystical encounter" and is inscribed into the "ideology of modernity."[24] Labour as belonging to the realm of psychology and leisure and not to the realm of commodities and work serves as the "justification of 'free' labor, badly paid or unpaid."[25]

While it is true that the privatization and psychologization of work belong to the ideological discourse of modernity, it is again important to remember that these legitimizing discourses of work only apply to particular propertied classes that can in fact afford unpaid labour. If the fact "that individuals should work is fundamental to the basic social contract," as Weeks asserts,[26] or, in Federici's words, if "to have a wage means to be part of a social contract" and this is a condition under which the majority of population is allowed to live,[27] then it follows that unpaid artistic labour is not viewed as part of that social contract. If artists have to have a second job to pay the bills, the second job only increases their exploitation. This is a point magnified by Federici when she argues that in the context of unwaged housework, holding a second job "simply reproduces the role in different forms."[28] Unpaid artistic labour ensures that art remains the privilege of the few whose job is not backbreaking enough not to leave them the energy and time to devote to art. On that basis alone, it should be remunerated, so as to allow members of all classes to have access to its rewards, both psychological and financial. The idea that one's enjoyment of one's work justifies one's exploitation is exactly what is wrong with capitalism at its base.[29]

Unpaid domestic labour may be the necessary condition for the accumulation of capital and the reproduction of the labour force,[30] but artistic labour has no such direct link to social reproduction. Nevertheless, as we saw in the previous chapter, it is essential for the ideological reproduction of bourgeois society's affirmative culture. Translated in contemporary terms, creative self-expressive work epitomized by a popular doctrine "do what you love, love what you do" is the bloodline of the neoliberal ideology that contributes to unpaid or poorly paid labour, not only in the arts but in other sectors too. Artists are the model workers, and it is precisely the ideology of autonomous art as divorced from the economy as well as its obscuring of artistic labour that is instrumentalized in neoliberal policies. The consequences manifest themselves in the depoliticization of labour issues in the arts as well as in an obscuring of class dimensions of arts (from the viewpoint of labour).

Drawing analogies between domestic and artistic labour has its explanatory strength because it demonstrates the mechanisms by which particular types of work get naturalized within the wage-conditioned economy that leads to exploitation. This helps us conceive of artistic labour and its poorly remunerated condition as a political question. Because it is done out of love and allows self-fulfilment irrespective of economic concerns, unpaid artistic work resonates with feminist findings about the assumed nature of housework, which women presumably do out of motherly love and/or their natural calling. To echo the feminist slogan "They say it is love. We say it is unwaged work,"[31] we could say that for the love involved in producing art, art workers have to relinquish payment for their efforts or accept modest and retroactive fees.[32]

In the sense that artistic labour remains to be understood as non-work, as an expression of inborn gifted, creative personality, it parallels the understanding of domestic labour as the natural attribute of a female subject. Feminized domestic labour has been historically conceived as women's natural calling, an extension of essentializing feminine traits. In the same way, artistic labour was established as non-work that originates in a subject's nature, inner calling, inherent artistic genius, or talent.[33] Domestic labour is the embodiment of femininity, and similarly, artistic labour is the embodiment of one's unique individuality, a notion that was historically masculine. Similar essentializing mechanisms animate domestic labour and artistic labour then, as one is understood as the natural inclination of women – a quintessential femininity and expression of love – and the other as the natural inclination of those who possess artistic genius, creativity, or, better yet, an ability to create. In both cases, particular skills are essentialized, declared, or culturally constructed as naturally stemming from the subject's essence or nature. Neither is defined as work; they are invisible in relation to the process of their production. Only the outcome (the clean house or the work of art) is allowed to be visible, in such a way as to obscure the work involved. Both are therefore economically devalued by being essentialized. Artists can thus be unwaged and happy, just like the domestic woman of yore. If there is an income, it only comes from a parallel form of employment that is not considered exploitation since the art or domestic labour are not perceived as labour intensive. Whereas the wage nexus would recognize the artist as a worker, the absence of payment makes artistic labour invisible under capitalism.

The essentialization of work to a particular type of subjectivity powered by the ideology of artistic genius and creativity is one key mechanism that engenders invisibility of art as a form of labour. Creativity as a concept has an influential history impressed in cultural discourses and practices.[34] It is thus not a surprise that it also affects the ideas of artistic labour, or better yet, the ideas that art is *not* labour. The attribution of creativity to certain gifted or talented individuals performs a key function in the institution of art and animates the paradox of unpaid artistic labour. It is grounded in philosophical ideas developed by white male bourgeois philosophers. Historically, the ideas of creativity got connected to artistic genius as an individual trait, an inborn faculty during the Romantic period in Europe. While creativity is another flimsy concept it has played an important role in establishing the institution of art, as well as the image of artist as a genius or extremely creative person in the West. Andreas Reckwitz explains that the Romantic period particularly in Germany, Great Britain, and France established the "aesthetic of genius" and attached it to the figure of an artist as an exceptional being who possesses a "faculty or power to invent."[35] Genius was designated an innate trait of exceptional individuals. "At the heart of the aesthetic of genius is the model of the subjective origins of novelty. The individual artwork is sourced to an individual, non-interchangeable 'creator' in possession of an out-of-the-ordinary soul. 'Genius' is the general title for these qualities of the psyche."[36]

What is more, the Romantic period reduced the idea of craftsmanship or even completely discarded it to make a distinction between an artist and an artisan. The artist was the inventor, creator; the craftsman was just doing high-skilled labour. Discussing the origins of authorship, Martha Woodmansee demonstrates that rather than the idea of craft what became important during the Romantic period's attempts to establish the exceptionality of artists' work was inspiration. But as opposed to inspiration coming from outside (from a muse or god etc.), it was now internalized, understood as originating inside in the writer. "'Inspiration' came to be explicated in terms of *original genius*, with the consequence that the inspired work was made peculiarly and distinctively the product – and the property – of the writer."[37] Together these notions of genius and creativity form the basis for an understanding of artists as exceptional subjects possessing creativity that exerts its impact on the perception of artistic labour in contemporary times.[38] In sum, what artists do is not work, it is creation. And needless to say, this was historically a very gendered notion, with men essentially being reserved access to this creative pool.

A demystification of creativity and its connection to the ideology of the artistic genius are profoundly consequential for a critique of artistic labour. Calling art labour then implies a rejection of artistic labour as the expression of creative genius or essentialized creativity and the social role that capitalism intended for artists. Indeed, in the twentieth century, artists heavily probed the ideologies of artistic genius and that of the author; some tried to divorce it from ingenuity and to establish art as labour even. In addition to the Duchampian gesture that characterized much of Western art in the twentieth century, which (among other implications) signalled that materiality of making is not what counts as art, that anyone can be an artist and any activity or object may count as art; another example rests with the historical avant-garde movements, specifically in Russian constructivism that was deeply engaged in redefining art for a new socialist society after the October Revolution. In general, as discussed in chapter 1, historical avant-garde movements were attacking all the cornerstones of the bourgeois institution of art and the idea of the author was one of them. However, in the capitalist context, their strategies of demystifying the author and exposing artistic labour as work had more ambiguous effects. The name of the author to this day performs an important function when it comes to art and its economic value. In other words, the ideology of exceptional subjectivity is one of the central mechanisms that establishes artistic labour as invisible work.[39]

The analogy between domestic and artistic labour does have an explanatory power as well as political relevance, especially for reconsidering how artistic labour is defined and exploited in capitalist society, but it only goes so far. While the parallels between domestic and artistic labour are striking, the differences between the feminist critique of domestic labour and my challenge to unpaid artistic labour may be even more important. A major distinction between domestic labour and artistic labour is the source that drives the essentializing rhetoric that mobilizes the subject. In relation to domestic labour, it is a collective, undifferentiated sexual difference that in the dominant view is at the origin of women's compulsion to clean and tidy. In these hegemonic views, women are not inscribed into domestic labour to distinguish themselves but rather as the oppressed collective entity that serves humanity. Not so with the artist, who is motivated by an individualist, original, special, and self-affirming inner compulsion that produces art. The domestic woman is selfless. The artist is full of a self that spills over on the canvas or a page, video, in a performance or a film, etc. What the artist has over the domestic angel of the house, then, is a self, but it is still not a self that deserves anything other than itself as reward. While domestic labour is selfless, aesthetic discourse manages to remove labour by making the self visible, just not the work. Women should not appear to have done anything in domestic labour so the labour can be rendered invisible. Artists work but because it is self-fulfilling that should be their reward.

Despite the similarities between the essentializing nature of artistic and domestic labour, the valences attached to inner and outer identities in relation to artists are fundamentally different from those attached to women. The woman's inner compulsions are externally assumed through gender conventions, but their supposed inner self produces not an externalized version of a unique and differentiated self but of gender conventions, of expectations aligned with femininity that assumes the lack of self, agency, and individuality. They are programmed, if you will, to produce the same outcome (assembly line, clean house, well-fed kids, happy spouses). Not so with artists. They are not to produce expected predictable outcomes because the externalized version of the self (in the art) is individualized and subjective, not predictable and conventional.

Even if the shared invisibility that makes it socially acceptable in both cases that this work is unremunerated since it is performed out of love, aspiration, and so on, there is a difference between love of self and love of other or family to whom women have to sacrifice the self. There is a choice element that has been withdrawn from femininity that art retains. Since artistic labour was historically reserved for white male subjects, the masculinity implied in artistic autonomy made the invisibility of artistic labour paradoxical. As such, Reckwitz asserts, the artist "assumed a special place. He was an exclusive type, thus implying a strange duality. On the one hand he was a socially identifiable figure providing the special service of producing artworks. But at the same time he was a socially exclusive figure, since not everyone can be an artist. Being an artist denoted by the words 'genius' and 'ingenium,' and these qualities tend to prohibit social inclusiveness."[40] On the one hand artist labour is essentialized and hence defined as non-work that is poorly, if at all, remunerated; on the other it is elevated as an act of creation and self-expression and thus admired and glorified.

While housework was degraded, artistic labour was exalted. For the woman, self-satisfaction, if there is any, follows the production of housework for others.

For the artist, it precedes the work that may later benefit others. Self before other is what distinguishes art from housework, which is others before self. For some sociologists, artistic labour should indeed be defined as "labors of love," which designates freely chosen, unalienated labour that "can be part of the worker's nature and allow self-fulfillment."[41] Because artistic labour is an expression of self and therefore comes naturally, it should not get paid, it is not work, it is self-expression, therapy, a benefit to the self that others may enjoy and benefit from retroactively, but primarily an uncontrollable, unavoidable oozing out of a self that should not be remunerated but admired. Still, as with gender, any form of essentializing definition contributes to exploitation. Other sociologists, such as Andrew Ross, define artistic labour as sacrificial labour – a form of cultural or mental labour that relies on the economic self-sacrifice of the worker.[42] It is a type of work for which workers are "inclined by training to sacrifice earnings for the opportunity to exercise their craft."[43] The fact that they find their work rewarding in other ways makes the economic sacrifice not only acceptable but expected! It turns it into a normalized practice. These gendered notions that (male) sociologists devise to discuss artistic labour therefore not only echo the initial feminization of artistic labour, they normalize artistic labour as a site of exploitation, as well as further disguise the class differences and material social relations that govern the production of art.[44] Artists may be inclined to give discounts or, if you will, be trained to make the economic sacrifice but the majority of them will have to make it up somehow, not to mention enormous debts that artists incur if they get professional training in art academies, especially in North America.[45] Furthermore, artistic labour understood as labour of love or sacrificial labour obscures the individualistic nature and the element of self-actualization characteristic for art.

The term invisible labour as devised by feminism then becomes a critical tool in unpacking the exploitation and gendered character of artistic labour. However, while feminists have criticized this predicament, the discourse of aesthetics and art theory uncritically perpetuates ideas about artistic practice as non-work or considers it in terms of decommodified labour or art's exceptional economy.[46] The question remains, however, from what class position are the ideas about the emancipatory function of such unpaid labour enunciated. Just because work benefits one or brings one self-fulfilment does not justify not rewarding it with payment. The fact that some forms of work have been relegated to leisure in such a way as to make them self-remunerative is one of the biggest ruses of capitalism; this has produced the cultural perception that doing the work of art in exchange for money is suspect. To which class does an artist in fact belong if they can afford unpaid labour without inevitably facing impoverishment? And to answer it with Ebert and Zavarzadeh's words, "The class question is the question of what is the relation to labor power. Those who have to sell their labor power to earn a living – producers of profit – are part of one class. Those who purchase human labor and take the profit from labor are part of another."[47]

In Pierre Bourdieu's terms, art relies on a disavowed or inverse economy. That is why an artist has to be established first independently and must have achieved success before they can extract a financial reward that is framed exactly as that, a reward rather than as fair compensation. Only when they have already made it can they have work commissioned. The alternative is not an option unless an artist wishes to be labelled "commercial," which immediately detracts from the value of their art. Bourdieu calls this process of establishing and legitimizing artistic value "consecration" and likens the practice to a religion that produces a belief in the symbolic value of art while concealing its economic value. The accumulation of value is based on generating symbolic capital, i.e., the process of establishing a prestige, authority, a name, or, simply, aesthetic value of an artwork or an artistic opus, and on proclamations of artistic genius. Through this circuitous consecration, the artistic value embodied in an artwork and the belief in the artistic genius therefore establish the mystique that becomes a guarantor for economic value. As a result, concurs Ross, "the name's value tends to increase with the formal estrangement of the artistic soul from the bargaining and haggling of the marketplace."[48]

Indeed, the institutional logic in the field of art connects the value of art to the artwork and not the labour of artists, even as, paradoxically, artistic subjectivity is a pivotal factor in determining the value of art. The creative talent embodied in an artist's name is an important part of the process of consecration. Once the artistic value is established and ripened, economic profits may follow.[49] In this ritual, a prominent feature of the paradox of art emerges: invisible artistic labour. Under the flags of the ideology of autonomous art and its flip side, its disavowed economy, we come back full circle to the tension between ideological and structural aspects of autonomy of art, and to issues of class character of art. The class character of art when considering (unpaid) artistic labour tells us that art-making is something that can be afforded to the propertied classes not the those that have to work to live.

I have shown that the analogy between domestic and artistic labour is an important lens through which to unravel how artistic labour is defined in a capitalist society and the function that its essentializing definition plays in its exploitation. The definition of artistic work based on the naturalization of artistic genius (i.e., an inborn trait) and supported by an idealized aesthetic autonomy still has purchase in the contemporary version of late capitalism; it is central for the oppression and exploitation of artists and the devaluation of artistic labour. But paradoxically the invisibility of labour was established precisely to elevate the fruits of artistic labour.

We can conclude that artistic labour is an economically devalued form of labour powered by the gendered ideologies of autonomy, artistic genius, and creativity as the key sociocultural mechanisms that naturalize or essentialize artists' skills and economically devalue their work. In other words, the emergence of an autonomous institution of art as a field where the work embodies creativity is the effect of the capitalist division of labour. Paradoxically it leads to an understanding and development of a social sphere where work is non-utilitarian, a free expressive activity available to gifted/talented individuals. What is more, the distinction of artistic work as the embodiment of autonomy and creative powers causes a contradiction: the exaltation of artists (which is a major difference between artistic and domestic labour) versus the economic undervaluation and exploitation of artists' labour (as with housework). The gendered association is strong enough to naturalize the unpaid nature of artistic labour but flexible enough to maintain a distinction between the selflessness of the domestic woman and the self-fullness of the artist. Both may be unpaid due to the invisibility of their labour but one is about the (gendered) norm and a recurring and predictable sameness, while the other is about uniqueness and an eminently recurring originality. Either way, the distinction impairs effective policy measures to eliminate such unpaid labour and to establish equitable welfare and social security provision for art workers. Here the dissolution of artists as workers that unfolded in the context of socialist Yugoslavia is a useful test case to expose the ideological developments surrounding invisibility. In my next chapters, I will reveal how the "deeper dispositif" (in Bologna's words) was also deeply ingrained in Yugoslav art, despite its socialist sociopolitical and economic system.

Chapter Three

The Making of Yugoslav Art Workers: Artistic Labour and the Socialist Institution of Art

In this chapter, I turn to the history of institutionalized art in the Socialist Federative Republic of Yugoslavia (SFRY) from 1945 to 1991.[1] The context of Yugoslavia is pertinent to my argument about the paradoxical status of invisible labour because it was one of the socialist countries that actually remunerated labour in all its forms, including artistic labour. And if I single out Yugoslavia from among all the socialist countries where that was also true, it is because the legacy of socialism there was inherently connected to its class origins in the proletariat (that is, propertyless working classes and peasants). The country emerged from an anti-fascist and plebeian revolution that while arguably problematic in some ways, was unique and different in light of the absence of a solidified bourgeois class. Because the country was positioned between the two Cold War blocs, it was neither Stalinist à la USSR nor liberal and capitalistic à la USA. Its ideological in-betweenness provided the adequate context to develop an idiosyncratic version of socialism, called self-management, in which art could thrive as a paid *and* creative practice for artists but also for the general populace. Here, I recount the stages of political economy and the cultural policies that instituted art as work and how that later came undone.

The socialist self-management principles and abolishment of private property as well as a commitment to emancipate human labour reconfigured the predicament of artistic labour under Yugoslav socialism. The paradox of art in socialist Yugoslavia that emerged during four and a half decades of the country's existence was animated by a larger, fundamental, and still unresolved question of the concept of art itself, especially as it was questioned in the twentieth century by the historical avant-garde movements that I discussed in chapter 1.[2] In this and the following chapters, I examine these movements' intervention and collusion with the existing ideas about the role of art in socialist societies. The understanding of the emergence of unpaid artistic labour in Yugoslav socialism is related to this fundamental tension between artistic avant-gardes and the revolutionary objective of socialism as well as global political and economic circumstances that were brought on by the October Revolution and by the First and Second World Wars. The West's sway was instrumental in this development.

Due to numerous and entwined reasons, the political project of socialist Yugoslavia reproduced the fundamental schism concerning the role of art in revolution that also defined the relationship between Marxist revolutionary politics and avant-garde art in the twentieth century. Explicitly, the question was whether art, through established formats and forms, should have the function of enlightenment and edification, or should it, by revolutionizing its own means of production, participate in the reinvention of social relations? Should art be an enlightened and perhaps provocative educator or an active participant in the establishment of a new (socialist) society? The tension between the ideals of the socialist revolution and the early twentieth-century artistic avant-gardes emerged practically from the outset and became explicit during the interwar years when the "actual needs of social revolution and cultural revolution [were] on one side, the interests of revolution in the art on the other."[4] This conflict had its particular version also in the history of postwar Yugoslav socialism.

The relationship between art and politics in the SFRY was constantly shaped by the questions about the new mode of production that would both ensure social prosperity and be different from capitalism in all respects – political participation, economy, and culture. Yugoslavia was grounded in a particular political philosophy of self-management, according to which anyone who built an alternative socialist society was considered a worker, and artists were no exception. In some interpretations, self-management strived to bring about disalienation and a new self-managed worker who would be liberated from the dehumanizing effects of the capitalist mode of production and as such would transcend the economic sphere.[5] The central goal of self-management was the emancipation of labour and the worker, to be achieved through a collective democratic ownership of the means of production, and the agency that workers would have in the decision-making process. This approach to management of the socialist means of production would consequently result in the abolition of wage labour and the division of labour.

In the polarization that defined the Cold War, and against Stalin's autocratic implementation of socialism in one country, Yugoslavia came to represent a different kind of socialism that raised hopes for the international political left. The art practices that emerged in this political option and that represented the heirs of the prewar historical avant-gardes, however, instantiated yet another split, which made them an alternative within the alternative, that is, cultural and artistic practices that advocated a more radical position with policies that the official or established left embodied in the League of Communists of Yugoslavia

(LCY). As a consequence of this struggle and position, it is an irony of history that the alternative art scene became the seedbed of precarious working conditions in the arts by the end of 1970s and during the 1980s. Importantly, however, the alternative was not a mere victim in this process; by the uncritical reproduction of ideals of art's exceptionality and autonomy the alternative also contributed in its own undoing. As such, alternative art practices stand as a case in point to explain the trajectory that turned artistic labour into invisible labour under Yugoslav socialism.

The split with Stalin and Yugoslavia's expulsion from the Cominform in 1948 represents the beginning of the era in which the Yugoslav political establishment created its own version of self-managed socialism based on public ownership and workers' management. Yugoslav socialism and its political economy was in no respect a homogenous socio-economic formation. It had several phases: (1) administrative socialism from 1945 to 1950 marked by bureaucratic centralized planned economy, (2) administrative self-managed socialism from 1950 to 1965 when planning and workers' self-management went hand in hand to secure economic and social prosperity, (3) market self-managed socialism from 1966 to 1971 when self-management was limited by market regulation and market competition, and (4) the ultimate phase of the disintegration of self-management and the restoration of capitalism from 1972 to 1989.[6] This economic development is significant to art because in this process, artists first understood as workers were transformed into artists as socialist entrepreneurs.

Concurrent with the development and transformation of the country's idiosyncratic version of self-managed socialism, its political economy, and its crises, Yugoslav cultural policy went through several phases or stages. There were three distinct cultural policy periods: the cultural policy of a centralized state (also called agitprop cultural policy[6]) from 1945 to 1953 that supported artists as workers, the decentralized cultural policy of social management from 1954 to 1974 that expanded workers' rights in culture and tested the limits of art as labour, and the cultural policy of self-management from 1974 to 1991 that resulted in the unmaking of art workers. In this chapter I discuss the first and the second periods, while the third stage or the unmaking of art workers is the subject of chapters 4 to 6. Underlying all three stages – the first being the stage of trial, the second the stage of expansion, and the third the stage of the crash of art as labour – was the concept of autonomy and art's exceptionalism. The institutionalization of art as labour was a progressive core during the first and second periods while the seeds of destruction were present.

The undermining of the socialist model of art in Yugoslavia was caused by external and internal forces. The external forces were induced by the hegemonic Western cultural model of bourgeois art and the pressure from the West to implement the liberal modernist ethos. The internal forces were provoked by a contradiction between the avant-garde demand to emancipate art from the institutional framework of autonomy and the socialist struggle to emancipate human labour. Yugoslavia created its socialist institution of art that was interesting precisely because it combined art as work and art as autonomy. While that singled out the system, it also caused its ultimate disintegration. This chapter surveys the conditions under which art as labour became possible and protected, as well as the elements that eventually contributed to the reinstatement of a capitalist and exploitative logic that rendered the labour of art invisible, paradoxically through the very idea of autonomy that had once been compatible.

Stage One: Artists as Workers

Yugoslavia developed a socialist version of a welfare state that was based on full employment.[7] The economic growth served two purposes, one "socialist" and the other "nationalist."[8] The socialist goal was to prevent mass unemployment and overcome underdevelopment while the nationalist goal was to break with economic and political dependence on foreign interests.[9] As the socialist pro-labour party, the CPY (the Communist Party of Yugoslavia), renamed LCY (the League of Communists of Yugoslavia) after 1952, legitimized the need for economic growth that was based in rapid industrialization and de-agrarianization of the country with the pledge to raise the living standard and secure subsistence for the entire population. Darko Suvin has noted that "both for pragmatic success as well as for steps toward utopia, all countries not having undergone a thorough bourgeois revolution found it imperiously necessary to rush into industrialization as the engine of urbanization and of a general rise in the standard of living."[10] Yugoslavia was no different. Significantly, all these developments included artists and contributed to creating an impressive cultural infrastructure.

The first period taking place during the early postwar years was a centralized state cultural policy combined with state-controlled and funded cultural activities (1945–53). During this period, all cultural institutions were nationalized and became part of public services. By expanding the modest institutional system that was established on the territory during the Austro-Hungarian rule and the Kingdom of Yugoslavia, the socialist government after the Second World War immensely enlarged the material foundations for cultural and art production in the SFRY. There were no privately owned cultural institutions in socialist Yugoslavia. Along with other social services in the sphere of reproduction, such as health, education, child and senior care, culture was, argues Močnik, also a "more or less non-commodified system of production and circulation" of public goods, which nevertheless "still had their 'price' (i.e., they had a value expressed in money) – a recognition that the law of value had not been abolished and was still functioning within the self-managed socialist society."[11] Similar to the Western European postwar cultural policy trends, the Yugoslav government understood art as an important element of cultural development and treated art as a public good.

All activities in art and culture and people working in culture were dependent on public funding. Until 1948, cultural institutions were financed directly through a special line in the federal budget. After 1948, each republic had its own budget through which ministries of culture and education in each of the six republics financed all cultural institutions based on the number of jobs or positions, that is, the number of employees.[12] Several versions of what can be considered a ministry for culture took on the role of organizing and administrating cultural production. The federal Ministry of Education (*Ministarstvo prosvete Vlade FNRJ*) took on the role of organizing culture from 1945 to 1946. Mostly it assessed the war damage, re-established prewar cultural institutions, and created new revolutionary cultural institutions. From 1946 to 1948, a federal Committee for Culture and Art (*Komitet za kulturu i umetnost Vlade FNRJ*) was in charge of implementing the cultural policy of the agitprop apparatus across the country. After the break with the Cominform, the committee was succeeded by a federal Ministry of Science and Culture (*Ministarstvo za nauku i kulturu Vlade FNRJ*) from 1948 to 1950 and by a federal Council for Science and Culture (*Savet za nauku i kulturu Vlade FNRJ*) from 1950 to 1953. Socialist authorities also organized the market for artworks by establishing policies and funds for the acquisition of artworks.[13] Various federal councils and cultural councils in the republics commissioned or purchased artworks.

The SFRY recognized artists as workers and as an integral element of the new socialist society, which included assuring their economic and welfare protection. Artistic work became understood as labour. Authorities established a number of centralized federal associations of professional artists (literary and visual art, music, theatre, film). They were funded by the state and their members acquired certain rights, such as tax exemptions, working studios and apartments, subsidized social insurance, and retirement contributions. The socialist labour policies establishing full employment coincided with the institutional framework of the autonomous arts that enabled art as a professional endeavour. This overlap ensured not only the emergence of art workers but also the practice of art as an economically viable form of professional work. Cultural policy guaranteed favourable working conditions for professional artists and strengthened the capacities for cultural production in terms of infrastructure. Moreover, this democratic dimension translated into access to culture, which enabled art appreciation and cultural engagement for the majority of people in their everyday life.

During the first period, artistic labour was integrated into the political economy predominantly in the form of full-time employment in cultural organizations, art academies, and high schools for applied arts. Art workers were also employed in primary and high schools, publishing houses, newspapers, and in radio and television. A very small percentage were not employees but operated as freelancers.[14] In order to protect the latter's economic rights as workers, authorities passed regulation prescribing author fees, the acquisition of artworks, and authorizing social security for freelance art workers. As early as 1946, authorities also passed a directive about author fees for writers, poets, scholars, and translators that later included fees for filmmakers and musicians.[15] While waiting for federal authorities to prescribe fees for other artistic disciplines, in 1947 the Ministry for Education in Croatia passed a separate directive about fees for theatre artists, which specified the amount of payment for a variety of typical artistic work, from playing a main part to being an extra or background actor.[16] In 1952, authorities finally added a contract ensuring social insurance for freelance writers, poets, and film production workers (screen writers, film directors etc.).[17] In 1955, this was extended to other art workers.[18]

In the immediate postwar years of SFRY, the interwar debate surrounding the avant-gardes and the role of art in the revolution came to a head in Yugoslavia. During the early 1950s, the heirs of the historical avant-garde movements emerged as the alternative in opposition to the doctrine of socialist realism and apolitical modernism. Some artists argued that revolutionary art needed to establish its own Marxist-leftist vision of art that should be aligned neither with socialist-realist doctrine nor with European modernism. These important voices in the Yugoslav cultural sphere advocated for "the construction of a uniquely Yugoslav left-leaning art."[19] Bojana Videkanić underscores that in the mid 1950s, writer Miroslav Krleža emphasized the importance of an "antifascist, anti-imperial discourse based on Marxist aesthetics" in building the Yugoslav version of socialism and its culture, which "meant rejecting the bourgeois aesthetic as well as the prescriptive, propagandistic art of the Soviets."[20] The doctrine of USSR socialist realism did not take root in Yugoslavia and the CPY did not embrace it as an official normative aesthetics or cultural policy.[21] After the Tito–Stalin split, the CPY relinquished the policy of socialist realism and declared a freedom of artistic expression, thereby, opening the way to a liberalized socialist cultural policy.

The heirs of the historical avant-garde art movements during the 1950s, for example Exat 51, who were the initiators of an alternative vision of art in socialist Yugoslavia, argued for a rejection of the traditional Western idea of the artist. Avant-gardist initiatives representative of alternative art, such as Exat 51, were concerned with the reintegration of art and life and with the articulation of the artist's role in society. They possessed optimism about building a new socialist culture in Yugoslavia. Exat 51 envisioned for the new

Yugoslav society a new type of socially engaged creative production based on a synthesis of all fine arts that would go beyond autonomous art objects intended for aesthetic contemplation and would blend artistic and political tendencies to actively build the material culture of the new socialist society.[22] For example, one of the most prominent features of the group Exat 51 was its opposition to the autonomy of artistic practice articulated in the group's manifesto, which declared "no difference between so-called pure and so-called applied art."[23] Exat 51 exemplified a break with the bourgeois understanding of art by demanding a "synthesis of all fine arts" and a different social role for art in the political, economic, and cultural transformation of Yugoslav society. Kršić argues that the avant-garde ethos of Exat 51's program was an indication that in Yugoslavia during the 1950s the "main conflict, therefore, did not take place between party dictated socialist realism and (individualistic, freedom espousing, that is, authentically 'artistic') modernism," but rather between the "bourgeois understanding of art" and an avant-garde, politically engaged art that embraced (geometrical, constructivist type of) abstract art.[24] The cultural phenomenon of Exat 51 signalled a possibility of "socially engaged abstract modern art" that would recognize not only that art and artists have an important role in the development of socialist society, but also that "they themselves were a project of social change and a radical transformation of the role and function of art in society."[25]

Attempts by Yugoslav artists to steer the understanding of artistic labour and the function of art away from the dominant bourgeois model of institutionalized art did, in fact, rely on the legacy of the interwar historical avant-garde art movements and their questioning of the autonomy of art. In Rastko Močnik's words, these attempts to revitalize the historical avant-garde movement's attack on the institution of art in the second half of the twentieth century "did produce certain features of a 'revolutionary' conjuncture: they were connected with the issues of their times, and 'politicised' in a way; they were socially innovative, and experimented with new organizational forms with which to support artistic, cultural, and generally symbolic practices."[26]

The questioning of the role of art in Yugoslav society had consequences for how artists saw their role and artistic labour. The Yugoslav political establishment was deeply engaged in building a political and economic alternative to capitalism; however its transformation of art as labour collided with the ideas of the autonomy of art as promulgated by the tradition of bourgeois culture and the revitalized power and influence of Western cultural and institutional models and networks. While Miroslav Krleža's ideas "provided an opportunity to create a potentially progressive alternative form of art production," hegemonic and seemingly apolitical formal modernism from the West nevertheless "became increasingly influential,"[27] not just in the realm of culture but also in terms of political economy.

Susan Woodward emphasizes that the LCY, after its split with Stalin, entered into "a Faustian bargain" with the capitalist West. "It [Yugoslavia] would maintain a strong military capacity independent of Moscow, including a critical role in defense of NATO's southern flank against possible Soviet movement west, in exchange for Western economic assistance and membership in global economic organizations such as the International Monetary Fund (IMF), with its access to World Bank loans, association with European trading blocs (the EFTA [European Free Trade Association] and the EC [European Commission]), and by 1965, the General Agreement on Tariffs and Trade (GATT)."[28] The defiance of Stalin and the strategic position of the country between the two Cold War blocs granted socialist Yugoslavia access to economic assistance and trade, but it was a Faustian bargain because it compromised the consistency of domestic socialist policies by relying on Western markets and capital.[29]

Along the lines of the Faustian bargain that defined the development of Yugoslav political economy (as a socialism that was paradoxically supported by a capitalist West), the rejection of the socialist realism doctrine and ensuing liberalization opened the doors for the liberal modernist ideology, which at that time was being forcefully imported by US cultural diplomacy.

Despite ideas to transform the organization of cultural production and its role in self-managed socialism, the organization of cultural institutions in Yugoslavia "was not changed to any great extent," maintained Majstorović, "but their activity was adjusted and geared to the new tasks."[30] The task was to create a Yugoslav culture, to democratize cultural production, and to make creative labour part of everyday life. Put differently, the organization of art production in the SFRY structurally resembled other European countries whereby "culture was identified with civilized habits and behavior copied from the European bourgeoisie."[31] In other words, the organization of art production during socialism was modelled after the institutional tradition of Western bourgeois culture. For instance, the organization of visual arts was fashioned on the French model,[32] wherein the art academies controlled and regulated everything from the artists' training to arts education and government commissions. The situation was similar in the performing arts and classical music.

Still, this embracing of traditional bourgeois cultural organizations such as theatres, ballets, and operas was not straightforward. There were several distinctive elements of what we can call the socialist institution of art, among them visual art cooperatives. These were established to help visual artists with art supplies and services that they needed to produce artworks, such as frames, moulds, and screen-printing facilities. By 1956, there were such cooperatives of visual artists in Slovenia, Croatia, Serbia, and in Bosnia and Herzegovina. Most of them were retail cooperatives and some employed collectives of applied art workers. Most had shops or galleries selling works of applied arts and visual arts. Visual arts cooperatives were under the jurisdiction of the state as economic units and were burdened with relatively high taxes, which resulted in the rise of activities that increased revenue and affected the initial mission to provide services for visual artists. They often had to resort to providing graphic design services for other companies or cultural organizations or to helping organize larger fairs or expos and so on. This felt to them like selling out. The central association of visual artists attempted to convince the authorities to implement a special law for visual arts cooperatives, which would lower their taxes at the same time as it would reify art's exceptionalism, a contradiction in terms.[33] Some art workers regarded cooperatives as the business branches of the centralized associations of visual artists. Others considered them as entities that should serve the needs of art workers and help them in securing a stable income based on the sales of artworks. Due to economic pressures and internal disputes among visual artists, both cooperatives in Ljubljana and Belgrade went bankrupt and were reformed or abolished by the early 1960s. Only the cooperatives in Zagreb and Sarajevo continued to operate. These are the perfect example of how difficult it is to think about the economy of art unburdened from Western ideals of art as an elitist practice. In this case, the progressive model of art cooperatives was undermined by financial exigencies on the one hand, and by the artists' resentment over the co-optation of their art for instrumental reasons of subsistence. They themselves were under the influence of Western concepts of autonomy and freedom rather than understanding their own art as a social practice for the new society.

Another unique feature of what made the Yugoslav institution of art socialist, in contrast to the conventional art of theatres, operas, ballets, libraries, museums, and galleries, was a vast network of cultural associations, called associational culture (*društvena kultura*), that embodied the ethos of the amateur mass culture. These cultural associations included a range of activities from the creative spending of leisure time to the preservation of folk traditions and experimental art production. The network of cultural associations was a particularly important aspect of socialist democratization of culture and was intended to raise the cultural and civilizational levels of society as well as ensure mass access to cultural production and appreciation. To enable public participation in culture, numerous culture houses (*kulturni dom*), where a variety of activities of cultural associations took place, were built across Yugoslavia. There were three types of socialist cultural associations: professional artists' associations (with regular public funding), independent art groups (with project funding), and the amateur culture associations that sponsored either cultural-educational or artistic activities for non-professionals and youth. The associations of artists (poets, writers, visual artists, performers, musicians, etc.) and art groups represented the professional sphere of art production in the SFRY. While the realm of associational culture was important for the development of many progressive ideas about art in the socialist society, it also unfortunately became the site for the mushrooming of precarious labour conditions. This was because the mainstream bourgeois art institutions were economically prioritized in the socialist system.

Researchers of Eastern European art often identify the radical art practices in postwar socialist societies that were not produced in the mainstream art institutions as *unofficial* art, or art outside/beyond the state system. Such designations are inaccurate in relation to socialist Yugoslavia. The consequences of the conflict with Cominform gave Yugoslavia the possibility of developing a new, alternative version of socialist society, due to which, oppositional movements were able to form much more explicitly than in the countries of the Eastern Bloc. Considering the organization of the cultural system in the SFRY, radical art practices were an integral element of the institutional design for art production, that is, the socialist institution of art. Often artists would work both in the public institutions and in the cultural associations. Ješa Denegri underlines that alternative art production "does not justify identifying the alternative route on the Yugoslav art scene with the phenomena of political and cultural dissidence such as were manifested in other parts of the real-socialist bloc, nor is the alternative route the opposite member in the binomial official/nonofficial art."[34] Socialist authorities in Yugoslavia did not ban these practices but created special organizational and legal structures, such as the network of cultural associations where the production of art by professional art workers, students, and amateurs took place.

Stage Two: Testing the Limits of Art as Labour

The second period engendered *pluralistic tolerance*, a specific trait of cultural policy that enabled an aesthetic pluralism by which authorities tolerated political critique to a certain extent, while the LCY maintained both a tacit ideological control over – and financial provision for – cultural and intellectual production.[35] The LCY proclaimed freedom of expression and artistic autonomy in the mid 1950s, an ironic twist for many who associate socialism with an autocratic regime. In conjunction with the rejection of socialist realism and the acceptance of cultural influences from the West, this attitude opened the door for the development of what Sveta Lukić termed "socialist aestheticism" (*socijalistički estetizam*)[36] – a modernist aesthetics represented by the mainstream traditional art institutions and supported by the liberal faction within the LCY. Art historian Lazar Trifunović, who elaborated and expanded the term beyond literature, noted that while socialist aestheticism "was sufficiently 'modern' to appease the general complex of 'openness toward the world'" it was also "traditional enough ... to satisfy the new bourgeois taste based in social conformism, and inert enough to fit the myth of a happy and unified community."[37] However, for the artists "it meant art's separation from social issues and reality."[38] Socialist aestheticism signalled a diversification in the field of cultural production where one faction of artists "sped through the process of 'revolution' to bourgeois art."[39] Nevertheless, due to pluralistic tolerance, the atmosphere of socialist aestheticism coexisted with more radical art movements and initiatives of the alternative art, which continued the political project of the historical avant-gardes to unify art and life, and to question the autonomy of art.

Until the mid 1960s, the coexistence of mainstream art promoting socialist aestheticism and alternative art promoting avant-garde ideas was a hallmark of pluralistic tolerance. After the social upheavals and student protests of 1968, however, a separation between these two cultural spheres emerged, which manifested itself both in economic and ideological terms. While external international political pressures on Yugoslavia's economic model were a central impediment to its existence, it needs to be emphasized that new forms of class struggle and the rising power of LYC oligarchy (what Suvin calls politocracy) played an equally important role in the reversal of emancipatory potentials of self-managed socialism as a political alternative. The issue was not just the division of labour but also, the commodification of labour and class stratification.[40] The problem of the emergence of class stratification arose early in the SFRY and was notoriously detected by Milovan Djilas in the mid 1950s, when he postulated the existence of a "new class," which swiftly led to his expulsion from power.[41] The Djilas affair was an indication of a phenomenon that Suvin terms "classophobia" or a denial of class that became apparent in particular during the mid 1960s.[42] Due to internal economic and political transformations as well as external geopolitical pressures, socialist prosperity in Yugoslavia was in crisis by the end of the 1960s.[43] This affected political and economic conflicts among the people, including cultural workers, students, intellectuals, and the factions within the LCY. Because tendencies of class exploitation and domination existed in socialist Yugoslavia, the social function of art reproduced a familiar structural position: it affirmed the status quo rather than brought about its reversal, or, better yet, a radical change of the class culture.

In search of a different kind of socialism to modernize the country and drawn to fashion this modernization according to a growing Western model of liberal democracy where art ostensibly remained autonomous in relation to politics, Yugoslav cultural policy embraced an autonomy of art that in turn limited avant-garde attempts to transform the social function of art. During the second period cultural policy recognized the economic needs of art workers but the attempts to radically redefine the institutional framework for art and its function in socialist society were limited and constrained by external (Western influence) and internal factors (opposition to the avant-garde).

The second period of decentralized cultural policy of "social management" (*društbeno upravljanje*) was characterized by the implementation of self-management as the alternative socialist system (1953–74). The first half of this period was economically characterized by the highest degree of economic growth, rise of employment, and the standard of living in general. This period witnessed an expansion and elaboration of policies for artistic labour but underlying issues related to autonomy were further amplified due to issues in the political economy. The mid-sixties (1963–5) were the turning point when the economic reform introduced market elements into the previously planned political economy of Yugoslavia. After 1965, economic planning was constrained while market regulation took precedence. In the long term, this impacted the transformation of art workers into socialist entrepreneurs.

While scholars like to explain capitalism by equating it with a market economy, and socialism by equating it with a planned or command economy, specialists on self-management point out that the juxtaposition between capitalism and socialism should not be mistakenly translated as the opposition between the market and the plan.[44] The use of market regulation in certain areas is possible if market competition does not function as a generalized and dominant principle of social organization.[45] In Yugoslavia, for a period, the balance between the plan, self-management, and the market contributed to social, cultural, and economic prosperity. This was particularly the case during "the twenty glorious years" that lasted until 1965, and when Yugoslav society witnessed an exceptional economic growth, a swift urbanization, and a "development of both [a] working and intellectual class."[46] A territory with long imperial and colonial oppression, the SFRY became the site of radical social and political transformation that turned an agrarian land into a relatively well-developed industrialized country, increased the standard of living, and fostered a vibrant cosmopolitan culture.[47] In this context, culture was not a mere commodity and artistic labour was recognized as paid work.

The LCY's inability to give up the idea of art as "an educator and a decent, illuminating friend"[48] impaired the transcendence of the bourgeois notion of art's autonomy. Moreover, due to the pressure to create its own version of art for Yugoslav socialism, the proto-bourgeois and the liberal factions of the LCY supported the idea of autonomous national art as a sign of liberalization and of a progressive society. "The seemingly neutral, autonomous, individualistic character of high modernism appealed to the Yugoslav state because it embarked on incorporating liberal political ideas into its self-management system."[49] Despite the LCY's commitment to finding a program of alternative self-managed socialism in Yugoslavia, the chances that artists would get the opportunity to implement a radical alternative vision of art and its social function became limited.

The initial phase of recognizing artists as workers appeared to support the avant-garde critique of the institution of art and, through the democratization of access to art, began a process of reintegrating art and life. A more radical transformation of the bourgeois institutional model of art was stalemated due to the unoriginality of the socialist institutionalization of art, which preserved a traditional understanding of its autonomy; it changed the rules without changing the game. The socialist welfare state took art away from the commercial pressure of the capitalist market and placed it under its wing. This curbed the avant-garde attack on art's traditional means of production and propelled what Marcuse termed the affirmative character of culture.[50] In the Yugoslav case, this was encapsulated in the phenomenon of socialist aestheticism.

By organizing the framework and financial support for art institutions and the associational culture, socialist authorities not only achieved a democratization of culture, increased literacy, and elevated cultural habits of the people, but also provided access to art production. The funding provided for associational culture thus enabled a germination of experimental artistic practice. While the socialist authorities supported the development of amateur mass culture, they simultaneously and through the same mechanism funded experimental art practices. For instance, an impressive production of experimental films and auteur films in the SFRY emerged due to a network of amateur cinema clubs in many cities all over the country.[51] Similarly, the production of modern and experimental dance was based in the realm of associational culture. As I discussed elsewhere, this had less favourable consequences for the professionalization of modern dance since modern dance was seen as a rival art form to classic ballet.[52]

Another impetus for development and financial support for art practices was the student and youth alliances, such as the League of Socialist Youth of Yugoslavia (LSYY)[53] and the Yugoslav Alliance of Students (SAY).[54] The organization of youth and student leisure time and its embodiment in student cultural centres was an important aspect of the socialist institution of art and funded through the university system in the major Yugoslav cities. One of the first student centres was Tribina Mladih in Novi Sad established in 1956; the Student Centre in Zagreb (*Studentski centar u Zagrebu*) opened in 1959 was another venue for non-mainstream practice that took place in *Galerija SC, Komorna pozornica (Teatar &TD)*. The Student Cultural Centre (SKC) Belgrade (*Studentski kulturni centar Beograd*) was opened in 1972 as a concession by the socialist authorities to students after mass student protests in 1968; in Ljubljana *Disko Študent* (later known as *Disko FV*) and ŠKUC, both founded in 1972, became important venues in the 1980s.[55] These channels and their infrastructure secured important support and funding for alternative art. For instance, student cultural centres operated art galleries, experimental theatres, cinemas, etc. Alternative art in Yugoslavia, therefore, emerged out of the vast network of associational culture and student/youth organizations. It competed with the art production of mainstream cultural institutions, which reinforced bourgeois ideas of autonomy of art and consequently established functions of art as realms for aesthetic contemplation. Despite alternative art's link to the historical avant-garde, it was not unsusceptible to the structural and ideological effects of the autonomy of art, which, in the second stage, became an underlying current.

The funding of culture was, however, subordinate to general fiscal concerns, and authorities determined the amounts and fixed the percentage to be allocated to culture and the arts. While self-management was introduced in factories and retail enterprises/firms in the first stage, social management became implemented in the realm of public services – culture, health, education, and so on. The workers' collectives in public services still had no say about the amount of funds except on paper. The funding remained constrained and top-down even though the terms for its implementation changed. "Social services were to be financed by firms (through direct grants, local taxation, their provision within the firm, or contract) so that expenditure on nonproductive activities would be governed by the limits of achieved productivity."[56] In the cultural sector, this meant that cultural workers did not manage culture economically since the funding was a matter of administrative budget distribution. Although culture also remained under ideological supervision,[57] cultural institutions had more professional autonomy in decisions regarding their artistic programs than in the previous stage. This autonomy would become a double-edged sword because on the one hand, it gave the semblance of pluralistic tolerance, while on the other, it could be revoked at any point. While at this point, this did not necessarily have economic consequences, it later would.

The second stage of cultural policy was administratively very complex as the SFRY implemented social – not state – ownership, self-management, and decentralization. The territories of each republic and the autonomous provinces were divided into communes that included one or more urban centres. There was a federal government body responsible for culture,[58] but the operational execution was in the hands of government bodies in each of the republics, that is, cultural secretariats and cultural chambers or councils. Despite the introduction of a communal system that aimed to organize the entire country territorially (as a network of communes) and not based on nationalities, cultural affairs during this period were administered by federal, republic, or provincial secretariats (i.e., transformed ministries of culture and education) and chambers of education and culture (*svet za prosveto in kuturo*). Secretariats ensured the enforcement of laws and legislative prescriptions and social plans, while they did not decide on the amount of financing of cultural institutions or activities. Chambers discussed problems pertaining to culture, adopted recommendations, and passed laws together with the general republic chambers (*republiški svet*). People working in the cultural sector, including artists, elected the majority of the chambers' deputies. This allowed more professional autonomy for culture.

Communal and republic cultural councils and secretariats administratively ran cultural policy while funding was secured by communal and republic budgets and special cultural funds were financed thorough specific taxes. There were three types of cultural funds: for advancement of cultural activities, for film, and for publishing. These special funds were instituted in 1957. The financing of cultural activities was therefore only indirectly connected to the federal level because the federal Fund for Cultural Advancement required that each republic create its own fund. The monies for the federal Fund for Cultural Advancement earmarked for each republic fund came from taxes from authors' rights fees. Redistribution of the monies of this fund was in the jurisdiction of communes, provinces, and republics. Some, but not all, republics passed special laws on the financing of culture, for instance in Croatia and Serbia. The monies for film and publishing were allocated based on special income taxes on cinematography and publishing enterprises. The funding for radio and television came mostly from subscriptions. The fund for the advancement of cultural activities was supposed to financially support cultural programs and projects and enhance the cultural offerings in each republic and both provinces. However, as cultural policy experts point out, it often performed the role of a reserve fund that covered the deficits of cultural institutions. Many cultural institutions struggled financially because the funding was dependent on the economic power of the commune (*skupnost/zajednica*), a generic term that corresponded both to city or town-level municipality.[59]

Yugoslav socialist authorities established a vast public cultural infrastructure in all six republics and both autonomous provinces that employed the majority of art workers and supported independent artistic labour. In the 1950s the number of cultural organizations, such as cinemas, libraries, museums, and art galleries doubled while the number of cultural and art associations increased five times. For example, Slovenia established 154 new cultural organizations, 95 of which were created by 1973[60] while Macedonia perhaps witnessed the most dramatic change, from 5 artists and 6 writers in 1945 to 105 artists and 120 writers in 1972, from two to eight theatres, from zero to eighteen museums, as well as the establishment of the first philharmonic orchestra, an opera, an academy of music and drama, a national and university library and so on, all in the same period from 1945 to 1972.[61] What is more, entire branches of cultural production emerged, such as cinematography, which did not exist before the Second World War.[62] Film production, including cinemas, publishing (of books, newspaper, magazines), including bookshops and printing houses, were organized as enterprises. In this respect, they can be considered a socialist version of cultural industry. Another element in this system was the entertainment industry, i.e., record companies (*Jugoton, Diskoton, Založba kaset in plošč RTLJ*) as well as concert halls. Radio and television were publicly owned. Although the main sources of revenue were public subsidies and mandatory subscriptions, radio and television also operated commercially and thus were considered "semi-commercial media enterprises."[63]

The second stage of cultural policy saw a rise in the number of professional art workers and an expansion of the access to art appreciation and art production in addition to an increase in international cultural exchanges organized either through state treaties or direct contacts between Yugoslav and foreign art organizations. Numerous international art events, such as festivals, took place and cultural life in larger urban areas became extremely vivid and cosmopolitan. Additionally, Yugoslav artists took part in renowned art festivals, exhibitions, biennials, and other art events across Europe and beyond.

The first stage had implemented minimal fees and social security for artists. In the second stage this became prevalent for the majority of art workers, especially freelance ones. While the majority of art workers were employed, artistic labour done independently was regulated as a form of autonomous or "traditional independent work."[64] The term refers to specialized freelance professionals, such as lawyers, athletes, and architects, who were socially protected by professional associations, such as guilds, chambers, or, in the case of the SFRY, through associations of professional artists and cultural workers in the fields of music, literature, visual arts, and film.[65] In the SFRY, laws and decrees were passed between 1955 and 1966 that regulated and protected artistic labour as independent work.[66] The funds for social security were paid from taxes on income from authors' rights.[67] The decrees pertained to social security, a retirement and disability provision for freelance art workers, and instituted subsidized social security for the independent labour of artists. They provided freelance art workers with similar protections as those enjoyed by employed workers. For instance, the independent art worker was covered for sick leave, pregnancy/maternity leave, disability insurance, and so on.[68] After 1965, when the jurisdiction and funds collected through taxes on author's rights were transferred from federal government to the six republics, Serbia, Croatia, and Slovenia regulated social security for freelance art workers via contracts between Social Security Institutes and artists' associations or cultural communities.[69] In the case of Slovenia and Croatia, funds were guaranteed via special laws either directly from the general budget or through the budget of cultural communities.[70] While Bosnia and Herzegovina, Macedonia, and Montenegro had no formal regulation regarding social security for artists, Montenegro financed the insurance directly from the republic's budget.[71] Public funds such as grants, fellowships, special honorary retirement pensions, and advanced purchases were also dedicated directly to independent artists.[72]

Creativity and labour were entwined because authorities understood culture as "a wide range of opportunities for the expression and confirmation of the human personality in all spheres of public activity."[73] In the words of the founder of cultural policy research in Yugoslavia, this implied a "reintegration of the hitherto alienated and divided spheres of human activity," and an aim to supplant "historically conditioned division of culture from the life, work and interests of the broadest strata of the people."[74] Yugoslav self-management's stance concerning the emancipation of human labour and creativity was related to the historical avant-gardes' aspiration to change the function of art in society.

Another example epitomizing left-oriented alternative art practice regarding artistic labour in socialist Yugoslavia came from the international art movement New Tendencies and an eponymous biennial exhibition that took place from 1961 to 1973 in the Zagreb Gallery of Contemporary Art. New Tendencies is another case of an art movement that was supported by a state-financed gallery but was "much too radical to be officially endorsed by the League of Communists of Yugoslavia."[75] Continuing the legacy of historical avant-gardes, this movement "was united by the desire *to abolish the artist as creative genius* and replace him with or her with the notion of visual researcher."[76] Based on Marx's criticism of commodity fetishism and "rooted in a deep democratic idealism," New Tendencies rejected the "artist as a producer of commodities for the art market."[77] Its aesthetics and politics developed in relation to ideas of participation, collectivism, science, and technology, envisioned viewers as co-producers of artworks, and thought of them as users.[78]

Nevertheless, the way in which this avant-garde ideal to transform the social role of art was implemented in Yugoslav cultural policy was through full employment that espoused a productivist logic specific to Fordism, that was in turn extended to traditional institutions of art (museums, galleries, theatres, operas, ballets, philharmonics etc.). The overlap of socialist labour policies and the institutional framework of autonomous art resulted in the artist as an employee. By securing funds for art projects, remuneration, and social security for art workers, cultural policy regulation acknowledged artistic labour as work that deserved payment and protection thus turning it from invisible to visible labour. The adoption of the Fordist paradigm based on standardization of production, stability of employment, and workers' consumption, however, limited the actual transformation of artistic labour into a form of emancipated labour.

Cultural policy regulation during the second stage secured artists' rights as workers; however, the decision about access to these rights was in the hands of professional artists associations and based on aesthetic criteria (artist training/ education, number of exhibitions, publication, performances, etc.). The artists had to demonstrate professional qualifications based on these aesthetic criteria, which in turn permitted access to workers' rights. Socialist labour policies and the aesthetic ideology of art concurred and were aligned during the second stage. Marxist ideals democratized artistic labour and mostly protected it from exploitation, but the social role of art remained caught in the structure of the autonomous artistic sphere and maintained its central pillars – the work of art, the figure of the artists, and aesthetic judgment. While socialist authorities championed culture as the cornerstone of self-management, they institutionalized it as a form of employment that was constrained by institutional rules of art and its separation in the autonomous social sphere. This situation created favourable working conditions for art workers but underlying were the seeds of undoing art as labour.

Culture was thus "a system of specialized and professionalized social activities," in which "workers cease living *for* creative work and begin to live *off* it," argued Zagorka Golubović.[79] In other words, artistic practices were confined to the autonomous artistic sphere wherein artistic labour was performed as a type of specialized professional work. The bourgeois idea of the autonomy of art was not renounced. Art workers did not give up their special social position and claim to genius, even though ideas of liberation of creative labour beyond the division of labour and institutional constraints of art were advocated by critical voices. One such articulation was offered by Golubović when she defined what a true self-management society in respect to art and culture entails: "All professional activities and professional groups must be eliminated, as institutionalized units of society and conditions must be created for human labour to become truly a *universal activity*." The latter was qualified in Marxian terms to mean the prospect for individuals to take on any number of activities for which they have talent and an elimination of "social and class considerations in the division of labor which bind the individual to a single activity for his entire life."[80] Moreover, Golubović also argued against the separation of social spheres. "Free associations" should therefore be created in such a way that they would "reintegrate the currently fragmented activities and spheres of life, such as politics, economics, art," thereby enabling an individual "to cease to be a partial being (*homo oeconomicus*, *homo politicus*, artist, etc.)."[81]

One of the main issues in developing an alternative social function of art in socialist Yugoslavia proved to be the bourgeois understanding of art, that is, the autonomous status that separates art from other social spheres. This viewpoint was paradoxically replicated in the dogmatic Marxist views concerning the base (or infrastructure) and superstructure. According to this view, culture is a part of the superstructure that pertains to the spiritual and not the material aspects of social organization. In her critique of this narrow and schematic understanding of culture in orthodox Marxist aesthetics, Golubović noted that "the concept of 'superstructure' holds culture to mean exclusively the objectivized attainments of mental activities," which positions culture as "secondary to infrastructure."[82] Culture, therefore, had only "a secondary, reflexive influence" as if material and spiritual aspects can be divorced.[83] While the labour of artists was paid and protected it was nevertheless considered an autonomous exceptional practice. Compartmentalizing art into the spiritual sphere means its separation from everyday life (autonomy of art). It also means that artistic labour becomes invisible and understood as non-labour. Moreover, autonomy of art obscures the class dimensions of art, and this was also the case in socialist Yugoslavia.

The effects of class divisions came in different forms: one of them was a growing opposition between available sources for alternative and mainstream art production. There was a constant discrepancy between the amount of funding dedicated to traditional cultural institutions and the funding for art production within the context of associational culture. The economic discrepancy overlapped with the division between mainstream institutions fostering socialist aestheticism and alternative art. This incongruity translated into a difference in the economic position of employed and freelance art workers – the key anchor for class division. Alternative art production, predominantly situated in the context of associational culture, was socially and economically unequal and disproportionately funded compared to traditional art institutions.[84] While scholars may interpret this division in cultural terms and interpret it as an opposition between official versus non-official or institutional versus non-institutional, or even by qualifying alternative art production as dissident art, such qualifications are misguided since practically the entire cultural production of the SFRY was funded via state appropriations; in economic terms there was no beyond-the-state redistributed funding (as there is no beyond-the-market in capitalist liberal democracies). The funding and organization of the socialist institution of art and art production was nonetheless unequal and disadvantageous for alternative art. For example, while art organizations, such as theatres, had actors and directors employed and production costs secured because they were a fixed annual budget item, independent theatre art groups had to secure project funding by applying for project money from cultural communities.

While cultural policy and ideological struggles in the cultural sphere during this period cannot simply be conflated with the political economy, these struggles were certainly affected by developments and crisis in the Yugoslav economy. For example, the policies of democratization of art lacked solutions for the ever-growing new generation of art workers. Moreover, some art workers did not want to work in the state art institutions that cherished socialist aestheticisms. Instead, they were more interested in the transformation of art and the expansion of the idea of emancipating artists' labour and human creativity beyond bourgeois art, artistic genius, and commodification of the traditional art object.

While the LCY insisted on the integrated development of Yugoslavia as a whole (that is, richer republics would help develop the entire country without slowing down their respective development), they abandoned this integrative and equitable plan after 1963. This coincided with the introduction of market reform in 1965. Throughout the 1960s the governments of the six republics quarrelled over investment and economic policies, which in the long run affected the rise of nationalistic identification in lieu of workers' solidarity and led to the formation of a nationalist ruling class in each republic. The top-down institutionalization of workers' participation and the subordination of the economy to market principles turned out to be detrimental for an emancipatory anti-capitalist project and the promise of new popular democracy based in social ownership. This was unsurprisingly also detrimental for the understanding of art as labour.

The internal social conflicts of 1965 became more visible due to LCY's decisions to redistribute economic surpluses and control over social ownership, which contradicted the principles of self-management. Social ownership promised new dimensions of popular democracy; however the political potential was "sapped by the apparatuses of social management," which Močnik likens to the contemporary category of "governance."[85] In the words of Suvin, by the end of the 1960s a full reversal "from going toward to going away from socialist justice and communist emancipation as well as economic well-being" took place, which "can only be explained in terms of a conflict of class interests between the growing oligarchy and self-government of the people."[86] After the culmination of the crisis in 1968, the coalition between the oligarchic politocracy, the working class, and the intellectuals was broken and self-management was marginalized.[87] While this point by Suvin is important, one should not lose sight of the larger geopolitical issues and Western pressures on Yugoslav economy.

The economic reform advanced the phenomenon of consumer culture in socialist Yugoslavia, a development that would transform the understanding of art from a site of production to a site of consumption. In his study of consumer culture, Branislav Dimitrijević nevertheless emphasizes that "left critical positions (mostly under the influence of the Frankfurt School) continuously recognized 'consumerist mentality' as an example of antisocialist behaviour, as a product of capitalist alienation and as a threat to the development of socialism."[88] Having recognized in the early 1960s that, as one philosopher of the neo-Marxist Praxis School put it, "forms of both economic and political alienation still exist in Yugoslav society,"[89] these left critical groups represented the alternative within an alternative Yugoslav socialism. They were the ones that articulated a leftist critique of Yugoslav self-management during the early 1960s to further the struggle for a self-managed socialist emancipation. Along similar lines and resisting the onset of consumerism, a number of art practices also articulated these positions: for example, the group OHO, or a similarly impactful group in the realm of theatre called Pekarna (Bakery) led by Lado Kralj.[90] However, the emancipatory aims of the Yugoslav political project got undermined by the ascent of liberal market economy precepts that were gradually imposed by the West. Due to dependence on Western markets and capital in combination with conflicts arising from the uneven economic development of the six republics comprising the country and a widening gap between the theory and the practice of self-management, a social and political crisis was unavoidable.

The dilemma over which route Yugoslav society should take, one going toward socialist consumerism, or the alternative, going toward a really participatory democracy that entailed "a radical democratization and later the withering away of the Party,"[91] was resolved by opting for the former. Lev Kreft, however, points out that "the shrewdness of socialist liberalism" lay precisely in its capacity to proclaim "every unwanted violence that refuted this liberalism as a consequence of the still living Stalinist core."[92]

Rooted in the antifascist liberation of the people and encapsulated in the slogan "Death to Fascism – Liberty to the People" (*smrt fašizmu – svoboda/ sloboda narodu*), the Party's leadership had initially played an emancipatory role in leading the Yugoslav people out of postwar devastation toward revolutionary political and economic emancipation with well-distributed gains for the entire population. They successfully stood up to Stalin to develop a self-managed socialism. However, by the late 1960s, they turned into a ruling class with several competing factions that alienated the working people and contributed to class stratification. The Party became an impediment to the emancipation of working people and the implementation of self-governance. In his penetrating analysis of class stratification in the SFRY, Suvin asserts that the "Party/State core" turned its initial "function of centralized leadership into the permanent class status of an oligarchic politocracy" by the early 1970s.[93] In this context, along with the development of class stratification, the socialist cultural system more and more clearly emulated the inequities of a bourgeois model and social role of art.

In 1965 the policies of full employment became an issue due to market reform and the rising pressures posed by the IMF and the World Bank. These institutions pushed for further market-oriented economic reforms and contributed to an exponential rise in unemployment. The rise in unemployment took place because the economy was unable to absorb the growing population. The economic differences between more and less prosperous republics were exacerbated and income inequalities among workers resulted in massive protests by workers and students by the end of 1960s.

The economic reform of 1965 represented a turning point because the implementation of market principles caused permanent economic instability and gradual disintegration of the self-management principles. Instead of expanding self-management to all levels of social governance, an introduction of market principles and decentralization of planning took place. Suvin explains that the process of decentralization meant two different things to various factions of the LCY. To one faction of the Party it meant "power to the republican and local leaders," and to the other faction "power to the self-managing working people."[94] The former understanding prevailed "with verbal and smaller sops for the workers, and much consumerism for the middle classes,"[95] thereby preparing the terrain for the misrecognition of art as non-work. Soon, the market principles would turn art workers from socially protected and supported workers into self-relying and unsupported entrepreneurs.

Stage Three: Disenfranchisement of Art Workers

By the early 1970s, the prosperity enjoyed by postwar generations and the rising consumerism propelled by market reforms that undermined the belief in the radicalization of self-managed socialism brought on a profound social conflict that played itself out in the following decade and a half. Following the 1968 student protests and the increasing numbers of workers' strikes and popular demonstrations, the LCY consolidated its rule by ousting the liberal faction, closing down and restricting platforms of critical dialogue run by neo-Marxist intellectuals and artists, and implementing a new constitution in 1974 with a promise of more direct self-management that was now implemented in all aspects (not just enterprises). This final third stage (1974–91), which covers the transformation of the art worker into an entrepreneur, will be discussed in detail in the next chapter.

Conclusion: The Contradictions of the Socialist Institution of Art

This chapter covered the first two stages in the making of Yugoslav art workers during which art as a form of labour was socially and economically protected and importantly connected to the swift industrialization and modernization of the country. Political factions of the LCY in power during postwar Yugoslavia developed an alternative brand of socialism and instituted a socialist welfare state based on economic ideas of full employment.[96] Production and labour relations within institutionalized art in the SFYR were protected first as a socialist ideal and second as a matter of state/national interest. The socialist institution of art was, therefore, a form of art and cultural production marked by deliberate attention concerning popular access to art and art workers' welfare. The Yugoslav socialist state created a production model for the arts that initially avoided unpaid artistic labour. During the first stage workers' rights and minimum fees were granted to artists, during the second stage these protections were expanded and elaborated to a broader circle of art workers. The labour policies of Yugoslav self-management opposed the traditional institutionalization of art by protecting art as labour yet at the same time they upheld artistic labour as an exceptional type of work that took place within the secluded autonomous sphere of art. The first two stages showed us that what emerged in Yugoslavia was a *socialist* institution of art, in which ideas of autonomy of art co-existed with a postulation of artistic labour as work. These two stages are important to fully understand the way in which the development in Yugoslavia was unique but also how it was still connected to important Western philosophical traditions that held sway on the understanding of art and artistic labour.

Considering the institutionalization of art in the SFRY, its central characteristic was a gradual affirmation and an adoption of a traditional European model of art production.

Culture and art were understood as a separate, relatively autonomous, social sphere that preserved the distinction between professional art workers, amateur art workers, and the non-creative audience. Granting access to art in various forms, the appreciation of art and the production of culture was not, however, limited to the wealthy. Through the network of cultural associations, people in the SFRY had access to creative work and expression that was not necessarily subject to the aesthetic judgment. Working people were encouraged to participate in culture, to form cultural clubs in their work places, or to collectively attend events such as theatre or music performances in professional art institutions.[97] Moreover, working people expressed their creativity regardless of the aesthetic merits of these expressions. However, the emancipation of human labour through affirmation of creativity and self-management remained an ideal that still needed to be realized through a full-fledged self-management practice in all areas of social life and on all social levels that was to take place with the passing of the new constitution of 1974.

The first two stages also exemplify that for two and a half decades after the Second World War exploitation of artistic labour in the SFRY was hardly existent due to the guaranteed remuneration and welfare provisions for art workers. By making art accessible to everyone and protecting artists' labour rights, the socialist cultural policy, to a certain extent, succeeded in undermining the practice of art as invisible labour. Nonetheless, underlying both stages was the concept of the autonomy of art, which contributed greatly to the crash in the final third stage. It was precisely because the *socialist* institution of art in Yugoslavia juxtaposed ideas of autonomy with the postulation of artistic labour as work that a tension emerged. This development was very much linked to the geopolitical power struggles and global economic conditions that affected Yugoslav socialist political economy and the socialist welfare state, including the protection of art workers. In other words, in no simple way did Yugoslav socialism fail on its own and in no way was capitalism and liberal democracy of the West the solution or a success. The only success the latter had was that it destroyed the alternative. I turn to these developments in the following three chapters that cover the third stage of the undoing of Yugoslav art workers. I discuss the unravelling of the contradiction between socialist labour policies for art workers and the increasing philosophical influence of Western art in chapter 4, while chapters 5 and 6 analyse the final decade that is exemplified by the breakdown of art as labour and the destruction of socialist Yugoslavia.

Chapter Four

The Mystification of Artistic Labour under Socialism

During the third and last stage (1974–91) the language of self-management became redeployed as a façade for (neo)liberal policies. Art workers were turned into self-sufficient, self-managed, and self-responsible socialist entrepreneurs – they became soldiers in an experimental frontline for the neoliberal transformation. This is when the progressive trends of the first two stages collapsed, no doubt because all underlying tensions impacted by the philosophical Western traditions of art and art's social role finally rose to the surface. I discuss the third period in this and the following two chapters because the mystification of artistic labour under socialism, especially during the final period reveals a contradiction present in Yugoslav socialism, which paradoxically reproduced, corroborated, and eventually recuperated Western bourgeois aesthetic and philosophical traditions. In this chapter I take a closer look at how the Yugoslav upholding of the autonomy of art and artists as workers, but exemplary, and therefore special kind of workers, turned art into an invisible labour by withdrawing employment security and many forms of social security and social protections. The housewifization of artistic labour in socialist Yugoslavia, and in particular of freelance art workers, during the third stage took place not only due to the marketization of self-management but also because artists of the postwar generations – with very few exceptions that are the focus of this chapter – saw themselves as creators and not as workers. I highlight those few examples of artists and intellectuals who articulated a critique of this recuperation from within. As I argued in chapter 2, this essentialization of artistic labour is detrimental because it divorces art as a productive social activity from other kinds of labour and turns it into an invisible labour. This is the transformation that became apparent during the third stage characterized by the process of undoing art as labour.

Due to the lack of available appropriate cultural and economic models and the concrete geopolitical constraints in which the cultural and social transformation epitomized by Yugoslavia took place, the socialist institution of art failed to live up to its revolutionary aims. The most telling sign of its disintegration was precisely this emergence of unpaid artistic labour during the third final period of cultural policy. Specifically, the emergence of unpaid artistic labour was, on the one hand, a consequence of the unrealized transformative potential of the alternative art movements, in particular their attempt to transcend the bourgeois institution of art, its autonomy, and art understood as commodity production. On the other hand, the emergence of unpaid artistic labour was related to the liberalization of market principles and the federal government's response to changes in the international economic conditions[1] that went counter to the aims of securing a rising living standard for all working people. The conflict generated a dissonance between the socialist provision of culture based on secure employment for art workers and an implementation of market principles in the field of culture, which began to redefine art workers as socialist entrepreneurs. While art workers were treated both as specialists endowed with creative powers and recognized as labourers that deserve equal rights with other workers, an implementation of market principles in the sphere of culture affected the demand for and provision of cultural goods.[2] On the heels of competition and existing divisions within the autonomous sphere of art, the working conditions began to deteriorate, and the process of class stratification and precarization in the field of Yugoslav culture began.

During this final third period (1974–91), the Faustian bargain that Yugoslavia had made with the West became manifest as the (imperial) devil came to collect its dues, especially at the level of political economy. After the oil crisis of 1973, the economy was further liberalized by market principles under the pressure of the IMF and the World Bank. Insidiously, "decentralization as a Trojan horse for marketization"[3] was allied with and enhanced by a nationalist ideology that enabled local rulers, especially in Slovenia, Croatia, and Serbia, to block policies on the federal Yugoslav level. Recent scholarship documents these formidable processes where on the one hand we can see a naiveté about market mechanisms displayed by socialist economists and on the other the insidious ideological imposition of liberal ideals by the American government.[4] On the heels of marketization the self-management encapsulated in the new Yugoslav constitution was intended to be the antidote. But, as Močnik underscores, the new constitution implemented in 1974, while attempting to eliminate the effects of market reform by instituting a principle of "free exchange of labor," consecrated "the most detrimental effect of the market economy by recognizing the nationalist composition of the state-party apparatuses and by transforming Yugoslav federation into a *de facto* confederation of nation states."[5] This was the beginning of the end for socialist Yugoslavia, assisted and orchestrated by the might of the imperial West wrapped in the foil of liberal democracy.

The third stage of self-managed cultural policy was marked by the official introduction of "social self-management" (as opposed to workers' self-management) in the public sector. In all areas of public services (non-industry or social service organizations), such as health, primary and secondary schools, higher education, science, culture, social welfare, the administrative bodies, in which social self-management took place, were called "self-managing interest communities" (SIC) (*samoupravne interesne skupnosti/zajednice*) and were comprised of two bodies, users and producers. In the field of cultural production, the "self-managing *cultural* communities" (SCC) (*samoupravne kulturne skupnosti/ zajednice*) replaced communal and republic cultural administrative bodies. Socialist authorities instituted SCCs in all republics and in the two provinces in addition to regional, city, or municipal SCCs.[6] In principle, self-managing interest communities redistributed the monies collected through deductions of the gross personal income of workers who were supposed to decide the percentage that an economic unit (i.e., Basic Organization of Associated Labour, or BOAL, for industry) earmarked for culture. The funds collected through this new form of taxation were deposited into the SICs that redistributed them. The SICs' funding decisions were based on the votes of the delegates representing *users* of particular public services, and delegates representing *producers* of a particular public service. However, the problem was that SICs depended on a commune's budget, economic power, and political will. In other words, the monies from personal income deductions were not the only resources allocated for culture (or other social services). The idea behind self-management as explained by Stevan Majstorović, the writer of the UNESCO report on Yugoslav cultural policy, meant that "the distribution of the surplus value is decided upon by the work organizations creating it, and that they also decide in a self-management procedure how they will use this surplus – to raise their personal income, expand production, purchase housing for their staff, satisfy social, cultural, educational, and other needs, provide recreation for their workers, etc."[7] He also noted that this is a "developmental goal" or "an end to be pursued" and not an actual practice because BOAL determine the redistribution "of only a part of the surplus, and not on the whole of it."[8]

All social service organizations, including art and cultural institutions, were now designated as a BOAL; this was also the name for the industry organizations, such as factories, etc. The only exception were cultural associations, which kept their names. The other official novum in the area of culture was that cultural workers were able to form temporary or permanent working communities (*radna zajednica/delovna skupnost*) to realize cultural projects or to develop a particular program.[9] The so-called free exchange of labour would now take place between BOALs, working communities, associations, and the working people. For instance, according to the Slovenian version of the Law on Free Exchange of Labour in the Area of Cultural Activity, the substance of this free exchange of labour was "individual cultural and other kinds of services."[10] Based on self-managing agreements (or contracts) workers in the roles of either producers (of services or other commodities) or users (of services or commodities) were supposed to negotiate and collaborate to realize programs and projects according to commonly determined needs. For example, in the area of culture, the SCC assemblies of users and producers were to determine a program of cultural development, activities, and projects in a particular commune, and decide on redistribution of funding.

By this point, the Yugoslav system generated hierarchies and relations of domination that were now regulated by a complicated system of self-management, which had lost its potential in the realm of industrial production already after the 1965 economic reform while it never fully realized its potential in the area of public services. The particular style of management embodied in the SIC was supposed to be the new Yugoslav alternative to the state apparatus, which "maintained the public services (health, retirement, social security, education, culture)" and "managed their domains in a more or less technocratic manner, whilst the properly political problematic of their mutual relations and of their insertion into vaster social systems (including the problematics of the special taxes that they collected, of the prices and the benefits that they supplied) was reduced to a sort of pre-established immanence that the alliance of communists took care of."[11]

While the scope of domestic and international cultural activities and the number of professional artists continued to grow during the third and final stage, the economic marginalization of the new generation of art workers became more obvious despite the domestic and international acclaim achieved by some Yugoslav artists. Despite revolutionary aims regarding the role of art and the emancipation of labour, the socialist institution reproduced inequalities and hierarchies among art workers. In the words of the director of the SKC in Belgrade, Dunja Blažević, the Yugoslav system of social management of culture was "a system of markedly state, bureaucratic structure, which [did] not resolve the existential problems of artists or the essential issues pertaining to the social function of art."[12] In other words, because a division of labour existed, artists were specialists on the one hand but becoming more and more precarious on the other.

These developments left a betrayed avant-garde whose sense of disillusionment began to be articulated in the 1970s. For example, artists producing alternative art that operated within the socialist institution of art but as a mutation of a bourgeois cultural system, articulated views about a betrayal of the historical avant-garde. In "Art and Revolution," Raša Todosijević pointed out that the bourgeois society in the West appropriated the historical avant-garde movements as their own history of art despite the fact that historical avant-garde movements were in fact anti-bourgeois and "spit in the face of that same [bourgeois] society."[13] While the "soviet avant-garde from the era of revolution was liquidated" and then, replaced by the "political blindness of 'artists' of socialist realism"[14] in the Yugoslav context, asserted Todosijević, a critique of socialist realism was "mainly based on a bourgeois liberal view of art, irrespective of declarative denials, even in the case of Marxist theoreticians."[15] He concluded, "It is no wonder then that these philosophers and theoreticians have turned to the *external appearance* of art. This decision, however, means imitating mystical and religious notion[s] of art."[16] Finally, Todosijević emphasized the irony that "art schools of socialist countries still study and practice the modernized art ideology of the nineteenth century" while they "view historical avant-gardes as some kind of anti-art, destruction and [the] downfall of the great European (bourgeois) culture."[17] The Yugoslav political establishment, in its desire to build an alternative to the Soviet state socialism, disenfranchised the politically engaged art workers since what it *socialisticized* was a fundamentally bourgeois model of the institution of art. I refer here to the fact that the Yugoslav political system made the institution of art socialist but did not transform its organizational framework and its key tenets: the genius artist, the work of art, and autonomy. But even this development was not unidirectional.

While cultural policy attempted to eliminate the separation of art and life and consequently the separation of the producer and recipient/audience (through the system of associational culture and emphasizing that all labour is creative), it also preserved an institutional art system that cultivated bourgeois ideas of aesthetics and considered artists as specialists. Creative labour in the realm of associational culture, also labelled amateur culture, was reserved for spare leisure time of all working people and the youth, as opposed to professional creative labour in the context of institutionalized art and the cultural and entertainment industry. In the socialist institution of art, a paradox of socialist cultural policy emerged. The latter established platforms and support for creation and art production, but it did not support a transformation of art's social function because it maintained the distinction and division of labour. This distinction produced inequality and class stratification among artists despite the aims of self-management to redefine creative effort, which in an ideal sense "no longer signifies various branches of art alone, but is identified with all types of creative manifestation – in physical labor, politics, social life, education, science, new solutions in social service, etc."[18] In the final analysis these contradictions contributed to the undoing of Yugoslav art workers and turned artistic labour into invisible labour. As we will see, it is precisely the exceptionality of creative work and the unique status of artists, which Yugoslav socialism maintained and glorified, that made artistic labour vulnerable to exploitation and disavowal as a form of labour.

Western philosophical tradition concerning art and in particular the autonomy of art held a sway also over the postwar generations of alternative art and critical theory in Yugoslavia. Western cultural models impacted the formation of the Yugoslav cultural system via various forms of well-documented Western cultural diplomacy. They also remained impactful because traditional art organizations, that is, museums, galleries, theatres, operas, and ballets that were established during the Austro-Hungarian rule and the Kingdom of Yugoslavia, were incorporated into the production model of Yugoslav socialism.

What is more, artists themselves were not particularly critical of the system of art or of the ways it reproduced the exploitation of labour and its invisibility. While a comparative analysis with the Western model of art production was available to Yugoslav artists due to intensive international cultural exchange, there were very few who went beyond the critique of consumerism and the problem of commodification of art to address the fundamental postulate of Western art and how it relates to labour. One such example was the work of Goran Đorđević, a Belgrade-based artist and a member of a collective of conceptual artists who during the 1970s ran the newly instituted SKC in Belgrade.

The Artist as Pseudo Subject and Creativity as Illusion: Goran Đorđević

Goran Đorđević most directly addressed the class character of art and sharply exposed the problems of art's institutional framework under Yugoslav socialism. A member of the circle of conceptual artists (known also as members of "new art practice") connected to the Belgrade SKC, which was established in 1971 as a form of concession to 1968 student protests,[19] Đorđević was the most consistent and deliberate critic of artistic creativity, and the nature of artists and artists' work. His interventions articulated one of the best critiques of the exceptional nature of the artist in socialist Yugoslavia.

Đorđević was not trained as an artist. He got his degree at the School of Electrical Engineering, and later (1982–3) was a Fulbright Scholar at MIT in the United States. Between 1972 and 1976, he became involved in the alternative art practice at the gallery of the SKC, where he was the only non-artist on the gallery's editorial board. After returning from the United States, he got a position as a lecturer at the School of Architecture in Priština. In 1983, he was accepted as a member in the Association of Visual Artists of Serbia, which granted him social and health insurance and retirement provisions as an independent artist. Since 1985 he has not been active as an artist, except briefly between 1988 and 1991 when he was a member of the Amateur Art Society *Jedinstvo* (Unity) under the pseudonym Adrian Kovacs.

From the outset of his engagement with art Đorđević was critical of the notion of creativity and creative genius. In an early interview from 1972 Đorđević underscored the notion of creativity as a theological notion. Creation is a phenomenon whereby something comes out of nothing (*ex nihilo*), hence, only an entity without a cause (such as a deity) can create.[20] The belief in human creativity is an illusion; the idea of art is a product of belief in this illusion. The fact that art is deeply connected to, and has emerged from, a belief in the illusory powers of creation and creativity of human beings puts art in the same category as religion, argued Đorđević. As such, contends Đorđević, it may be analogized with Marx's views on religion as "opium of the people" that serves the ruling class.[21] Considering that this passage is often misinterpreted, it is important to highlight a close reading of Marx's views of religion by Jan Rehman. He points out that many interpretations missed Marx's point that religion is as a "'sigh of the oppressed creature' and *as such* the 'opium of the people.'"[22] Instead most readings understand these two contentions by Marx as separate, an either-or position. Put differently, religion is an opium of the people precisely because it is merely a sigh "without an analysis of the existing conditions of exploitation and oppression" and as such has paralyzing effects for resistance to these exploitative conditions.[23] This is an important interpretation of this notorious passage from Marx because it points to the problem of resistance and the diversion from any analysis of people's existing conditions of exploitation. In this sense we can also understand Đorđević's claims about religious tendencies of art and the ways beliefs in creativity affect the exploitation of artists. Đorđević pointed out that the naturalization of art as creation is flawed because it robs the art worker of a strategic position to negotiate the power relations within the institutionalized production of art. In this sense Đorđević asserts: "I never understood myself as an artist nor that what I was doing then was art (in a positive sense). For me it [his work] was a kind of subversion toward this illusion (of creativity)."[24]

Đorđević's initial postulation about creativity and art as a form of illusion resulted from logical thinking; his experiences confirmed his hypothesis.[25] In the texts published in the mid-1970s, he wrote: "Art as 'creative' activity (by, of course, 'exceptional' men) serves as yet one more 'proof' of the justifiability of given class relations."[26] Artists are on the one hand human beings who are conditioned by a number of economic, social, biological, and psychological factors, and on the other hand ideas of creativity represent artists as the opposite of that, as someone possessing god-like qualities, such as creation. Since dominant cultural perceptions of art in the West reproduce these views, Đorđević contended: "Art in its real and practical function was *and remains* one of the instruments of the ruling class in the process of the forming of consciousness and in the process of governing the majority. Revolutionary change of the social order is primarily conditioned by qualitative changes in the relations of production. Thus the control over labor and its fruits would be fundamentally altered."[27] Creativity is therefore both a theological and an ideological notion that imparts the class character of art and serves as the fulcrum of exploitation.

While his text "On the Class Character of Art" was published in 1976 in *The Fox*, a journal edited by the Art and Language group, the initial title, "Art as a

Form of Religious Consciousness," dates back to 1975, when it was published in Serbo-Croatian to accompany the exhibition *Oktober*, organized by the SKC Belgrade. The *Oktober* exhibitions and events were organized by the SKC gallery as alternatives to the annually organized October Salon in Belgrade, which, in view of the many artists working on the alternative scene, represented the growing hegemony of bourgeois cultural values in Yugoslav society. However, Đorđević's critical position concerning creativity was unique on the Yugoslav alternative art scene and gained little traction among his peers. "For them, it was a non-issue, they were simply for some other art, and not for overcoming art."[28] The illusory character of creativity, and in turn, the notion of artist as genius creator "was not a topic that was discussed at the time, probably because it questioned the basis of the existence of art itself and the purpose of one's work."[29] Artists were not willing to raise issues with the precepts of art, or, if you will, the illusions that perpetuate art, even if these principles were a known source of their oppression in economic and social terms.

By the mid 1970s, Đorđević developed a critical stance toward alternative art itself, since he noticed that interventions by conceptual artists produced little effect on the functioning of the cultural institutions and the art market. The alternative art practices that got called "the new art practice" during the late 1960s and early 1970s,[30] were ironically not new since they did not pose a decisive challenge to the ways in which art institutions or the art market operated. Even less did they challenge the mystification of artistic labour. In 1979 Đorđević concluded that the "new art practice" represented "a new tradition."[31] This position had a two-fold meaning. It pertained to a critique of the new art practice's lack of awareness that its members were delegated into the politically ineffectual sphere of autonomous art on the one hand, and on the other hand, it indicated a lack of criticism of the institutional exploitation and the ontological position of the artist within this system.

In Đorđević's terms, the artist is a "pseudo subject" in the art system. He enunciated this concept in 1977 after he was invited to exhibit his work at the Belgrade Triennial of Yugoslav Art but was ignored by the organizers when he asked about the budget of the exhibition and the distribution of financial resources. This demand came out of the growing realization that a number of people in art organizations, including the SKC, were paid for their work, but those for whom the centre existed and who created its artistic program did not get a penny. Moreover, he realized that every exhibition had a budget that was based on the works of participating artists.[32] In his text, "The Subject and the Pseudo Subject of Artistic Practice," published together with his letter to the organizers of the Belgrade Triennial, Đorđević asserted that while the entire system of art depends on and gains its social justification through the existence of artists and their labour, a true definition of an artist's work is in fact "anything that is accepted by the art system (or one of its parts)."[33] Consequently, "the art system (specific people in specific social positions) emerges as the only real and complete subject of artistic practice (in the material sense as well as in the sense of actual social power), while the artist and his art work have the role of a *pseudo subject*, a marionette and an unavoidable instrument of the art system."[34] In turn this predicament of subservience has profound consequences on the pecuniary aspects of artistic labour, and hierarchical and oppressive social relations in the arts. Đorđević argued:

> Since the art system practically disposes with the entirety of material resources allocated by the society for artistic activities, the artist is forced to accept the relations and rules of behaviour prescribed by this system. This concerns not only the division of material resources through which various and numerous directors and curators of museums and galleries, members of diverse committees, councils and boards, critics, professors, secretaries etc. provide for their existence thanks to the existence of something called art work, but also to practically exclusive right of decision about the division of the rest of the material resources dedicated to the organization of artistic activities.[35]

In other words, the institution of art has an enormous social power and the artists in this system are its weakest link since they are practically dependent on the art system. Đorđević contended that the artist is not autonomous in relation to the art system, and is rather its direct outcome, which minimizes the possibilities for a substantial transformation of social relations within the institution of art.

> Since the time when art became a form of social practice, the art system had seen significant transformations due to the pressure of changes in the basic social structure. Some of its parts became inadequate and were replaced by new ones. Many of its components altered its role and meaning. However, the relations between the art system and the artist/art work, and between the art system and society, remained practically unaltered until this day. The art system represents a very powerful and specific form of social parasitism that in addition to self-reproduction of its vital parts (including forms of collective and individual consciousness), also produces the direct reason for its existence: the artist. It is understandable that the majority of people who belong to the art system aim to strengthen or maintain the material and social power relations. They do so with all available (not insignificant) means and with a great dose of arrogance. I think that in the current situation, and depending on the concrete conditions, it is only justified to organize or support only those activities in the context of the art system that represent its real diversion.[36]

One such diversion became an organization of the international strike of artists in 1979. As opposed to Đorđević's stances on creativity, which he

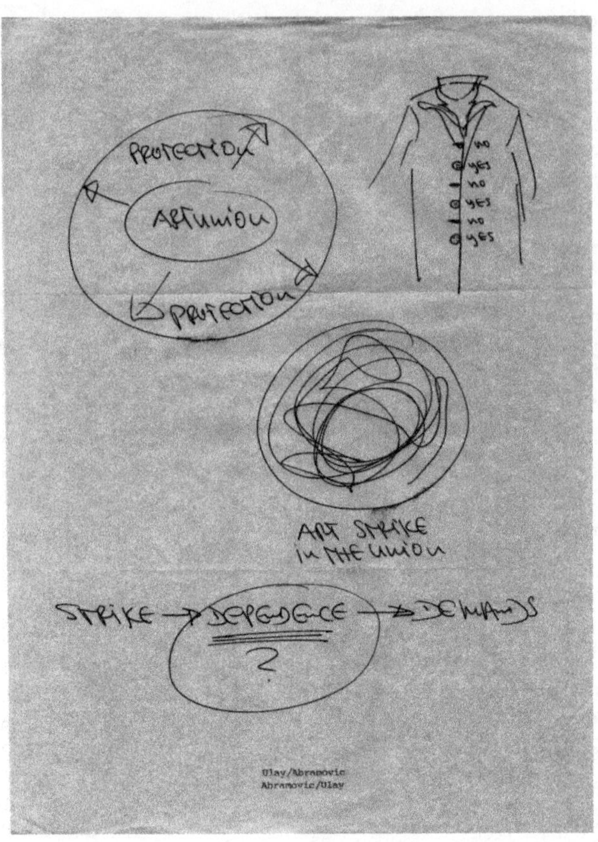

4.1. Goran Đorđević, International Strike of Artists, postcard with a response to the call for an artists' strike, Belgrade, 1979. Courtesy of Goran Đorđević.

made at the beginning of his engagement with alternative art practices, the proposal for an artists' strike came out of several years of experiences and observation of both the Yugoslav and the international art world. By that time, the editorial board in the SKC in Belgrade had also changed and with the change a strong trend of depoliticization in artistic practice came about. As some scholars allude, that was due to a conflict – between the artist and curators – about the radical political position pertaining to the critique of art as ideology.[37] The artist that demanded a radical political critique of the ideological aspects of culture and art (such was no doubt Đorđević's position) were stranded and excluded from the visual art redaction of SKC

Belgrade where depoliticized bourgeois attitudes toward art prevailed. One scholar therefore maintains that "Đorđević was the artist who never fitted in the art movements because the subject of his examination was precisely the ideological consequence of these movements."[38] In other words, artists were not ready to question the system and their pseudo subject position within them.

protection	No
art union	Yes
protection	No
	Yes
	No
	Yes

art strike in the union

strike → <u>dependence ?</u> → demands

Ulay/Abramovic

Abramovic/Ulay

According to Đorđević, artists should reject and surpass art not only as a form of consciousness but as an actual activity. A radical position by an artist should, he argued, refuse the bourgeois institution of art and strive for "qualitative changes in the relations of production," which would result in the transformation of the "control over labor and its fruits."[39] Art institutions, not artists, control both. Therefore, artists should deny providing "material support to the parasitic mechanism and system of institutions that seek and have the right to possess these alienated means thanks to the existence of the results (products) of artistic activity – the work of art."[40] Đorđević's call to arms took the form of an international artists' strike. Not only were Yugoslav artists invited to participate, but so were artists around the globe. Unfortunately, the response was mild and did not result in a coordinated action. Đorđević only received about forty responses two and a half months after sending the invitation.[41] Morale turned out to be low and the strike, concluded Đorđević, appeared to be a utopian vision rather than an actual alternative.[42] Nonetheless, the strike was understood as a refusal to participate in the exploitation of artists' labour and was a clear symptom of artists' paradoxical position in the institution of art.

HENRYK GAJEWSKI
00-950 WARSZAWA,
P.O.Box 744, POLAND

for Goran Đordević
project of
artists strike

There is no time for
artists strike. There is
nothing to do with art.

NOW
is better to concentrate
on problem

WHAT KIND OF WORLD
WE OFFER TO OUR CHILDREN

if we, conscious "artists",
have enough energy and
ability to influence
human culture today

4.2. Goran Đorđević, International Strike of Artists, postcard with a response to the call for an artists' strike, Belgrade, 1979. Courtesy of Goran Đorđević.

Đorđević's interventions need to be contextualized within the larger socio-economic conditions of late 1970s and 1980s Yugoslavia. In the cracks engendered by the relentless implementation of market principles and commodification, it was becoming clear that the socialist welfare state and its protection of the artist as worker was undergoing a gradual but steady transformation whereby ideas of subsistence and artistic labour were splitting up. Đorđević's solution was, however, not a call for payment or a wage precisely because material conditions for art workers in socialist Yugoslavia were relatively good until the early 1970s. His critique was directed at the entanglement of the (socialist) institution of art and the (capitalist) market that orchestrates the exploitation of artists' work. Đorđević's critique of artists who are seen, and also saw themselves, not as workers but as creators, uncovers the ideological mechanisms enabling the exploitation and consequent precarity of artistic labour. Mainstream socialist museums or galleries were exhibiting similar patterns as art museums and galleries on the other side of the Cold War divide, and saw young artists as a source of relatively cheap labour to provide content. Đorđević asserted, "the fact is that the artists of this orientation [i.e., conceptual art] could freely exhibit, but it is also a fact that for years there has been a strong process of economic exhaustion and the choking of all those phenomena in the arts that carried elements of criticism of traditional art and culture in general."[43]

Đorđević's call for strike had something in common with the tactical, utopian dimensions articulated in Federici's *Wages against Housework*. Federici points out that the demand for a wage is not a demand for a lump of money but needs to be seen as a political perspective that allows for the demystification and subverting of existing social relations in order to reimagine them. Vital to such a subversive move was precisely divorcing housework from its understanding as a natural inclination in female subjectivity. The power of this move in the context of art is embodied in Đorđević's description of the artist as a pseudo subject. In this sense, Đorđević's idea of a strike functioned as a provocation and as a test of whether a collective struggle is possible among those artists that are already critical of the institutional context of art in Yugoslavia and abroad. It tested whether a collective struggle aimed against the hierarchical art system and the marginalized, exploited, and instrumentalized function of artists in the system was even possible. A call for a strike was a strategic test of artists' readiness to question or demystify the institutional system and its theological presuppositions as a means of transforming the existing social relations in the arts. Very few artists were, however, ready to question their position and participation in the reproduction of artistic labour's mystification.

21 MAR 79 PO BOX 1001 NY, NY 10003 USA
DEAR GORAN DORDEVIĆ — THANK YOU FOR
YOUR CARD — THANK YOU ALSO FOR YOUR CLEAR
HAND & MASTERY OF ENGLISH — THE PROBLEMATIC
OF ART IN THE UNITED STATES IS DIFFERENT FROM
THAT IN EUROPE — ART HAS NEVER BEEN A PART
OF THE NATIONAL LIFE HERE EXCEPT AS AN
INCIDENTAL DIVERSION OCCASIONALLY IN FASHION —
THIS WAS TRUE OF THE 1960'S BUT IS DEFINITELY
NOT TRUE NOW — ON ONE OF RICHARD NIXON'S
WHITE HOUSE TAPES HE WARNS HIS DAUGHTER TO
STAY OUT OF ART MUSEUMS & GALLERIES BECAUSE
THEY WERE FULL OF JEWS & HOMOSEXUALS — THE
AMERICAN NATIONAL BUDGET FOR ADVERTISING
IS $43,000,000,000 WHILE THE NATIONAL BUDGET
FOR FINE ART IS CERTAINLY LESS THAN ONE
THOUSANDTH OF THAT ($43,000,000) — ART SEEMS
TO BE NECESSARY TO ARTISTS HERE BUT TO NO
ONE ELSE — THAT DOES GRANT A KIND OF NEGATIVE
FREEDOM — FROM WHOM WOULD ARTISTS BE
WITHHOLDING THEIR ART IF THEY DID GO ON STRIKE
? — ALAS, FROM NO ONE BUT THEMSELVES — "THE
SUPERSTRUCTURE IS AUTONOMOUS, BUT THE
ORGANIZATION OF THE MEANS OF PRODUCTION IS
DETERMING." K. MARX — THE BLESSING OF SPRING
TO YOU — BE WELL @ carl andre

GORAN DORDEVIĆ
III BULEVAR 106/15
11070
N. BEOGRAD
YUGOSLAVIA

4.3. Goran Đorđević, *International Strike of Artists*, postcard with a response to
the call for an artists' strike, Belgrade, 1979. Courtesy of Goran Đorđević.

Middleton Cheney
19 Aug.

Dear Goran,

Thank you very, very much for the parcel of social realist literature you forwarded to me. It will be most useful + I appreciate the amount of effort you put into collecting it.

If I can return the favour – let me know.

As for your 'art strike.' I would not take part in an international art strike. If the artist is alienated from the results of his practice, its up to the artist to take steps to change this, not to blame entrepreneurs, [illegible] capitalists.

Finally, two things: I don't have the financial flexibility to boycott the art system.

Second in the art + language record, there is a song 'Don't talk to sociologists.' One line is:

'Don't unite artists, if it makes you think there is a rational core to their activity, and not one maintained by force and violence.'

Best wishes + thank you again!

Mel Ramsden

4.4. Goran Đorđević, International Strike of Artists, postcard with a response to the call for an artists' strike, Belgrade, 1979. Courtesy of Goran Đorđević.

Hervé Fischer
143, boulevard de Charonne
75011 PARIS

Dear Goran Dordevic,

Of course I like very much your proposition of a strike and I do accept to participate in it.

I ask for permission for publishing your letter in the book I am just now finishing in writing, called: <u>The art history is finished.</u>

I send you here with a french text from a performance I made February 15th.

Give me information later about the organization of your idea of strike.

All the best,

Hervé Fischer

4.5. Goran Đorđević, International Strike of Artists, postcard with a response to the call for an artists' strike, Belgrade, 1979. Courtesy of Goran Đorđević.

What we see here is the emergence of a class-determined idea of art under socialism, which was criticized by Đorđević as well as a few other critical intellectuals in Yugoslavia. In his text "On the Class Character of Art,"[44] Đorđević proclaimed, "In countries that are building socialist relations in society, not only is the class character of the artistic consciousness not understood, on the contrary this consciousness is upheld and asserted."[45] Zagorka Golubović provided a similar reading of art under socialism when she argued: "The class character of culture in socialist systems is revealed in a double limitation of culture. First, culture has a class-interest function (the existing system is identified with this class interest) rather than having man as a human being as its goal. Second, culture performs the function of socialization *in accordance with a class conception of socialization*, preparing the individual for life in a given system in its existing state.... In other words, culture aids in the formation of the *conformist personality*, in fact, the nonconformist is the creator of true culture."[46] Golubović maintained that "in Yugoslavia, cultural nonconformism has not yet reached the point of radical opposition to the practice of assigning culture a special place in society and reserving it for particular social strata." However, "this nonconformism is still *class conformism*," she asserted.[47]

Self-management's emphasis on the idea of all labour being creative did not eliminate the structures through which art production operated as a separate autonomous field that became an exclusive concern of professional and political groups in larger urban areas. If self-management's goal was to liberate labour from constraints of capitalist exploitation and commodification of labour, it developed a blind spot in terms of understanding artistic labour and the institutional organization of art practices as an autonomous sphere. This merely emulated and recuperated Western bourgeois aesthetic and philosophical traditions. For example, Stipe Šuvar, a sociologist and at the time the secretary of culture and education in Croatia, clearly expressed this problem, when he wrote in 1975: "It seems that the misunderstandings that occurred at the beginning of the development of socialism, that also trouble our contemporary society, which is still a relatively young and underdeveloped socialist society, mostly stem from the fact that what we call culture has been inherited from the bourgeois society as a set of institutions, as a system of values, and as a form of traditional structure of cultural creators."[48] The socialist institution of art was culturally conservative in the sense defined by Yugoslav cultural critic Predrag Matvejević. It was "inclined to reproduce or emulate bourgeois models in art and culture rather than to engage in creating new alternative ones."[49]

Along with professionalization came also elitism. For instance, Šuvar admitted: "Even today, we are mostly concerned about the fate of traditional, inherited cultural institutions and the traditional content of their work. And this is still the focus of our cultural policy. This is also the focus of the traditional consciousness of cultural creators and the majority of intelligentsia."[50] Golubović echoed this view resolutely by noting that in the cultural sphere "the major demand [was] not for the *elimination of the professionalization of culture*, but for freedom for professional cultural activities."[51] Despite an awareness of a "need to create an enlightened public," art workers "fail[ed] to make any great efforts to close the 'unbridgeable' gap between professional 'creators' and 'non-creative' consumers."[52] Golubović was critical of this divide when she noted that there is "quite evident disinterest of many creators of so-called 'high-culture' toward the penetration of 'mass culture,' and its disastrous effects on the general population."[53] One of the reasons for this condition was, in Golubović's view, a demand to expand "the circle of 'culture customers'" and a lack of "struggle for the provision of the conditions and the means to make culture a daily need and a way of life for all."[54] This means that ideas of emancipation of human labour whereby culture would become a way of life was in contradiction not only with the idea of cultural consumption and commodification of culture, but also with bourgeois ideals of art's autonomy.

In her analysis of the social role of culture under socialism Golubović asserts that culture in socialism still has and affirms a class character. "Instead of allowing culture to perform its function as mediator between utopia and reality, to act as a field for expressing creative dissatisfaction and rebellion and to serve to revolutionize reality, the authorities in existing socialist countries demand that culture submerge itself in reality and that culture be employed exclusively in the service of reality (affirming reality and not criticizing it), declaring utopia an undesirable and useless sphere of dreams."[55] Golubović's critique points out a contradiction between utopian dimensions of culture that should lead to the general emancipation of human labour and put an end to alienation versus the reality of socialist societies in which she saw a tendency for culture to be used as an apparatus to affirm rather than criticize reality. Should culture be allowed to perform its function, this would allow an open critical debate, or as she phrased it, "a cultural contestation – in philosophy, the humanities, and some of the arts – [that] serves as a dynamic factor in socialism."[56] Surely, her position on culture being used as an apparatus for affirming reality was affected by the disillusionment in building true democratic forms of self-management in Yugoslavia during the final third stage of cultural policy, where LCY also reinstated certain forms of censorship. Despite disillusionment, Golubović stressed two crucial steps that would need to be taken to overcome the problem of class character of culture and emancipation of human labour: "To eliminate the class system it is not sufficient to abolish the economic conditions which produce it, but it is essential in addition to transcend the class functions of culture and to return to culture, long impoverished by class society, a rich human significance."[57] In other words, economic conditions that produce class exploitation need to be abolished but so too we need to critically examine the class character of culture that reproduces the division of labour epitomized by professionalization and elitist tendencies of culture.

These elitist and individualistic tendencies connected to ideas of creativity as we saw have a lot to do with the historical philosophical foundations of art and ideological dimensions of art's autonomy established by bourgeois societies. As I showed in chapters 1 and 2, art in the West was historically established as an individualistic activity of talented genius, or if you will, creative subjects presumably unburdened with matters of subsistence. These Western aesthetic and philosophical foundations are based in bourgeois ideology of autonomy that obscures art's class provenance. They also obscure the structural compulsion of wage-labour specific for capitalist class society and are in conflict with a Marxian understanding of emancipation of human labour in general. When and if labour is emancipated, it will also be creative but the designation "creative" may then become obsolete or irrelevant. For the present moment, however, it is politically problematic to defend and promote an essentialized understanding of artistic labour as an expression of creative self because it affirms an individualistic exclusive ethos that lends itself to exploitation and problematic hierarchies that govern our reality. In this sense, it was Golubović who already in the 1970s incisively argued that the nonconformism of cultural workers under socialism was in fact merely the means to achieve "*personal* affirmation in the domain of culture" and as such was boiled down to "expressions of particularist aspirations which either completely exclude or relegate to second place the aspiration of general human emancipation."[58]

Golubović and Đorđević's critique have two things in common. They are not only critical of the economic conditions that generate class systems and exploitation, but they also both brought to the fore the reproduction of class system in culture. Culture both under capitalism and under socialism was burdened by class character and bourgeois ideology, which is exemplified in the individualistic and exceptional ethos that is ascribed to artistic labour. This contributes to an elitist understanding of art and culture. Under the flag of creativity, the class character of art is not only neutralized, it is also depoliticized. Creativity joins all art workers of different socio-economic backgrounds under a mirage of a classless banner. Calling art labour however offers a tactical vantage point for rejecting the understanding of artistic labour as essentialized creativity and the social role capitalism intended for artists. Moreover, I argue that an essentialized creativity also contributes to artistic labour's exploitation and reproduces merit-based systems of class and economic exclusion. These developments were also present in the third stage of the transformation of artistic labour in Yugoslavia, although they were not subject to wider cultural debate.

Art workers were seen and also saw themselves as creative individuals, which made them vulnerable to exploitation. As I detailed in chapter 3, socialist cultural policy of the first and second period created special policies for independent art workers. However, the status of employment and the hierarchy between the traditional art institutions and associational culture dictated a concomitant ladder of the valuation of artistic labour. The work of an artist was appropriately remunerated only in the traditional cultural institutions where artists were employees. In principle freelance art workers were paid and the valuation of artistic labour was not guided by the principles of a Western style art market but by state regulation and welfare protection. The economic rights of art workers, however, were filtered through a merit-based logic of aesthetic quality that was governed by the autonomous (socialist) institution of art. The socialist cultural policy thus ironically established status inequality and hierarchy.

This predicament caused a tension, especially in light of the economic crisis. The vulnerability of the Yugoslav political-economic model, which was increasingly dependent on Western markets and conditioned by the economic downturns, especially after the oil crisis of 1973, profoundly and negatively impacted the social organization of employment and the pledge of the LCY to ensure full employment and a rising standard of living. The Yugoslav political project of emancipation of labour resulted in self-management that, instead of empowering the management of workers, served to rationalize the cost of labour and discipline workers; it increased the level of market competition and dependence on foreign loans and investment. These dynamics resulted in the rise of unemployment among the low-skilled working class at the expense of securing skilled labour. As Susan Woodward explained, "Unemployment was high (and largely structural), but it was largely invisible. It consisted of persons shunted off to the individual and household sector of the economy, including women and retirees; young people who had no employment status into their late twenties because they could not find even a starting position; and a huge temporary exodus for work abroad."[59] This situation exacerbated regional economic inequalities between the northwest republics of Slovenia and Croatia, and the poorer southeast republics of Macedonia, Bosnia and Herzegovina, Montenegro, and the southern part of Serbia.

The division between art workers employed in the cultural institutions with full economic rights and independent art workers was in fact similar to the division between the workers working in socially owned firms and associations (socialized, or public sector), and those who performed individual and household labour in agriculture, small crafts, and trades (a quasi-private or individual sector). Woodward explains that the system of economic rights belonged only to the former.[60] "The social organization of employment in Yugoslavia thus defined individuals' economic, social, and political position, rights, and prospects."[61] Moreover, "one's economic and social prospects depended on the economic base of one's locality and republic (including its capacity to finance education and social benefits, to invest in employment generation, and to keep tax levels low)."[62] While the LCY promoted the emancipation of labour with self-management and raised the standard of living, the Faustian bargain that the SFRY struck with the West inevitably sabotaged the potentials of the self-managed economy.

In the context of art, the distinction was manifest in the gradual economic marginalization of the alternative art practices. The imbalance that emerged between mainstream art institutions and alternative art practices, not only affected the available funding but also working conditions. In other words, the class differences in the sphere of culture emerged due to an ongoing shortage of resources caused by the economic crisis and the growing number of art workers. While artists in Yugoslavia did not pick up on Đorđević ideas to examine the class character of art nor his idea of an artists' strike, some of them did address the emerging economic inequalities and developed a pragmatic strategy to address them within the existing system of art production. I now turn to another rare example of such an initiative that emerged among a collective of Zagreb-based artists: Podroom.

A Contract for the "Free Exchange" of Artistic Labour: RZU Podroom

Radna zajednica umjetnika (RZU, working collective of artists) Podroom existed between 1978 and 1980 in Zagreb as an alternative art space and collective to the dominant socialist art institutions. Initially, Dalibor Martinis, a visual artist and graphic designer, used the space as a studio. Later, he joined forces with several other artists and Sanja Iveković, who later on became an internationally recognized artist, to turn the studio into an artist-run space.[63] The name "Podroom" was a pun: a combination of the Croatian word "pod," which means "under," and the English word "room," which when read together sounds like *podrum*, the Croatian word for basement. The artists involved with Podroom were some of the key figures of the Yugoslav new art practice. Most of them worked with and exhibited in the gallery of the Zagreb Student Centre and the Contemporary Art Gallery (*Galerija suvremene umjetnosti*) and were connected with other artists of the alternative art scene in Belgrade, Ljubljana, and Novi Sad. Like the artists of the Belgrade Student Centre, the artists of Podroom criticized mainstream aesthetic trends and the institutional design and dynamics of the Yugoslav art scene. For example, Mladen Stilinović wrote that galleries in Yugoslavia comported themselves "as an authority and manipulated artist work," while the artists' aim was to gain control over their work because the "work primarily represents the artist, and only secondarily (or never) a gallery."[64] Moreover the group of artists gathered in Podroom questioned the unequal economic and social position of independent art workers.

In 1980 Podroom artists published their critical stances on the working conditions and the power dynamics of the Yugoslav art scene in *Prvi broj* (The First Issue), a magazine intended to be a periodical. However, only one issue was released, which coincided with the dissolution of the RZU Podroom.[65] In the magazine, we can find some of the rarest and most explicit engagements with the socio-economic situation of the artists that belonged to the alternative art scene in the SFRY. Whereas Đorđević's stances were radical and characterized by an anti-art attitude, the artists gathered around Podroom developed a more pragmatic, though also critical, attitude toward art. In the words of Boris Demur, another member of Podroom who published his views in *Prvi broj*, culture in Yugoslavia had been regarded "in romantic terms, but the point is to penetrate the gallery system as an economic structure."[66] Artists of the new art practice based in Zagreb were acutely aware that despite new attitudes toward the social role of art, its forms, formats, and modes of presentation, they inevitably confronted a powerful institutional system of art that had already began to integrate critical art practices. However, the socialist institution of art integrated these new attitudes without changing its hegemonic modus operandi, which was increasingly based on invisible labour and disallowed artists control over their work. In a group discussion about Podroom published in *Prvi broj*, Martinis pointed out how the "new or so-called avant-garde art that expressed with every work a new attitude and new relationship to the social role of art" became inevitably assimilated "through time and coordinated efforts of various institutions … into the existing conventional system." Hence, he added, "the fact that this [i.e., Podroom] is called the basement and not, for instance, a contemporary art gallery or modern art gallery, is not a guarantee that the same thing will not happen here."[67]

In order to confront this powerful mechanism, the Podroom group embraced a new stance toward socialist cultural policy directed in favour of an emancipation of artists' economic conditions and control over their labour. One such attempt, which the Podroom group discussed, was the need for an artist's contract that could be used with galleries.

Demanding a "fair socioeconomic relationship" for independent artists who did not want to produce art objects for sale, Dalibor Martinis and Sanja Iveković drafted the artist contract that was published in *Prvi broj*.[68] The idea was to have a "collective position on how to relate to the institutions, the system."[69] Moreover, the contract was drafted in such a way that it would be applicable to "everyone who considered herself an independent artist."[70] Or, as Martinis put it, "We insist on a socioeconomically fair relationship and not on some exclusive relationship toward a particular aesthetic attitude."[71] Nonetheless, the artist's contract did not became standard during the existence of the SFRY because not enough artists demanded its use.[72] According to Martinis, "although the sociopolitical system called for self-management, most were not ready to question its implementation. Also, compared to any other socialist country, the openness to contemporary art (architecture, design, film, etc.) in Yugoslavia was on an enviable level. Therefore, the artists felt that the situation was quite good as it was."[73]

The contract, relating "to the conditions of public presentation of an artwork by an artist in organizations of associated labour in the field of culture" outlined the responsibilities between an artist and a gallery concerning the realization of an artwork (regardless of its medium or format), reimbursement for work that included the author's fee for the conceptualization and realization of an artwork, exhibition fees, and costs related to the installation, documentation, promotion, and a catalogue or publication.[74] In addition to securing payment for artists' labour, the purpose of the contract was a fair distribution of the responsibility and control between an artist and a gallery. Martinis explained: "We maintained that as producers of cultural goods we should be remunerated for our work. We (I mean the group of artists around Podroom) made works that were immaterial (video, performance, text) and where the act of work/ production and exhibition were often inseparable. Accordingly, we maintained that the act of exhibiting should be appropriately remunerated because the institutions lived precisely by exhibiting art."[75]

In the preamble to the contract, feistily titled "*U galerije s ugovorom!*" (In the Galleries with a Contract!), Iveković and Martinis proclaimed that art is about sharing an experience and not owning objects. In artists' own words, "The social recognition of the value of artists' labour cannot be affirmed in a sales act because art is not socialized through the purchase of an artwork, even if the buyer is a public institution, but by means of the public communication of the creative process."[76] Considering the existence of numerous cultural institutions that employ cultural workers, they maintained that Yugoslav society perceived "artist's work as socially useful."[77] Thus, Iveković and Martinis argued, "There is only one possible form of exchanging the artistic labour with the labour of those who enjoy art: an exchange of an equivalent of the artist's labour (which is an artwork, or another form that is an evidence of this labour) with the equivalent (for example, money) of the labour of the user [i.e., viewer] of an artwork."[78] However, they underlined that this logic does not imply any aspirations "toward the principles of capitalist societies, in which the exchange is realized through market process and laws" because "spiritual values cannot be owned but only communicated."[79]

As I mentioned above, some republics implemented laws that specified the substance of the free exchange of labour in the field of culture explicitly as a "service," not just as an (art)object. The service was supposed to be the basis for determining the amount of compensation.[80] However, the implementation of self-management in the field of culture did not function well, first because the apparatus of governance was convoluted, and second because of the effects of austerity measures imposed on Yugoslavia by Western financial institutions. In theory, the *providers* of cultural services (art workers) and the *users* of cultural services (audiences) were supposed to negotiate their needs and programs based on these needs. This theory of self-management had been profoundly compromised, especially, after the LCY suppressed the social and student movements and rejected a revision of self-management that would lead to direct democracy and workers' control. Self-management and the free exchange of labour in the field of culture was now a legal fiction. Despite its idealistic design it was subject to the reality of the economic resources and power of a specific locality as well as to the established cultural hierarchy of art institutions and hegemonic aesthetic tendencies.

While in theory self-managed socialism and the idea of associated labour implemented by the 1974 constitution continued to recognize the social value of artists and their work as labour, the practice of socialist art institutions undermined the idea of artistic labour. Iveković and Martinis argued that socialist society "doesn't acknowledge the visual artist's act of exhibiting, that is, the public presentation as a moment in which an artist exchanges labour with the public, but forces him to secure his material existence via the market (by selling art artworks)."[81] The Yugoslav institutional system obscured artistic labour since it "require[d] the artist to fabricate objects in order to sell them on the market."[82] Furthermore, Yugoslav "society regularly [paid for] the work of all other collaborators (curators, translators, reviewers, museum guards, cleaners and others)" except artists.[83] The paradox of unpaid artistic labour could not be articulated more precisely. It is ironically echoed in the anecdote about the miserable payment of artist labour that I described in the introduction of this book.

The relations between an independent artist and the socialist institution of art therefore did not have much to do with the constitutionally proscribed laws and policies on the free exchange of labour since art institutions did not see artistic labour as work. "On the contrary," contended Iveković and Martinis, "the act of exhibiting [was] considered just as an opportunity that the society gives to the artist for the affirmation of his work and through which [artist's work] can increase the price. This is revealed in an unwritten (sometimes even written) rule that, after the close of the exhibition, the artist should donate at least one artwork to the institution which 'enabled' the exhibition."[84] The artist should provide not only the art institution with specific content, but should also donate the result of her labour without compensation since this will supposedly raise the value of her artwork. All that is left, then, is the promise of artistic glory that may increase the value of the artist's work on the market. The institutional logic of Western art that was emulated and replicated in the case of Yugoslavia overrode the ideals of socialist labour policies. While artists were the providers of content for art institutions, and understood themselves as "the subject[s] and initiator[s] of action,"[85] the socialist institution of art did not

PRVI BROJ

PRVI BROJ je prvi broj kataloga
radne zajednice umjetnika (RZU)
PODROOM.Sam naslov ukazuje na
neki niz brojeva to jest na
ideju o kontinuiranom izdavanju
ove publikacije.
RZU PODROOM nije galerija već
jedan oblik umjetničkog djelo-
vanja.Velik broj naših radova
ne može se realizirati u gale-
rijskom kontekstu jer je upra-
vo njegova negacija i zato smo
od početka nastojali otvoriti
sve alternativne mogućnosti
unutar kojih bi naš rad potpu-
nije funkcionirao.
Brojevi kataloga trebaju biti
jedna nova alternativa.
Kao i u radu PODROOMa, tako i
u radu na Brojevima kataloga
uvažavamo apsolutnu individu-
alnu slobodu i odgovornost u
radu i prezentiranju rada
stvaraoca.
Brojevi kataloga su otvoreni
svim potencijalnim suradnici-
ma, a uređuju se na principu
dogovora svih zainteresiranih.
Sadržaj svakog novog broja
(kao i ovog Prvog) odražava
aktualne probleme, interese i
preokupacije umjetnika člano-
va RZU PODROOM kao i onih koji
će se uključiti kao suradnici.
Troškove tiska namirujemo iz
uštedenih sredstava koje je
SIZ kulture općine Centar do-
dijelio RZU PODROOM za 1979.
Prvi broj je besplatan.

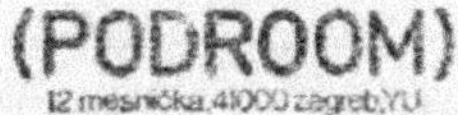

(PODROOM)
12 mesečka,41000 zagreb,YU

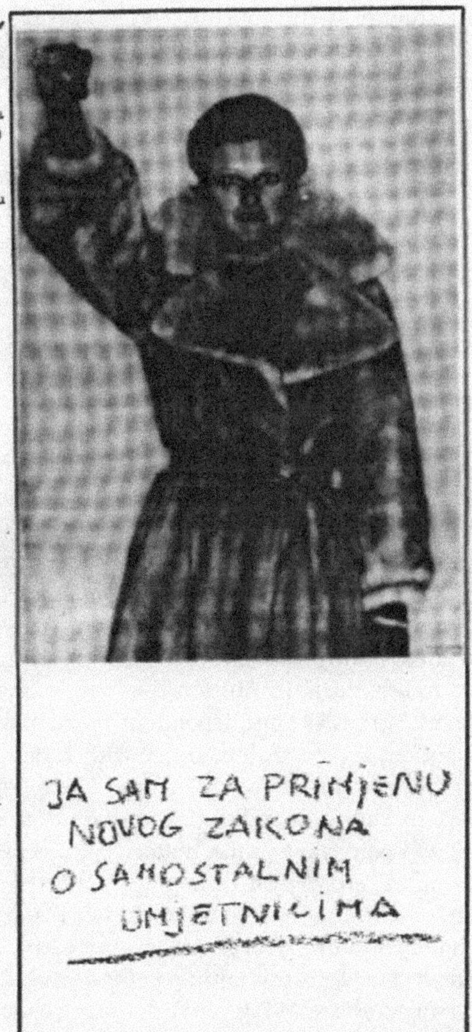

3

4.6. Page three of the magazine *Prvi broj* published by RZU Podroom,
Zagreb, 1980. Courtesy of Dalibor Martinis.

embrace or practice relations of "exchange of labour." Even worse, it obscured the actual labour.

To prove their point, artists offered in *Prvi broj* a quantitative and an artistic exemplification of artists' socio-economic conditions and inequality. The third page featured a peculiar image. A model dressed in fur coat and heavy, expensive-looking jewellery was assertively raising her right hand as if she was protesting. Underneath her image was a handwritten demand: "I vote for the change of the new law for independent artists."[86] The republic of Croatia was the first to implement the special Law for Independent Artists in 1979 proclaiming in article three that "independent artists have in principle the same socioeconomic position, rights, and responsibilities as the workers in the organizations of associated labour. Artists earn income and settle income obligations according to the law."[87] This statement was a legal fiction that artists in Podroom quickly demystified.

On page six, Iveković and Martinis published a chart with a long, discombobulated title: "An Indicator of the Relationship between the Income of an Independent Visual Artist and Their Actual Personal Income as well as the Personal Income of a Worker in the Field of Culture." The chart compared the monthly income of an independent freelance artist (*samostalni likovni umjetnik*) with that of a worker employed in a socialist cultural institution (*radnik u kulturi*).[88] The comparison was based on an index of 10,000 Yugoslav dinars (*din*), which represented the average net income of a senior employee in a cultural institution that would have had comparable educational qualifications as an independent visual artist. According to the chart, an independent artist was left to live with 2,190 dinars, which was only 20 per cent of the net amount of her income. She spent most of the sum on copyright taxes, rent utilities and insurance for a working space, contributions to sick leave and paid leave funds, materials for art work, administrative costs, travel expenses, etc. A full-time employee in a public cultural institution had the net amount of 10,000 dinars at her disposal. In addition to covered welfare benefits, an employed art worker earned five times more than an independent artist.[89] Commenting on the economic situation of independent artists during the late 1970s and 1980s in Yugoslavia, Iveković recounted: "We received no fees for artistic labor, we were pleased that cost for materials and production were paid. We received good fees for graphic design of posters and catalogues that were commissioned by institutions, such as Contemporary Art Gallery or theatres. These were our only sources of income."[90] This was quite a paradox; an artist creating for a press or a mainstream theatre was paid, but when they provided services in the form of more or less ephemeral artworks, their labour became invisible. The mystique of creation took the wheel and thus began the (hi)story of precarious working conditions for freelance art workers in Yugoslavia.

POKAZATELJI ODNOSA IZMEĐU PRIHODA SAMOSTALNOG LIKOVNOG UMJETNIKA I
NJEGOVOG STVARNOG OSOBNOG DOHOTKA RAD I OSOBNOG DOHOTKA RADNIKA U KULTURI

index: 10.000 din mjesečno
(ovaj index je izabran ne zato što odgovara najčešćim prihodima samostalnih
umjetnika, već zato što odgovara osobnom dohotku radnika u kulturi, kustosa
ili voditelja zagrebačke galerije i sl.)

radnik u kulturi	samostalni umjetnik
PRIHOD	
10.000 din	10.000 din.
RASHODI	
	1) porez na autorski honorar (16%) ....1600 din
	2) troškovi radnog prostora (30 m²) ....
	a) najamnina 400
	b) struja 150
	c) grijanje 250
	d) telefon 250
	e) održavanje 400
	3) bolovanje .... 200 (7 dana u god)
	4) godišnji odmor 830 (8,3%)
	5) materijal za rad 1500
	6) komunikacija djela (priprema djela za izlaganje) 200
	7) administriranje (korespondencija, pošt. troškovi) 400
	8) naobrazba i informiranje (časopisi, katalozi) 600
	9) putni troškovi 300
	10) troškovi reprezentacije 100
	11) osiguranje prostora i djela 150
	12) ostalo 150
ukupno: 0.000 din	ukupno: 7.810 din
NETTO DOHODAK	
10.000 − 0.000	10.000 − 7.810
10.000 din	2.190 din

ako samostalni umjetnik ostvari prihod od 100.000 D. njegov stvarni dohodak i manji.

priredili S.Iveković/D.Martinis

6

4.7. "An Indicator of the Relationship between the Income of an Independent Visual Artist and Their Actual Personal Income as well as the Personal Income of a Worker in the Field of Culture," a chart on page six of the magazine *Prvi broj* published by RZU Podroom, Zagreb, 1980. Courtesy of Dalibor Martinis.

The SFRY's implementation of social security for freelance professions including art workers was a sign of democratization and a result of larger social struggles that strived to change the "arrangement of the classic welfare state of the Fordist era, which was bound together with productivist mass production and consumption."[91] Nonetheless, the democratization of culture in the SFRY produced inequality in the economic value of artistic labour. While social security and the income of art workers employed in public institutions were secured, the freelance art workers were entitled only to the minimal social security and relied on the meagre public funds available for their art projects. Although self-management encompassed the idea of a free exchange of labour, which would, in principle, enable a fair remuneration of art workers' actual labour (though not the artwork itself), this idea never came to fruition. Clearly, the disparity in the quality of social security and income between the employed and freelance art workers would not get resolved during socialism. In fact it continues to present issues in the post-socialist era.[92]

In sum, alternative art practices had ironically become the seedbed of precarious working conditions and unpaid labour. In this chapter we have seen that very few artists took issue with the effects of Western bourgeois understanding of art and autonomy, its relation to the class character of art and consequently with the exploitation of essentialized understanding of artistic labour. Whereas postwar Yugoslav cultural policy resulted in a fairly open institutional framework for the arts that was aligned with the postwar European cultural-policy trends of democratization, its paradoxical organization is still apparent. It is visible in the ambivalent understanding of artistic labour that remains partially based on the belief that art is the product of artistic genius as conceptualized by hegemonic Western discourses of aesthetics. Since socialist cultural policy declared art as a public good and granted social security and workers' rights to employed art workers as well as to the independent artists, we could say that the socialist welfare state secured a relatively fair "labour market" for art workers, but could not transcend the detrimental effects of autonomy. While the concept of autonomy was underlying during the first two cultural policy stages, it contributed to a gradual crash in the third stage. Despite the fact that artists and intellectuals in the mid to late 1970s offered critical paths to transform the socialist institution of art by pointing to art's class character and the invisibility of artistic labour, this line of critique faded during the 1980s when artistic labour was finally divorced from universal labour rights and became based on ideas of artistic exceptionality. The divorce of art and labour was amplified by the crisis in the political economy of the 1980s. The transformation of art into an invisible labour, however, cannot be confused or conflated with economic crisis. The detrimental influence of the Western aesthetic traditions and ideas of autonomy had an important effect on this change. The lack of critical engagement with exploitative relations in the socialist institution of art and Western aesthetic traditions merely amplified the problem. In the following two chapters, I turn to these developments that took place during the crash of the final decade of Yugoslavia's existence and the violent breakup of the country.

Chapter Five

Art Workers and the Hidden Class Conflict of Late Socialism

During the 1980s the political economy of the Yugoslavian state reached its ultimate crisis. As one scholar put it, the country had arrived at a state of total "moral, economic, socioeconomic and national" crisis, which "put into question both the self-management system and the republican governments at the very moment that austerity and debt repayment became the main goals of the federal government."[1] The generations of the last decade of Yugoslav socialism responded to this crisis with a new wave of artistic and critical practices, which advanced a critique of the existing socialist cultural and political institutions and of their ideology of self-management. This was the third stage discussed in the previous chapter, which, although it was characterized by the unmaking of Yugoslav art workers, initially had promise. Indeed, it held the potential to build on the radical critique of the influential Western model of bourgeois art and its central postulates: autonomy, genius artist, and invisible labour. By the 1980s, however, the potential was completely undermined. The 1980s represent a complete debacle, and the following two chapters will discuss the decade's effects on the ideals of art as labour and its ultimate undoing.

During the final decade of Yugoslavia's existence, issues of class character and unpaid labour in the arts were marginalized in critical discussions. What emerged instead was a new agenda epitomized by an ideal of establishing "civil society" under socialism. This was promoted by the movements known as "the 1980s alternative" (*alternativa osemdesetih/osamdesetih*). Alternative to what, however, became the real issue. They claimed to be oppressed ideologically, which is extremely ironic since they were free enough to be able to offer their criticism of socialist ideology. While the LCY increased censorship and ideological control of oppositional movements after 1972, it also intensified the implementation of market principles as the cure proscribed by Western financial institutions. As these alternative movements of the 1980s mounted their critique of overly oppressive ideology of socialist self-management, they failed to realize that the problem was not too much socialist self-management but not enough of it. In these final two chapters, I break down this dynamic from two viewpoints that both follow the process that transformed art workers into self-relying socialist entrepreneurs. One trajectory presents the analysis of the transformation of labour-related cultural policy which took place parallel to the critique of socialism and planted the seeds of neoliberalism in the field of culture. The other trajectory pertains to the critique of socialist state apparatus voiced by the 1980s alternative. These alternative art practices and their ostensibly new models of cultural production were undermined both by their uncritical attitudes towards art and autonomy and the transformation of labour policies in art.

An examination of the stakes raised by the 1980s alternative culture offers a rich avenue to explore the problem of artistic labour and the ways in which the lack of critique of Western art and the autonomy of art affected the deterioration of working conditions of art workers. On the one hand, the alternative cultural and social movements during the last decade of the SFRY's existence represented yet another attempt to establish an alternative or improved version of socialism. The 1980s alternative was not against socialism; it was for its reform. On the other hand, the 1980s alternative also embodied the conflicts that led to the breakup of the federation and the transition to neoliberal capitalism. This chapter juxtaposes the cultural politics of the 1980s alternative (and its focus on civil society) with the unexamined spontaneous absorption of liberal ideology (the realization of personal freedom). This conflict with its exclusive focus on the critique of repressive state apparatuses affected the final transformation of art into invisible labour. I examine the ways in which the political and economic transformation of the 1980s as well as implicit class struggles impacted the status of artistic labour, its remuneration, and the working conditions of art workers.

Certainly, the 1980s' artistic practices were an offshoot of the conceptual art and countercultural practices of the 1960s and 1970s and the ethos of the avant-garde. They were embodied in the phenomenon that, in the broader social discourse, came to be known as the alternative culture of the 1980s or simply "the alternative" (*alternativa*). Used as a proper noun, the term "alternative," along with its variations (such as alternative culture or alternative scene or subculture alternative) was a vernacular concept of the 1980s, even though the various groups using the term did not hold equally radical left political positions. The term had in fact two points of reference, one narrower and one broader. In a narrow sense, the "1980s alternative culture" designated artistic and subcultural practices that emerged in the context of associational culture and youth cultural centres and not in the dominant socialist art institutions. They were frequently supported by student and youth organizations and their venues (student cultural centres and galleries) and media (for example, Radio Študent, *Tribuna* newspaper etc.). More broadly, however, "alternative movements" pertained to a variety of feminist, LGBTQ+, pacifist, and ecological social movements, including the art groups and intellectual production of the left-wing neo-Marxist, Lacanian, and poststructuralist orientation. Finally, the term alternative culture as I use it in this and the following chapter stands for the one final stage of development of the phenomenon called "alternative art practices" in the previous chapters. That is, a host of postwar leftist art movements linked to the ethos of the historical avant-gardes, but also to the activities and atmosphere of neo-avant-garde movements, the new art practice of the 1960s and 1970s, the student movement (1968–72), and the political and cultural practices of communes that emerged in Yugoslavia during the late 1960s and the first half of the 1970s.[2]

For the most part, the critique of the social and cultural institutions of the late 1980s Yugoslav socialism took place in marginal rather than mainstream venues, most notably in temporary or ad hoc public spaces. These platforms established the context for a new articulation of politics that aimed to reform self-managed socialism; this is partly the reason why they were called "alternative." Even though ever more pronounced class divisions of the 1980s socialist society engendered a renewed social critique, issues pertaining to economic stratification were not at the forefront of the debates among the alternative culture movements. Instead, the cultural and political criticism of the new generations focused on the critique of the oppressive socialist ideology. This took place in the cultural and theoretical milieu that was saturated with poststructuralism, neo-Marxism, and psychoanalysis and was also influenced by Althusser's theory of ideology as a material practice. But as they were focusing on the ideological discourses they ignored the economic processes. The fact that "economic relations and practices are completely saturated with ideology," and vice versa, that even "purely ideological practices are to an extent ... economic" was mostly disregarded.[3] This allowed an uncritical absorption of liberalist ideology that has in the final analysis – and including a crucial reliance on the nationalistic rhetoric – put some of the final nails in the coffin of the Yugoslav socialist project. Put differently, the critical discourse of ideology that reproduces particular material economic relations was not complemented by an analysis of the ongoing transformations of late socialist economic relations, which was profoundly crossbred with liberal ideology and a particularly naïve understanding of market mechanisms.[4]

The issue of unpaid artistic labour during the last decade of Yugoslav socialism can be understood mostly as a problem of a growing crisis of the welfare state and the rising tension between art understood as a form of labour and art as commodity. In the SFRY, art and culture were part of the public service system that provided general social welfare,[5] which was proclaimed economically unsustainable by neoliberal ideologists in the late 1970s when the capitalist mode of production entered a new cycle of global crisis and signalled the coming of the post-Fordist era. Since 1965, when it began to introduce market mechanisms, Yugoslavia was increasingly unstable and its debt kept growing. "The trouble for 'really existing socialism' in Europe was that ... now socialism was increasingly involved in [the world economy], and therefore not immune to the shocks of the 1970s," asserts Eric Hobsbawm as he emphasizes the historic irony of this situation.[6] "The 'real socialist' economies of Europe and the USSR, as well as parts of the Third World, became the real victims of the post-Golden Age crisis of the globalist economy whereas 'developed market economies,' though shaken, made their way through the difficult years without major trouble, at least until the early 1990s."[7]

The liberal hegemony has affected a generalized public opinion in North America that likes to think of socialism as an alien political system, out there, that developed and failed on its own, in isolation from capitalism's triumphalist ascension. The socialist East was defunct and the superiority of liberal West proved to be the solution.[8] Nothing could be further from the truth and the Yugoslav case helps reveal the role the West and its political model played in the demise of socialism whose more egalitarian premises threatened capitalism's reason for being. Scholars have revealed these impactful dynamics in various areas of Yugoslav economy and culture.[9] My discussion, however, focuses on the role Western influence had on the transformation of art as labour, these impacts were intellectual and philosophical as well as economic.

Two global processes marked the period of the transition and the violent breakup of the socialist Yugoslavia and the formation of new nation-states on its territory: the transformation of the capitalist accumulation from the Fordist (industrial) into the post-Fordist[10] (post-industrial) mode, and the rise of what scholars came to term neoliberal rationality[11] to emphasize that neoliberalism is not just an economic policy but a system of thought, attitudes, and values that shape the mode of government and culture.

What was characteristic of the Golden Age of Fordist capitalism in Europe and North America before the ascent of neoliberalism were high-profit margins, full employment, and the construction of the welfare state. Yugoslavia experienced a similar and even more fascinating miracle that was brought about by intensive industrialization and urbanization, and became a welfare state on the periphery, built on the industrial mode of production and consumption. "On the one hand, the people were consumers of the welfare state, on the other, they provided the consumption that enabled capital accumulation."[12] In such a way, a part of the surplus value returned to the workers in the form of a social wage or social security. Labour and social rights provided by the welfare state were a "social wage" (a guarantee of a minimal level of tolerable exploitation) through which a state turned workers into "consumers of its social services."[13] Yugoslavia, as a welfare state, was therefore upheld by mechanisms of social solidarity (free public education, health, social services, and inter-generational solidarity in the form of the pension system) that ensured an undisturbed reproduction of labour. When the global economic crisis hit in the mid-1970s (sparked by the 1973 oil crisis), "the Fordist model of accumulation with its 'cheap' methods of increasing productivity (Taylorism and mass production) had reached its limits, profit rates declined, and cyclical movements increased in strength, although even in periods of recovery, growth rates were modest and unemployment remained high."[14] In the following decades, profit rates increased again, primarily due to stagnating real wages and decreased company taxes "that were financed primarily by cuts in social expenditures,"[15] that is, by a deconstruction of the achievements of the welfare state.

These processes brought an increase in social differences and inequality to Yugoslav society, particularly among generations of students; unemployment among educated youth increased after 1972.[16] While it was one of the demands of the 1968 student movement in the SFRY that "high-school youth and university students be given the constitutional classification of 'worker'" which would grant them rights to participate in economic decision-making,[17] this demand was never met. Regardless of the increased number of labour strikes, and the fact that at least some artists discussed their working conditions, the issues of class stratification in the field of art were largely unaddressed because the critique of the socialist ideology took centre stage. For instance, the issues of a limping socialist economy manifested in a lack of funds and spaces for the alternative culture, and no investment in new cultural infrastructure[18] shifted the ideological battle. The shift manifested itself in the form of a state and party repression of the alternative culture. The LCY used ideologically constructed prejudice to quell the subcultural and countercultural movements that grew in number, particularly after the protests of the student movement from 1968 to 1972.

In the 1980s such was the case with the punk movement and the Nazi Punk Affair that erupted in socialist republic of Slovenia. The Nazi Punk Affair began in the 1980s when news reporter Zlatko Šetinc published an article in the newspaper *Nedeljski Dnevnik* that insinuated that the punk scene in Ljubljana had Nazi tendencies. The authorities then arrested some of its members and organizers and later released them. Igor Vidmar, a prominent figure on the alternative scene and one of the subjects of this repression, claimed – with an appropriate dose of sarcasm – that the affair was "a campaign for 'the final solution' of the question of punk in Slovenia, and for a removal of this ideologically impure lump from the healthy tissue of the Slovene national youth."[19] As early as the mid-1970s, when the LCY's liberal faction was ousted, and much more so after Tito died in 1980, the Party became ideologically repressive and intolerant. Struck by panic when it had no leader with authority and could no longer control the economy, society, or the rising nationalism, it used administrative bureaucratic means and prohibitions to clamp down on new generations with no prospects. Even though such repression did exist and the actors were sometimes investigated, questioned, and even briefly imprisoned, society was still permeated with pluralistic tolerance. In addition to advocates of national bourgeois culture there were also the voices of the alternative culture. The central tenets of the alternative scene during the last decade of the SFRY's existence were the legalistic defence of human rights and freedom of expression, criticism of the dominant ideology, and, later, the discourse of civil society.

"Civil Society" – A Nonsensical Political Program of the 1980s Alternative?

The 1980s alternative scene used and often attached its political struggle to reform Yugoslav socialism by employing the notion of civil society. The notion of civil society is problematic because it is not neutral. It denotes residents of a state, or the people, but it erases the perspective that enables us to see people living in unequal material conditions. The political program of establishing a civil society in the SFRY was a questionable tactic in the design of an alternative to socialism. While the notion of "civil society" had ample resonance in 1980s Yugoslavia, its use was fraught if not oxymoronic. This is why the issue of the political vision of the 1980s alternative remains puzzling.

If the generations of the 1960s fought for implementation of self-management as a form of democratic popular management of the commons and the economy, the generations of the 1980s transformed this into a fight against the repressive and ideological state apparatus (however, it would probably be more accurate to say the party authority). In a reflection on the legacy of student movement in Yugoslavia philosopher Darko Štrajn maintains that the 1968 student movement gave birth to a new strategy of resistance that became important for the 1980s alternative movements. In his words, this new strategy was "a leap from previous dissidence, which was heroic, but unfortunately ineffective, and wanted to provoke the regime with the 'truth,' to a public action that called upon legal rights and freedoms explicitly without the fear of secret surveillance. This 'style' of action later became the main characteristic of the civil society movement."[20] The civil society movement therefore did not have class differences and economic inequalities as its main points of contention or anchorage for struggle, rather the repressive and ideological state apparatus was the issue. Little attention was paid to the geopolitical struggle that ravaged between the East, the West, and the Nonaligned (anticolonial) Movement, the founding member of which was also Yugoslavia. Even less attention was paid to the rise of neoliberalism. Neoliberalism had since the 1980s become a normative system or an "existential norm of western societies," which is exhaustively discussed in the study by Dardot and Laval.[21] During the 1980s the seeds of this new existential norm were implemented in socialist Yugoslavia as well.

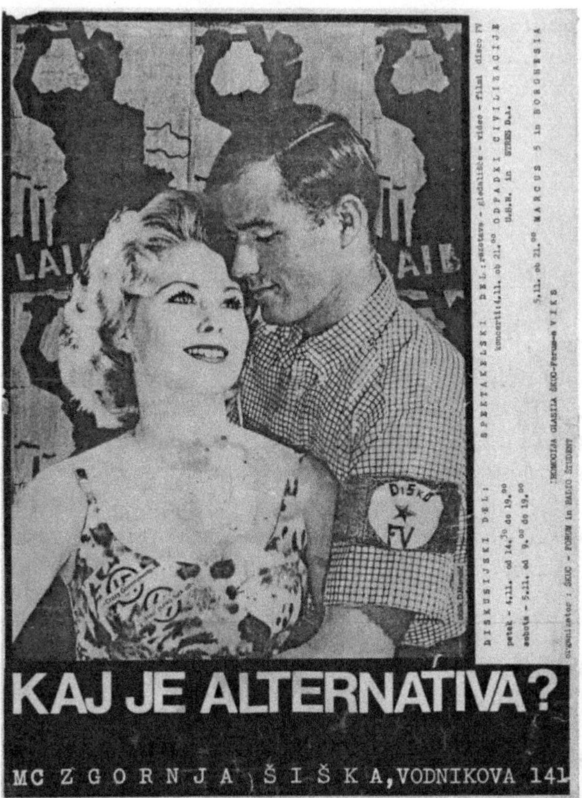

5.1. Dušan Mandić, "*Kaj je alternativa?* (What Is the Alternative?)" poster for a symposium at Disko FV, Ljubljana, 1983. Courtesy of Dušan Mandić and FV Archive at MGLC – International Centre for Graphic Arts Ljubljana.

In socialist Yugoslavia the notion of civil society and alternative were connected and inherent in the advent of new social movements in the 1980s, which, for the most part, emerged within youth and student structures. Indeed these movements adopted the term "alternative culture" (*alternativna kultura*) or simply "the alternative" (*alternativa*) from the student movement. Sociologist Tomaž Mastnak, one of the key figures of the 1980s alternative culture and who dedicated his academic research and activist work to the concept of the civil society,[22] maintains that the notion of the "alternative culture" or "alternative scene" was introduced at the symposium "What Is the Alternative? (*Kaj je alternativa?*)" in November 1983, at Disko FV, then situated in the Šiška Youth Centre in Ljubljana.[23] This in his view is where these notions merged or came into association. Prior to this symposium, the discourse and debates about civil society in the context of socialist countries was mostly confined to academic circles in Slovenia and had yet become one of the slogans of the alternative. The debates about "civil society" were connected to the intellectual discussions in other countries in the Eastern Bloc, where the idea of promoting civil society was in fact the ideology of the political opposition that demanded democratization.[24]

In the Yugoslav context the discourse of the civil society was ambivalent. Today Mastnak frankly admits that the discourse of the civil society was conceived of as a program, albeit an unusual one, since it "was characterized as searching for an 'alternative' socialism, a 'freer, more democratic socialism'"[25] that positioned itself against the state. The opposition to the state was contradictory in the context of Yugoslav self-management in that in its ideal scenario it aimed to abolish the state apparatus. Rastko Močnik thus contends that the notion of civil society was "hardly anything more than a political catchphrase" because Yugoslav self-management represented anti-statism and sought to "eliminate the state and directly organize the society in such a way that a 'pluralism of self-managed interests' could be enforced through its institutions."[26] Therefore he argues that from this viewpoint and this "political horizon … there would be nothing 'alternative' about asserting the 'civil society' against the 'state.'"[27] Not only was this slogan not revolutionary, it was lacking a position informed by the rising class differences in socialist Yugoslavia and detrimental in its ignorance of the role that the state has in the political economy of a socialist society. Nonetheless, the discourse of the civil society in Yugoslavia, and particularly in Slovenia, where these discussions were articulated to the greatest degree, was understood as an opposition to the state, epitomized by the Party or, in Mastnak's words, to the socialist bourgeoisie.[28] However, what was not addressed in this program was the economic and class inequalities that characterized Yugoslav society. While the dominant groups within the LYC may have earned the term red bourgeoisie, the alternative movement's lack of class analysis and an investigation of the political economy is jarring from our present moment. Partly that was a consequence of the movement's middle-class provenance and the fact that it was based in Slovenia, the most prosperous republic that enjoyed almost full employment. Economic hardship was not an issue for these generations of intellectuals and cultural workers, oppression by the state or party bourgeoisie was.

In other words the generation who participated in the student movement of the late 1960s and remained politically active afterwards in the 1980s saw social issues as a problem of power and authority of LYC that arbitrarily violated its own laws and limited the rights and freedoms of the people. The struggle of what we could call the New Left under Yugoslav socialism took place in the form of a struggle for the "pluralization of lifestyles,"[29] that should have translated into softening the oppressive nature of socialism but not eliminating socialism. However, the tactics lacked an analysis of existing political economy and the rise of the neoliberal project. In a recent essay on the effects of the discourse of civil society on the politics of the 1980s alternative culture, Mastnak acknowledges that while the endorsement of civil society "was not [fuelled by] anti-socialism, or anti-communism," socialism nevertheless became "the collateral damage that came out of falling in love with civil society," which was in turn affected by an imprudent, spontaneous absorption of liberalism.[30] By the 1980s, the demands of the 1960s Yugoslav student movement, which demanded economic justice and true self-management, became the basis of a movement for an alternative that strived to reform the existing socialist system and assert human rights and the rule of law.

The conflict of the 1980s was based neither on an analysis of the class composition of the SFRY, nor on a discussion of the differences in working conditions, economic equality, and emerging new forms of labour (in which post-Fordism coincided with neoliberalism). It was marked by a discourse that criticized the dominant self-management ideology and classless notions, such as a civil society and basic human rights.

Additionally, as Močnik showed in his later analysis of Yugoslav socialism, the reason that an actual transformation of socialist self-management did not take place during the 1980s lies in the destructive strategy of the Party's leading faction, which played the national (read: nationalist) card. In turn the working classes – the industrial/Fordist workers – shifted their support to the goal of strengthening the national economy, that is the economy of each of the six republics comprising the SFRY rather than the country as a whole.[31] The nationalist ideals were also affecting the field of cultural production, in which ideals of a national culture that were deeply connected to bourgeois culture and the art canon became important anchors that tore the country apart. Ideals of national culture assisted in articulating the divergent national identities as the ideological foundation of the new nation-states that emerged after the breakup of the SFRY. Slovenia, as the most economically successful republic where liberal elites were particularly interested to break off from the rest of Yugoslavia and join the liberal West, was indeed the most skilful in employing the nationalist card through a performance of victimhood of the historically oppressed Slovene nation. Other republics of the Yugoslav federation that were also ethnically more mixed that Slovenia, however, were not able to escape or avoid the inevitable nationalistic carnage and violence that was in fact underpinned by growing economic inequalities between the six republics.

The peculiar socialist concept of unemployment – a symptom that is otherwise characteristic of social stratification – undoubtedly affected this state of affairs. While unemployment became a structural problem in Yugoslavia from the mid-1960s onwards, it was socially invisible.[32] As Susan Woodward established in her seminal study, in the SFRY unemployment meant "to be without means of subsistence" and was, in principle, preventable with a guaranteed minimum wage and protected smallholdings.[33] Woodward showed that unemployment was not an indicator of "penury or proletarization of classic industrialization."[34] The Yugoslav population was not stratified with regard to "vulnerability to unemployment," but with respect to "disposable income."[35] "The problem of joblessness was supplanted by that of living standards."[36] Unemployment was socially invisible, because it was understood as "voluntary or short-lived, a choice for leisure instead of work made according to household standards of consumption."[37] The socialist understanding of unemployment consequently affected the perceptions of employment. In this sense, young people with a certain level of educational qualification were automatically expected to obtain employment. Moreover, it was a common understanding that a good job and a better standard of living were dependent on the quality of one's educational qualifications (higher education equalled a higher living standard) rather than the number of actual, available jobs.[38] However, the fact remains that job creation and access to a job became scarce, even in republics such as Slovenia and Croatia, that had until the mid-1980s, enjoyed full employment. For example, in Slovenia, the number of employees in public cultural institutions between 1978 and 1988 only increased by approximately 24 per cent (or 730 employees),[39] while the number of students that pursued education in cultural professions and at various art academies[40] – who represented a reserve army of cultural workers – kept rising.

The social resistance focus of the alternative culture shifted from issues of economic inequality and class stratification to questions of freedoms and human rights, demilitarization, and the rule of law. The situation was a consequence of the obscuring of class conflict within self-managed socialism and the social and political invisibility of unemployment. Reflecting the symptom of a concealed economic inequality in self-managed socialism, the discourse of civil society that emerged in the arena of social struggles was riddled with contradictions. It primarily dealt with limiting repressive state apparatuses and implementing the rule of law. There was no critical examination of the relations between the state and the economy among the 1980s alternative culture. Mastnak asserts that the protagonists of the alternative culture "had absolutely no clear idea about ... the role the state was to have in relation to the economy – which was not surprising because they, as a rule, had nothing sensible or informed to say about economic matters."[41]

The alternative culture's views about the opposition between the state and the civil society were overly simplified. As noted by Stipe Ćurković, equating the state with "a sum of repressive apparatuses" on the one hand, and the civil society with a "sphere of potential realization of the individual's freedom" on the other, "neglected the differences between the mandates of different state institutions."[42] This equivalence "put repressive apparatuses and the institutions of common social reproduction, such as the publicly funded health and education systems, in a continuum."[43] In this rendering of the opposition between the state and the civil society, the history of labour struggles for a social wage is invisible and the "contradictions that permeate the civil society disappear as both the subject of critique and as the object of political problematization."[44] The discourse of the civil society overlooked the issue of economic inequality that stemmed from altered forms and conditions of labour and employment through which "the working people of Yugoslavia" (*delovno ljudstvo/radni narod Yugoslavije*) had access to subsistence. The political struggle of the 1980s alternative was limited and shortsighted as it grounded itself in ideas of civil society. Clearly it was a generational struggle of highly educated urban youth without prospects but it articulated itself as a movement demanding human rights while it naïvely forgot that the socialist worker remained a cog in the machine of an economy pressured by international capitalism and the neoliberal offensive. In sum, the conditions in late socialism were marked by the crisis of the socialist welfare state and a host of internal political battles for an alternative to socialism. It was a generational struggle, united by its demand for human rights with disregard for waning economic and workers' rights. This struggle had its parallel in the alternative culture's disregard for the transformation of artistic labour.

The Emergence of the Socialist Art Entrepreneur

The alternative culture of the 1980s had no political, artistic, or class homogeneity: they had different political orientations; some members came from small towns or rural areas, and others from richer urban areas; some were dancers, others performers, street artists, and conceptual artists etc., few of whom would have agreed on the quality or merit of the art they produced. Despite the differences among the groups of alternative culture, the non-nationalist ethos of the alternative culture stood in opposition with the conservative ideals of (bourgeois) national culture.[45] Močnik for example maintains that various groups that made the alternative culture of the 1980s were "the formulations of potentiality that the federal socialist Yugoslavia could be" and "what its creative and productive possibilities were."[46] However, Nikolai Jeffs points out, that in socialist Yugoslavia, "not all of the social heterogenization of the eighties took place on the battlefront between the alternative culture and the official, or dominant culture," rather, heterogeneity, ideological divisions, and conflicts also characterized the alternative scene of the 1980s.[47]

From a contemporary perspective the function of the alternative culture in the breakup of the socialist self-management system can be understood as a decade-long eruption of social forces that adopted idiosyncratic practices to pierce the heavy armour of the single-party system and its discursive and administrative repression, with the intent to liberalize it. By doing so, the alternative culture bypassed the issues of class stratification, impact of neoliberal ideology, and the dismantling of the welfare mechanism that took place against the backdrop of the change from the Fordist paradigm of the capitalist mode of production (based on factories and wage labourers) to the post-Fordist paradigm and its endemic forms of labour. In the post-Fordist paradigm, mass employment of workers was replaced by an army of the self-employed, who became "divorced from the social conditions of production,"[48] that is, from the social protection enjoyed by industrial workers and workers in liberal professions, which was established and provided by the socialist welfare state.

In the process of the breakup of Yugoslavia, a part of the socialist working class within the alternative culture ended up in precarious working conditions. Such dynamics were parallel to the political defeat of the Western working class in the late 1970s that was "a consequence of technological restructuring, the resulting unemployment and the violent repression of working class avant-gardes."[49] The path to these new labour conditions was paved by reforms designed in the 1980s that prepared the ground for the introduction of an entrepreneurial logic in the field of art and culture, for instance, with specialized laws for independent artists and cultural workers that were implemented in several republics in the socialist Yugoslavia.[50] The socialist cultural policy integrated freelance artists and cultural workers into the mechanism of the welfare state by embracing the concept of independent work, which regulated the conditions for artistic labour and ensured that art workers, along with other workers of liberal professions, were socially protected.

In Slovenia, Croatia, and Macedonia this regime was ostensibly upgraded with the Law for Independent Artists in both Croatia (1979) and Macedonia (1982), and the Law for Independent Cultural Workers in Slovenia (1982).[51] As argued by some researchers in Slovenia, self-employment lowered the rate of unemployment and represented an alternative to employment in a period when there was a lack of resources for job creation.[52] In other words these laws were a mechanism through which freelance art workers became self-employed creators or sole proprietors after the breakup of Yugoslavia. The laws signalled the coming of the second-generation independent work[53] and the precariousness endemic to it. From the point of view of cultural policy makers, the laws in all three republics were introduced to improve the socio-economic circumstances of independent cultural workers. In this sense Slovenian law went the furthest by expanding the list of cultural professions that the law encompassed. In Croatia and Macedonia it only pertained to independent artists. In Slovenia, however, the law pertained not only to independent artists but also to other "cultural workers," such as film workers, translators, and all other cultural workers who "create cultural values" to freely choose and independently perform cultural and artistic labour by working as a socialist version of a sole proprietor within the framework of the free exchange of labour.

Shrouded as they were in the discourse of self-management ideology all three laws proclaimed that independent art workers "have equal socioeconomic position and in principle equal rights and obligations as the workers in the organizations of associated labour."[54] However, the laws planted the seeds for the introduction of the entrepreneurial logic, regardless of the fact that in the early 1980s, mechanisms guaranteeing social security were still functional. As early as 1987, researcher Marjana Bele symptomatically noted that each independent art worker was in fact "a one-person OAL [organization of associated labour, i.e., a socialist enterprise]" and that we may consider them as "'free enterprise' type of people," who "steer, oversee and carry out the labour process. They search for clients. They do everything that, in the organizations of associated labour, is specialized, distributed among numerous workers, and divided into several work processes."[55] In contemporary terms, independent cultural workers are sole proprietors or independent entrepreneurs, or, in even more up-to-date terms, they are self-employed, that is, workers that "are external suppliers who do not receive a wage or a salary sufficient for their own reproduction, but are paid according to performance."[56] These workers, as Sergio Bologna ironically indicates, live "at their own expense."[57] They need to secure work and then cover all the expenses of the labour process including their own reproduction as opposed to employed workers where the employer covers part of the social reproduction and also secures the work. Couched in the language of freedom and creativity, these workers were defined as enterprises but because of the weakening socialist welfare state this in fact signalled their proletarization. The gist of the transformation is that the self-employed workers not only "become both entrepreneurs and proletarians, but entrepreneurs *as* proletarians, that is, they oversee and manage their own human capital in competition with all other proletarians-entrepreneurs."[58]

As discussed in the previous chapter, the price of such freelance life in the 1980s was detailed plainly in *Prvi broj* (The First Issue), in which Sanja Iveković and Dalibor Martinis presented a comparative table of labour costs for an independent artist and an employee in a cultural institution. These laws' misleading introduction of an ostensibly revolutionary autonomy and freedom of cultural production that is reminiscent of the pre-capitalistic artisanal mode of labour was, in fact, a regression. While the welfare state guaranteed a social wage for employees, the new laws for independent artists and cultural workers transferred the costs of social security onto the backs of the art workers. For example, the Croatian Law for Independent Artists explicitly stated, "The tributary for the contributions to the health, retirement, and disability insurance is each independent artist personally."[59] The production autonomy of art workers paradoxically normalized the idea of self-care and personal responsibility for an individual's social protection as the state diminished its role in welfare provision. This was a two-fold problem. First, the socio-economic situation was altered globally due to the 1970s recession and the ascent of neoliberalism. Next, this affected the economic foundations of the welfare state in its socialist form. It was difficult to expand social welfare mechanisms that would enable life beyond the structural pressure of labour while the country was pressured by IMF and other Western institutions to embark on austerity measures to repay its debts. The autonomy of artistic labour no longer meant the freedom to self-organize the working process and time, which previously was made possible by socialist state financial support of art production and generous welfare provision for independent artistic work. Rather, independent work became a false choice that the state organized in line with the neoliberal entrepreneurial logic of competition and a race for increasingly stagnating, limited public funds. In their study of neoliberal rationality Dardot and Laval underline that the very characteristics of neoliberalism are "unprecedented techniques of power over conduct and subjectivities"[60] and individuals' submission to the pressures of competition. "Neo-liberal governmentality is based on a *global normative framework*, which, in the name of liberty, and relying on the leeway afforded individuals, orientates their conduct, choices, and practices in a new way."[61] This new way is based in competition not solidarity. Under the guise of improving art workers' socio-economic circumstances, these tendencies were part of the ethos of the Croatian and Macedonian Laws for Independent Artists and the Slovenian Law for Independent Cultural Workers. They all paved the way to transfer the responsibility for social welfare onto the shoulders of individual art workers. Neither the emerging entrepreneurial logic nor the implied recomposition of the working classes were the subjects of the alternative culture or social movements of the 1980s. The debates remained powered by the discourse of civil society, civil liberties, and freedom as the pivotal point of social transformation. This outcome is no doubt so visible from today's point of view since the aftermath of the struggle for alternative socialism was won by neoliberal capitalism. The reason why this blueprint of neoliberal logic needs to be exposed in the context of Yugoslav culture of the 1980s, however, is because it was powered by ideals of autonomy and creativity, the hallmarks of the Western bourgeois model of art, which was, as we saw in the previous chapters, emulated in the socialist institution of art.

The institutional shield of the welfare state still appeared functional during the mid 1980s, hence the political antagonisms did not manifest as class stratification. Conflicts in the field of art and cultural production were, therefore, struggles for recognition and entitlement to equitable terms of existence for alternative art practices in the socialist institution of art – and not a struggle against the idea of art as an autonomous social sphere. For example, artist Neven Korda, co-founder of Disko FV, an important art collective of the alternative culture, claims that the 1980s can be seen as a period when "alternative cultural practices were searching for a way of inclusion in the dominant culture."[62] Nikolai Jeffs concurs and adds that during the 1980s, the alternative art scene was in a dilemma whether to "transform itself into a counterculture and preserve its oppositional, uncompromising, but also socially isolated status" or to become part of the mass culture and take the risk of "being instrumentalized by the ruling elites" or, even worse, to "reproduce the same relations of power and authority that [it] initially opposed."[63] While the apparatus of traditional socialist cultural institutions had undoubtedly sustained its hegemony, the 1980s alternative culture established itself as a new avant-garde that demanded social recognition and space but without questioning the presuppositions of Western art. According to art historian Barbara Borčić, who was, from 1980 to 1985, one of the three leaders of the Ljubljana student cultural centre, the ŠKUC Gallery, the alternative scene was "an institution of difference vis-à-vis the ruling ideology and cultural policy" that fought "for alternative art practices and their social recognition in the face of what was officially considered as art, a confrontation with the cultural stereotypes, myths, taboos, contemporary technology and mass-media procedures."[64] In other words, this was a struggle for different kind of art and not against art as a Western bourgeois institution. In a way these artists continued the struggle of the new art practice from the late 1960s and 1970s and were still in fact trying to become another version of what Đorđević called "the new tradition." This eruption of creative forces by younger generations in the 1980s had its prehistory in 1968, when the authorities suppressed the political demands of the student movement, but as a concession, the LCY dedicated infrastructure for their creative endeavours. While student cultural centres became crucial platforms for the younger art workers, by the 1980s a drought of financial support became an issue due to the deepening Yugoslav economic crisis. Hence, the legal regulation of cultural labour was an attempt by cultural policy to solve the issue of the reserve army of cultural labour and the problem of job creation in the field of culture.

The 1980s alternative culture was a cacophonous, distinctly heterogeneous social phenomenon. It was defined by differences that did not hinder political action, but established surprising alliances and culminated in the demise of the Yugoslav project, and the formation of individual nation states. As the discourse of the civil society gained hegemony and nationalism escalated, alliances and coalitions that came into existence, especially after 1988,[65] proved problematic. After the breakup of the SFRY, when former socialist republics became nation-states, social cohesion fell apart. Neoliberal policies, or rather, accumulation with dispossession[66] in combination with disintegration of social solidarity, took over. In Mastnak's words, this was a period when the civil society came into power. "The coming of civil society to power was the overture to the catastrophe that saw no end in sight" even though the usurpation of power by the civil society was "a counterpoint to the expectations that had fueled the civil social movements."[67] In the following chapter I detail the contradictions that shaped this outcome. One part of the equation was related to the alternative culture's attempts to implement new production models into the realm of the socialist institution of art, the other can be seen as its counterpart that was exemplified by the cultural policy, which in attempts to solve employment issues disenfranchised new generations of art workers by turning them into socialist entrepreneurs.

Chapter Six

The Contradictions of 1980s Alternative Art

This chapter focuses on two different approaches to the alternative production model; the first rejected the socialist institutional model of art and aimed to exist in a parallel universe as it were, and the other wanted to reform it. They both failed, for reasons that will be detailed here, to unveil the process through which the artist as worker was transformed into a socialist entrepreneur in a way that contributed to their own undoing and the end of labour rights. The 1980s alternative art scene in advocating for new production models of culture did not consider, for instance, the class stratification and the legislative transformation of the working relations of freelance art workers. While these movements aimed to redefine Yugoslav socialism and its system of cultural production by criticizing socialist ideology, they failed to address the deteriorating working conditions of art workers and to critique the Western notion of art's autonomy, which affects the invisibility of artistic labour. The process which, during the 1990s, resulted in a transformation of the protagonists of the alternative art scene into members of the post-socialist precariat of self-employed cultural entrepreneurs paradoxically took place through the obscuring of art as labour on the account of artistic autonomy.

The 1980s saw new attempts to introduce an alternative model of art production. The majority of these attempts found an inspiration in the practices of the historical avant-garde, neo-avant-garde, and conceptual art movements, but they were not necessarily concerned with the critique of the autonomy of art that was reproduced in the socialist institution of art. For example, while Đorđević's work that I discussed in chapter 4 and his writings on the artist as a pseudo-subject were read by members of the 1980s alternative culture, his critique in the form of a direct attack on the mystifications of art did not create a larger movement, at least not for the strategy of a radical direct confrontation with art that was based on the deconstruction of the nature of artistic labour. Đorđević's radical critique, although moderated, was, however, significant for the development of institutional critique advanced by alternative artistic practices. The attitudes of the 1980s alternative culture, as this chapter argues, did not question Western art and were not in conflict with the autonomy of the institution of art that would have affected the subservient status of art workers and that would have questioned the presuppositions about artistic labour as invisible work. Rather the 1980s alternative culture was a platform for a critique of the rigidity and conformity of mainstream socialist art institutions; they were for a new and different kind of art but not ready to question art. The alternative culture criticized socialist art institutions and put forth a plethora of divergent demands that would establish and de-marginalize alternative art practices in Yugoslavia. If I borrow Zagorka Golubović's words, the alternative culture of the 1980s "represents a struggle for *personal* affirmation in the domain of culture, through the choice of orientation, style, and theme in individual cultural work,"[1] and as such continued the agenda of the new art practice from the late 1960s and 1970s, that is, to use Đorđević's words, to become "the new tradition."[2] While the struggle for the affirmation of a different understanding of art and the interests of the new generations of cultural workers in socialist Yugoslavia was no doubt a legitimate and relevant agenda, the issue, as viewed from the point of labour exploitation in the arts, was the misguidedness of the method or strategy. The strategy "protests against the existing system, but within the framework of the system's basic presuppositions."[3] It questioned the rules but not the game itself. The labour point of view was lacking and contributed to the undoing of art as labour.

In this political battlefield the alternative culture chose two distinct approaches to the cultural politics of the 1980s. One approach was parallel institutionalization; the other was reform through a critique of socialist cultural institutions. Neither of them pertained to the invisibility of artistic labour. The first approach attempted to create a parallel system of art organizations that would support interdisciplinary art forms, such as performance, street art, dance, and video, and the multidisciplinary cross-section of visual art, theatre, music, and architecture. However, this strategy struggled due to financial marginalization, naïve ideas about the market, and an anti-state attitude whereby the welfare mandate of the state was ignored on account of the critique of state oppression. The second approach was that of reform through a critique, in which the idea was to occupy the mainstream socialist institutions, reform them from the inside, and use their resources to establish a new international vision of avant-garde art. However, it also failed because the system was not willing to support new artistic expressions that were not espousing a clear nationalist ethos. Since the "new tradition" did not affirm "national" tradition through culture, it did not stand a chance. Finally, the cultural policy changes of labour regulation for art workers established a formidable platform through which socialist institutions were able to rely on outsourced labour of independent artists and cultural workers. Considering the larger economic crisis and looming neoliberalization, art workers lost the safety net of the socialist welfare state.

I have chosen just two examples from the multitude of artistic practices on the 1980s alternative scene to discuss the two approaches to alternative production models. These two examples, both based in Slovenia, are Disko FV and Scipion Nasice Sisters Theatre (SNST), because they illustrate the key problems of Yugoslav cultural policy that have persisted and have been exacerbated since the country's breakup. These issues include the inaccessibility of infrastructure for emerging art practices, inequitable production models for artistic and cultural practices of new generations, the prevalence of traditional bourgeois national(istic) cultural institutions, and the lack of available funding for alternative art practices, all of which affected the working conditions of art workers already in the 1980s. The trajectory of the two examples and their approaches to alternative production models is juxtaposed by the socio-legal transformation of art workers into socialist entrepreneurs, which affected the conditions for artistic labour in the SFRY and its aftermath. Both cases are from Slovenia also because they are linked to the only newly built socialist infrastructure during the 1980s – Cankarjev dom (CD). This impressive cultural infrastructure emerged as a harbinger of neoliberal rationality's reign in the realm of cultural policy: the exploitation of outsourced artistic labour. CD, which was and still is a public cultural institution, is one important agent of the neoliberal policies that were already bourgeoning in the 1980s. CD was very open to the aesthetics of the alternative culture and included these practices in its various programs, from dance to theatre to video art and performance. The case of the SNST and the production of their monumental performance *Baptism under Triglav* serves as a case in point, but also as a symptom of what the *novum* of the production models of alternative culture was. In other words, CD rose as the new dominant institution, open to alternative artistic practices but engendering an exploitative relation embodied in the practice of outsourcing underpaid artistic labour for its artistic programs.

The Case of Disko FV: Parallel Institutionalization

Theatre FV 112/15[4] (later called simply FV) was one of the alternative art groups formed in Slovenia in the context of the ŠKD Forum (Student Cultural Association Forum) in the first half of the 1980s and featured artists, performers, musicians, and club organizers. The theatre group considered itself a "punk theatre" that aimed to "rescue the past from servitude to the bureaucratized apparatus of the ideology of the state, as it then existed."[5] Korda, one of the co-founders, explains, "the FV 'conglomerate' belonged, above all, to the counterculture, the underground."[6] The first FV performances took place in Disco Student (*Disko Študent*), a student disco located on the campus of student housing in Ljubljana.

The collective of artists initially functioned foremost as an experimental theatre group FV 112/15 that saw the disco club as an expansion of theatre beyond its traditional contexts.[7] "The disco [was] a part of the show or vice versa, the show [was] a part of the disco."[8] Shows or evenings comprised a collage of quotes taken from various artworks and media and the appropriation of symbols of the self-managed socialist everyday life, and in which the ironic attitudes toward bourgeois culture played an important role. In an interview for the journal *Problemi* in 1982, Zemira Alajbegović, one of the co-founders, explained: "Our theater activity is somewhat contradictory – we're taking a stance, albeit not a firm one, inside the theatre tradition, but our work is to a much greater degree influenced by the production of mass media, which represents our most important frame of reference."[9] The theatre was performed by different means, and it left the traditionally designed dark box with a stage/ramp that distanced the audience in order to become a space of collective experience. Concerts, video projections, conferences/ symposiums, exhibitions, and theme events were all part of the disco. Besides organizing the evening disco "shows," Theatre FV soon expanded its work on other activities, including a nightclub program and video production (which also established and included documentary work) as well as music, performances (Borghesia), and the production of vinyl records and audio tapes (FV Label).[10]

In all its locations from 1981 until 1985 when it lost its space, Disko FV greatly contributed to the formation of the socializing milieu of the alternative scene. The art workers and participating audience took over the various public spaces and contributed to "democratization of forms of sociability, art and politics,"[11] not only through support and production of alternative art practice but also by asserting LGBTQ+ rights and the right to non-normative sexuality and lifestyles in general. According to Alajbegović, FV's practice was that of utopian activism.[12] Or as Korda maintains: "The disco was all about making it possible for high culture to enter the space of mass culture. To do this, FV first had to create such a space, adapt it, and of course, constantly maintain it. It was about facilitating a 'place of descent,' and not about presenting a given project. The project was something that merely used the 'place of descent' for its setting."[13] The spaces created by the collective were thus crucial to the rise of the alternative culture and new social movements in the SFRY that struggled to transform the Yugoslav socialist culture.

The FV's method of establishing the space for alternative art practices was that of parallel institutionalization and not a transformation of the existing socialist art institutions. FV understood the mission of the 1980s alternative culture as a matter of "establishing a parallel, self-sufficient world," which was "directed toward 'naive freedom,' toward a 'utopian model of coexistence in the dominant culture.' In terms of the place of production, the place of creation, and the place of representation or consumption, it was directed away from theatre, away from galleries, away from 'official' music labels, and away from television."[14]

After the first two seasons (1981–2, 1982–3) Disko FV moved from its initial location in Disko Študent in the basement of building four in the student village, a complex of student housing in the Rožna Dolina neighbourhood, to the Šiška Youth Centre. According to Jeffs, Disko Študent was "closed under pressure from the authorities."[15] In Šiška (another neighbourhood in Ljubljana), the Disko FV team created the program and new members joined the team so that the program had three different nights (Disko FV night, heavy metal night, and a night for hardcore punk). Korda maintains, "The club in Šiška was the fullest realization of FV's idea of a club. Especially during the period when we were able to use the auditorium of the district community on a regular basis each week," since it had the capacity to hold four to five hundred people, which was in addition to a bar and disco in the basement.[16] The team of Disko FV was managing weekly programs, and the Šiška venue became the site for various art projects (for example, exhibitions by other members of alternative art practices), symposiums, gay and lesbian festivals, of and for artists living in Ljubljana, from other parts of the SFRY, and from abroad. Moreover, the Disko FV team organized presentations of the "Ljubljana alternative scene" in other cities in the SFRY.[17] However, the life of Disko FV lasted only one season at the Šiška Youth Centre (1983–4). After FV lost the use of the auditorium, the final seasons of Disko FV (1984–5) took place in the basement of a building on Kersnik Street 4, that FV named K4. Since the entire building on Kersnik Street 4 was transformed into the Centre for Activities of Youth, FV could move its activity into the basement. Over three weeks, the team turned the neglected basement into a club, which became yet another version of Disko FV and the share of public grants for the theatre group was used to open the new disco club. "This was [FV Disko's] third incarnation, or exercise in style, this time a variation on the 'squat'.... Here everything needed to be done, from the wiring and plumbing to the furnishings, organizing the space, the walls, the stage, and the audio system."[18] For example, the artist Dušan Mandić fashioned a visual image and also made large graffiti on one of the walls in the disco. The program of the K4 maintained its multidisciplinary nature, from various DJ music nights, to film nights, video art screenings, exhibitions as well as their emancipatory political stances towards the oppressive dominant cultural trends, norms, and behaviours.

So decisively linked to the creation of a new cultural space, the decline of Disko FV was symptomatic of the loss of access to public space. As early as the mid-1980s, this situation revealed not only that "the policy of denying and preventing access to and/or management of spaces" had replaced "the policy of repressing alternative subcultures and subpolitical actors," but also that "(non) availability of spaces is one of the structural problems" of alternative art practices and that it is, in fact, trans-generational.[19] The availability of space or access to it was part of the alternative's political program and its struggle to redefine cultural production in urban centres. In addition, the demand for space was tied to the changes in cultural policy that should have redefined the institutional organization of the socialist cultural production. The effects of these struggles were amplified in the 1990s and were undoubtedly affected both by the breakup of the SFRY and the unsuccessful demands to reform self-managed socialism.

In his interpretation of the FV, which he calls "the third scene," Jeffs stresses that the managerial takeover of Disko Študent was a key moment for the group, which was then able to expand its activities and supposedly incorporate a new model of cultural economy that was "independent of any subsidies from various official bodies."[20] However, the facts provided by Korda in his detailed contribution on the operations of FV do not support such an interpretation. Disko FV's economic organization was in part based on subsidies and on the infrastructure of the ŠKD Forum, as well as on "finding a balance between the public and private sectors" by offering services and funding the creative work through ŠKD in addition to public subsides.[21] However, public funds were extremely limited. In the 1982 interview for the journal *Problemi*, Alajbegović explained that the "conditions under which theatre groups (and music bands) perform[ed] in Forum [were] catastrophic in terms of space and miserable in terms of finances. At best, they [sufficed] for running a poor theatre or recital club."[22] What then, characterized this ostensibly new model of cultural economy? It was based on meagre subsidies, self-funding (via selling tickets and drinks at the bar), and unpaid labour. It was, in fact, quite similar to the economy of art production in the era of neoliberal capitalism.

Similar claims about new models of cultural production are featured in scholarly discussions and historic interpretations of the 1980s alternative scene.[23] In a somewhat perverted logic, these interpretations identify revolutionizing features and the autonomy of art production as independent from state and public funding. Selling goods and services is not a new model of art economy. It is merely an inevitable (though obscured) fact in the institution of art that is founded on a disavowal of economy and the invisible labour of art workers. The issue here should not be that public funding be provided by the welfare state. On the contrary, the issue should be that there is equal access to public funds and spaces for new art production and the deconstruction of cultural hierarchies and traditional institutional models of art that sustain inequality and the exploitation of art workers.

The Case of NSK's Theatre SNST: Institutional Transformation through Critique

In the political battles for an alternative socialism that took place in the last decade of the SFRY's existence, the theatre productions of SNST, one of the founding groups of the larger collective Neue Slowenische Kunst (NSK), represents another case of how alternative art practices struggled to transform the field of socialist cultural production. While the SNST emerged in the context of 1980s alternative culture, it developed a different strategy to establish a new production model for alternative art practices. In contrast to the parallel institutionalization, the SNST's method was based in critique of the existing stratification of the socialist institution of art wherein alternative art practices were marginalized. Specifically, the aim of the SNST's critique was the network of socialist theatres, which emulated the nineteenth-century bourgeois European theatre model and served as the bastion of nationalist ideology.[24] It should be noted that cultural policy in socialist Yugoslavia turned sharply towards the concept of national culture in the mid-1970s, specifically after the new Constitution of 1974, which recognized "the nationalist composition of the state-party apparatuses," and thus transformed the "Yugoslavian federation into a *de facto* confederation of nation-states."[25] This meant that each republic was developing its own national cultural policy and priorities. For example, the idea of a national Slovenian culture as the constitutive part of Slovenian nationhood was used as an ideological operation that covered the underlying liberal, market-oriented transformation of the political economy, along with a nationalistic ideology, which in the end resulted in the violent breakup of the SFRY and the creation of nation states. The SNST's form of institutional critique within Yugoslav socialism was directed at the paradoxical unoriginality of the socialist institution of art, which embraced the bourgeois institutional model rather than develop a new avant-garde cultural model.

The SNST was established on October 13, 1983 by three art and theatre academy students: dramaturge Eda Čufer, visual artist Miran Mohar, and theatre director Dragan Živadinov. Their names became known only later, once the SNST self-abolished in 1987.[26] The SNST ceremoniously announced its existence in *The Founding Act*, in which they declared that they were a theatre without a stage; this statement was not merely philosophical but also factual. *The Founding Act* proclaimed what appeared to be an impossible program: to occupy "the space of any performing arts institution" in a span of four years with an exact timeline of production activities that would end with an act of self-destruction.[27] The central creative program involved three theatre performances dubbed "retrograde events" that epitomized the phases of the SNST's program of transforming the socialist theatre. While the group "emerged from the underground and had no institutional background or communication networks on which they could rely to promote their work,"[28] it is a remarkable coincidence of history that the SNST, in fact, realized the transition from the margins to the centre, as they announced in *The Founding Act*. The first two self-funded and self-produced theatre performances took place in private spaces for less than thirty audience members who were invited by mail or contacted individually. The first, *Hinkemann*, was held in 1984 in an apartment in Ljubljana; the second, *Marija Nablocka*, was held in 1985 in a design studio undergoing renovations. Both performances were invited to Zagreb and to the Belgrade International Theatre Festival (BITEF). Even more, after seeing the first performance, *Hinkemann*, Goran Schmidt, the artistic director of the Theatre and Film Department in CD, suggested that the SNST move the performance "to one of the new centre's roughly built basement spaces, and advertise the performances through the centre's own network of contacts."[29] Schmidt had seen the SNST's first *Retrogarde Event Hinkemann* and ascertained that they were a young, educated, well-prepared, and aesthetically innovative group capable of realizing an unconventional large-scale performance for the large new stage.[30] Additionally he proposed that the SNST create a performance for Slovenian Culture Day, one of the most important holidays in Slovenia, to be staged in CD. The holiday celebrates the cultural origins of the Slovenian people by commemorating the death of its greatest national poet France Prešeren.[31] Consequently, the SNST's third and last performance, *Baptism under Triglav*, had its premiere in 1986 at the newly built cultural and congress centre in Ljubljana in the largest venue, Gallus Hall, which seats 1,500 people.

Through the strategic use of totalitarian imagery, the iconography of the historical avant-gardes of the 1920s and the Wagnerian format of the *Gesamtkunstwerk*, the SNST's monumental theatre performance, *Retrogarde Event Baptism under Triglav*, confronted the implicit nationalistic tendencies within Slovenian society in general, and theatre institutions specifically. The approach with which they provoked their antagonist – the text-based national theatre model – was to stage an aesthetically radical performance with practically no spoken words or stanzas from the actual text, France Prešeren's "Baptism on the Savica." The SNST did not dramatize the storyline of this Romantic epic poem depicting the central myth of the Slovene national identity in any classical way. Instead they replaced the storyline by creating "a distinctly rhythmic, visual, and musical-stage spectacle that was impossible to classify as theatre, opera, or ballet, although it borrowed elements from all these art forms."[32] Exploiting the poem's topic of baptism, which the SNST interpreted as a form of crossing or shifting paradigms, they created an abstract visual and musical performance, since the "central aim was to visualize the moment of baptism" in the realm of aesthetics and history of art rather than in the religious-political sphere. The SNST's temporary occupation of the central stage with this sophisticated visual theatre, however, caused a general uproar and polarized the art world. Some members of the art and intellectual circles, particularly in Slovenia, accused the SNST of formalism. Others reproached the SNST for instrumentalizing alternative culture and falling prey to the allure of mainstream institutions.[33] Some were more perceptive. Alenka Zupančič, for example, argued, "Scipions [laid] the entire burden of 'politics' on the side of the theatre called 'audience'" and had thus produced "the greatest possible provocation."[34]

Part of the SNST's enigmatic appeal certainly lay in the group's appropriation of an authoritative attitude reminiscent of the grandiose utopian language and mode of operation of historical avant-garde art groups. In the SNST's first manifesto, written in a form of a letter, the group notably stated, "Theater does not exist between the Spectator and the Actor. Theater is not an empty space. Theater is a State."[35] By repositioning and redefining the relationship between the (national) theatre and the (nation) state, the SNST was not subscribing to the civil society's anti-statism. On the contrary, the SNST staged the usurpation of power in an attempt to take over the state and its dominant cultural institutions. "By insisting that transnational 'retrogardism' (or the revitalized spirit of the avant-garde) and *not* the national culture would be the most appropriate cultural model for a socialist state, the SNST sought to usurp the Yugoslavian state's cultural ideology and impose itself as a transcendental, 'real' socialist authority in its place."[36] Even though many members of other collectives comprising the NSK were part of and collaborated with other groups and spaces of the 1980s alternative culture, the SNST did not perform in the spaces of the alternative scene. Instead, it created its own strategy and demanded central stage for the production of new urban aesthetics and culture right at the heart of the socialist institution of art. Ultimately, seen in retrospect, the political struggles for the new form of theatre that occurred during the disintegration of socialist Yugoslavia had paradoxically little effect on the political economy and the new production models of art. This becomes clear as we investigate the production context of the SNST's *Baptism under Triglav* in CD.

CD[37] was one of the largest investments made by the authorities during the last decade of socialist Yugoslavia intended both for political congresses and cultural activities. The CD building was constructed between 1978 and 1983 in the face of severe economic crisis, and despite the federal authorities' ban on investments in social activities in all of the Yugoslav republics. The cultural-political document, "The Foundations of the Cankarjev dom Program," from 1980 states that this ambitious architectural undertaking was the expression of working people's and youth's appreciation for art and culture, which is an essential part of a self-managed socialist future.[38] As Aleš Erjavec and Marina Gržinić suggest, "The initial planners of the CD on the one hand had to fight with politicians who saw it [CD] as a representative national (and congress) building and on the other hand they had to struggle with public opinion that proclaimed the project to be megalomania."[39] At the time, CD had the largest and one of the best technically supported stages in Yugoslavia. It was in Gallus Hall that the SNST performed *Baptism*.

Despite its primary function to serve the needs of the LCY, CD played a crucial role in the cultural policy realm because it was an institutional *novum* in the cultural landscape of Yugoslavia. The building was in fact a multidisciplinary cultural centre that could have accommodated the altered methods of production for contemporary art and possibly established a new model of art production in socialist Yugoslavia. Its Theatre and Film Department signalled a possible change in the theatre's production paradigm, and presented the possibility of launching a new production model for the culture of younger generations. Although CD is known today as an intermediary cultural institution that imports and presents international as well as local performing arts, music, dance, and film, at the time of its inauguration, the possibility existed for CD to perform a very different function, that of a production house. This possibility rested with the artistic director of the CD's Theatre and Film Department, Goran Schmidt, appointed in 1984, whose aim was to support local art production by investing in the creation of new theatre/performing arts pieces.[40] Before Schmidt's arrival, CD functioned as a stage for the presentation of imported guest performances, what Gržinić and Erjavec call "a cultural factory."[41] Schmidt believed that a cultural institution of CD's weight needed to have its own productions and should not be used only as a guest stage for international ones. He persuaded the management of CD to stage local productions and was thus able to put the new theatre poetics of the SNST to the test by proposing that the group prepare "a slightly less conventional commemoration of Slovenian Culture Day."[42]

The production of *Baptism* received funds that gave the contractually hired director or project leader the means to organize the whole production and ensure the performance was realized.[43] For a brief moment, rebaptism of the paradigm of national theatre coincided with the idea of the institution as a production centre that would provide the possibility of an interdisciplinary, multimedia aesthetics for new artistic generations and thereby redefine the format of production relations in the field of culture. An important facet of the new mode of production of contemporary art was that the funds necessary to carry out the performance were provided by the state. Even though the artists entered a contractual agreement with the institution, we should not underestimate the fact that *Baptism* was carried out exclusively with public funds, that the authors of the performance received payment, and that the producer did not dictate how work should proceed even though Schmidt chose the theme of the performance. This was not a co-production, where a team of artists would have to secure a portion of the funds or where the institution would rent its space and technicians and declare the rentals as its financial investment in the production, as is mostly the case today. CD, however, played the role of producer of *Baptism*, but only for approximately one year.[44] The support for a different concept of production and for an alternative art project,[45] introduced to the state institution and the cultural and political horizon of self-management socialism by Schmidt, ended when funds for CD's theatre productions were cut.[46] The funding cuts also made it impossible for the congress centre to become a contemporary production centre. The cultural and political problem of funds and spaces for alternative artistic production and different production models remained unsolved after *Baptism*. In time, CD became a parasitic structure that offered its space and technical services through co-productions with either other national institutions or actors of the alternative culture but did not provide funding. It became a paradigmatic structure of cultural entrepreneurship that set up its program via outsourced labour – poorly paid or unpaid artistic labour.

This is precisely the point where the problem emerges. In the 1990s we see an even clearer cross-section of the absence of investment in spatial infrastructure for alternative cultural production and a growing reserve army of cultural workers. Alternative productions had no access to space, but they did have artistic potential that the existing infrastructure of national institutions could partly exploit for little expense. This meant, firstly, that the alternative artistic practices could not appropriately develop and reinforce the new production model as they had no access to infrastructure and, secondly, that their productions were mostly a product of self-exploitation when produced outside of institutions. All of this led to a clear class stratification that was reinforced with labour regulations for freelance artists, such as the Law for Independent Cultural Workers in Slovenia, by which individual art workers were designated as the protomodel of outsourced contractors for institutions and had from the very onset no privileges in terms of access to certain social rights, benefits, or to public space infrastructure. While access to culture and art production in the SFRY was democratic, the crumbling welfare state mechanisms, which had previously secured rising living standards and high levels of social security, revealed the underlying issues with the institutional model for art production. This went hand in hand with the changes in the laws that established new rules for accessing social security for independent art workers.

These two cases show that while artists on the alternative art scene of the 1980s were struggling to implement new production models and struggling for their particular form of art to take a more central or dominant position, they took the welfare state for granted. Meanwhile, cultural policy was, unbeknownst to them, turning them into socialist entrepreneurs. These precarious workers would now have to buy into the myth of self-reliance that shifted the responsibility for social welfare from the state to the individual. While they were concerned with what art they were making, their working conditions were being altered in ways that would make them bereft of the very rights they were taking for granted.

Undoing Art as Labour:
Laws for Independent Artists and Cultural Workers

The economic conditions of 1980s Yugoslav socialism made it impossible for independent cultural workers to earn real income equal to that of workers in organizations of associated labour, or to have equal access to public cultural infrastructure. In theory, the laws for independent artists and cultural workers should have regulated the working conditions of freelance workers, who, in legal terms, were to be given "equal socioeconomic status to workers in organizations of associated labour,"[47] and ensured that they could legally provide cultural services. Misleading and grandiloquent formulations, however, declaring that the socio-economic status of the independent art workers must be equal to that of employees, did not mean that the rights of independent art workers were guaranteed simply because they worked. Even at that time, art workers formally paid social contributions themselves. During the 1980s not all of them were entitled to social protection covered by public funds. For example, in Slovenia in 1984, there were 749 independent cultural workers in total, of which 485 (65 per cent) were entitled to subsidized social contributions. In 1989, only 715 (31 per cent) of a total of 2,321 registered independent cultural workers were entitled to the same subsidy.[48]

The underprivileged socio-economic status of independent art workers was revealed in a study from the late 1980s, which showed that contributions for health and pension insurance were calculated on the lowest insurance rating base.[49] What's more, the results of the study indicated that "independent cultural workers [did] not participate in sufficient numbers in the self-management processes of organizations of associated labour, which [could] freely use the surplus value of their work," because independent art workers were subject to "less favourable conditions for social security benefits (sick leave, maternity leave, pensions)."[50] Independent art workers were frequently deprived of other benefits as well, such as apartments, consumer credits, and additional professional training and only had access to a limited amount of funds, as allocated by the Cultural Communities (that is SCC in the area of culture).

Even in 1980s Slovenia the Law for Independent Cultural Workers not only resulted in inequality between full-time employees and independent art workers, but was also a sign of a broader neoliberal social transformation – that is, the training of entrepreneurial subjects that both see themselves, and function, as enterprises – that had already begun during the last decade of Yugoslav socialism. One of the more efficient methods that the neoliberal governmentality used to reform the political economy was to change the society and its relations by undermining "the institutions and rights which the working-class movement succeeded in establishing from the late nineteenth century onwards" and by resorting to extra-economic violence.[51] Paradoxically in Yugoslavia, this took place under the banner of self-management whereby the language of the new constitution was redeployed as a cover for neoliberal policies and ethos.

Although the legislation nominally required equal treatment of independent art workers and full-time employees, the redefinition of the legal nature of employment relationships set off the process whereby independent art workers gradually lost their labour rights and social protection. The cultural policy of

1980s socialism intervened by means of a legal administrative measure, that is, the Law for Independent Cultural Workers, which established a new form of cultural labour that was radically different from the safe haven of full-time employment. The law did not protect freelance art workers, but left them to fend for themselves. Hence the socio-economic situation of independent art workers was neither better nor equal to their peers employed in BOAL.[52]

In his study of neoliberalism Michel Foucault points out that neoliberal ideology rests on a new concept of human labour, one that occupies the opposite extreme of Marx's definition of labour power as commodity. In neoliberalism, labour power is seen as "capital-ability" and, as a consequence, the worker is seen as an "enterprise for himself."[53] The worker is the one generating capital, therefore, in later years the term "human capital" became a popular notion employed in a variety of misleading ways. The absurdity of the term "independent entrepreneur" and how problematic it is to apply the notion of enterprise onto an individual was well explained by Sergio Bologna.[54] In economic theory, an entity is defined as an enterprise if it is composed of the following three elements: capital, labour, and management. An enterprise then is by definition an organization and a micro-system that employs technology and human intelligence to generate large quantities of commodities and surplus value. Bologna's rhetorical questions: "How could an 'independent entrepreneur' manage all this work?" needs no commentary. However it does reveal the transformation of a labour relation into a business relation.[55] "In order for an employment contract to become a business contract, the worker needs to be redefined as enterprise."[56] Dardot and Laval concur, the category of independent entrepreneur (sole proprietor) is a "psychological and social, even spiritual entity," by which a "work contract" is undermined and, ultimately, the "wage relation" is gradually dismantled.[57] What is more, "the individual's activity in its entirety is conceived as a process of self-valorization."[58] This applies to art when we finally take off the rosy glasses of artistic autonomy. The institution of art is not autonomous or separate from economic processes, it is in fact its own economic system even if ideological discourses gloss over these processes. There are contractual relations that govern art work and artistic labour as a type of service. Redefining art workers as enterprises is thus both absurd and detrimental for their socio-economic status.

Although the social rights of independent art workers were not abolished (officially, payment of social contributions was obligatory under the Law for Independent Cultural Workers), the new legislation introduced an unjust principle according to which the independent art workers were required to self-fund their social security, while the employer or the state were free of this obligation. It is therefore not true that all citizens had access to social protection under equal conditions. A study in 1987 revealed that interviewees (independent art workers) were most concerned about "insufficient social security, inadequate social insurance," and the "unequal socioeconomic position of independent cultural workers in comparison to workers in associated labour [the socialist enterprises]."[59] Rights to social security became an incentive, and as such, subject to competition. This seemingly harmless change meant that during the last decade of the SFRY there was no longer a just redistribution of "goods in accordance with a certain regime of universal rights to life – that is, health, education, social inclusion, political participation," which was characteristic of the paradigm of the welfare state.[60] Rather, the change signalled a different role of the state that invoked "the calculating ability of subjects to make choices and achieve results, which are posited as conditions of access to a certain well-being."[61]

The laws for independent artists and cultural workers can therefore be understood as the first sign of neoliberalization of labour regulation in the field of culture. In theory, they gave art workers the possibility of freely choosing their projects and organizing their own work. In reality, however, institutionalization of self-employment organized – in the name of freedom – the activity of cultural workers and at the same time limited their labour rights and the access to a social wage, which they henceforth had to compete for on the market of artistic labour. This is precisely the logic of neoliberalism. In opposition to dogmatic liberalism, it introduces a new way of justification that reinforces competition and the enterprise as the new generalized form of society – the entrepreneurial subject.[62] Neoliberalism "means precisely the shift away from the principle of *laissez faire*," however, not towards state redistribution and welfare planning, to be sure, but towards a public policy of "establishing, developing and maintaining a competition-based economic order using both legal and repressive means."[63] New forms of labour that, among others, emerged with the laws for independent artists and cultural workers, gradually increased the level of economic uncertainty and the "*social fear*" that arises due to the proliferating logic of personal risk-taking.[64] The latter triggered "a 'chain reaction' by producing 'enterprising subjects' who in turn will reproduce, expand and reinforce competitive relations between themselves."[65]

The cultural policy of 1980s socialism reacted to the problem of a growing number of cultural workers by inventing a new form of labour that was drastically different from the protected full-time employment. When Marjana Bele conducted an empirical study in 1987 about the working conditions of independent art workers in Slovenia, it was clear that "the number of registered independent cultural workers [was] increasing every year despite the predictions that it will slowly stabilize."[66] During the last decade of socialism, the conditions and possibilities for cultural workers to earn income were better compared to the era after the breakup of the SFRY. For instance, the tax on royalties[67] for independent work was lower, and cultural communities or professional art associations could subsidize the contributions for social insurance.[68]

However, the fact remains that independent work posed a greater risk than full-time employment, both in terms of making a living and the quality of social security.[69] Independent cultural workers were not on the market of "free exchange of labour" (*svobodna menjava dela*), but on the market of competition that was built on inequality and was regulated by the state through new labour legislation.

The laws for independent artists and cultural workers set up the conditions for second-generation independent work in the field of culture and reduced the pressure on employment in the cultural institutions. The convenience of neoliberal policies was also provoked by the fact that "simple class-reproduction started precisely at that historical moment [the 1980s] to turn" the Yugoslav working-class youth "into a superfluous industrial reserve army."[70] Youth unemployment in Yugoslavia began to increase as early as the mid-1970s and had escalated by the time the federation broke up. Additionally, the rate of unemployment in the SFRY was obscured by those workers who left for (temporary) work abroad and eventually came to be known as *gastarbeiters* (guest workers).[71]

Inequalities were not levelled out under the measures of socialist cultural policy in the 1980s, but proliferated. This was the effect of neoliberal rationality, but was also brought about by the structural effects of the autonomy of art. The institution of independent artistic work was fundamentally connected to the autonomy of art in all three cases. The exceptionality of artistic work, in socialist terms the "artist's specificity" (*svojskost umetnika*), represented the basis on which artistic work was integrated in and regulated by the cultural policy of the socialist welfare state. In the 1980s socialist cultural policy reinforced and upgraded the hierarchy of artistic exceptionality – something that had thus far been in the domain of the institution of art – through the discourse of artistic value and by neutralizing welfare policies. The contradiction of unpaid artistic work re-emerged. Artistic exceptionality became the foundation for basic social protection. Independent art workers had access to social protection, not because they were working, but because they were exceptional. The protection was less substantial and based on merit, that is, an assessment of artistic achievements. While the initial intervention of the socialist welfare state's cultural policy into the realm of the institution of art resulted in protection for art workers, the rise of neoliberal rationality subordinated this protection to merit and prevented equal treatment.

Although alternative artistic practices were inspired by the historical avant-garde movements of the early twentieth century as they attempted in various ways to democratize the socialist institution of art and create new production models, the structural issues of the autonomy of art remained a blind spot. The radicalization of artistic procedures, non-hierarchical working methods, interdisciplinary integration and incorporation of alternative art practices into the domain of the institution of art, and the attempts to create new parallel organizations did not address the structural position of art in society or the mode of production based on the invisibility of artistic labour. The alternative did not address this perspective, even if the "desire for having one's own space and funding for producing work" was its impetus.[72] While some recent interpretations claim that the 1980s alternative scene produced new modes of cultural production, there is in fact little evidence to support an emergence of a new model of art economy. With hindsight, it becomes clear that the deconstruction of welfare mechanisms and the waning of the commitment to a fairer redistribution that marked the Yugoslav political project, eroded the working conditions of art workers.

The Alternative as a Symptom of the Breakup of Yugoslavia

These two case studies show why the 1980s alternative culture, or the alternative scene, and the divergence that was characteristic of it, was a symptom of the breakup of Yugoslavia. What this alternative stood for is particularly evident from today's perspective. The reality after the end of the socialist state of Yugoslavia does not even remotely resemble a reformed self-managed socialism enhanced with human rights but is, foremost, the dominion of neoliberal rationality that uses the ubiquitous logic of entrepreneurship to break down social ties of solidarity and accelerate socio-economic differences of a once much less class-stratified socialist society.

In the last decade of socialism, when criticism of the dominant ideology led the authorities to ironically distance themselves from their own ideology to a certain degree, various portions of the political spectrum saw social turmoil as a possibility for reform and an alternative socialism. According to cultural theorist Boris Buden, "Really existing socialism suddenly appeared as something that can be reformed, expanded with the ideals of freedom and general socio-economic well-being. As if communism's long repressed and abused utopian perspective had re-opened at its core."[73] From today's perspective, the actors in the final act of the crumbling Yugoslav socialism, including Buden, perceive this past as a "drama of the new foundation of society," which had no clear outcomes and therefore appeared as a "radical politicization of everything existing," because the drama questioned the fundamental axioms of the forms of social life. "'What is it that makes us members of a society?' Is it social justice or cultural identity, god or private property, 'our values' or 'their fear'?"[74]

The issue with the 1980s alternative was the political horizon on which social struggles took place before Yugoslavia broke up. Socialism and the welfare state were a given. The fact that they were based on labour, or the function that the state performed in this economy by guaranteeing that surpluses were, for the most part, redistributed according to the principle of solidarity, were not taken into consideration. In other words, what the alternative did not consider was that the basic foundations of social existence in the SFRY lay in public education, health services, pension schemes, and labour rights provided by the same socialist authorities who those fighting for a civil society had attacked so fiercely. On the contrary the struggle took place on the level of democratization, which had its own characteristic liberal foundation. In the words of Viktor Misiano discussing the period of the fall of the USSR, "Democracy was understood not as the product of self-organized social movements, but as a direct byproduct of the liberal market economy."[75] In fact, democracy and the freedom of human rights were at stake. As Buden asserts, during the final years of the SFRY: "Everyone believed in democracy, regardless of how they understood it. For some, it simply denoted a general healing power of parliamentarianism and the democratic public, for others, it meant the self-regulated potential of a market economy. Communist reformers saw in democracy the opportunity for communism to make a fresh start. Anti-communists also believed in democratic freedom, by which they meant nothing democratic – only the freedom of their nation, race, or god, or rather, the freedom to hate a different nation, race, or god."[76] As noted by the Italian philologist and historian Luciano Canfora, democracy is an ideological notion that is characteristic of liberal capitalist states.[77] Canfora's critical analysis of the notion of democracy sheds light on the discourse of "democratization," which occurred in the 1990s in connection with the process of Yugoslavia's demise and reveals how it is problematic in its entirety. Let's take Slovenia as an example, since it was not directly affected by the bloodshed that took place in most of the other republics of the SFRY during the 1990s. In Slovenia there was no process of democratization after it gained independence from the SFRY. In fact, it was during the socialist 1980s that "the Yugoslav alternative triggered important struggles linked to the freedom of expression (Article 133 of the federal criminal law criminalized "verbal injury") and other human rights (particularly in connection to the Belgrade judicial process against the organizers of the Free University 1984–5)."[78] Founded on the idea of a nation as the identity community,[79] Slovenia fully consolidated its position as the liberal "democratic" capitalist state on the tail of exacerbated socio-economic differences and by stripping 25,000 people of their residency – Slovenia's "erased" citizens – in the process.

The struggle of the 1980s alternative culture appears politically naïve, which was the effect of a poorly considered class conflict of self-managed socialism. Indeed, the "hegemonic consciousness of liberal-democratic capitalism as the unanimous winner of the Cold War" set a clear framework for the alternative's naïveté.[80] Buden expressed the contradiction of this position accurately, not to mention poetically: "The cry from the East 'There is no socialism without democracy' is echoed by the cynical reply from the West: 'There is no democracy without capitalism.'"[81] In other words, the naïveté of betting on civil society and cultural emancipation, which characterized the 1980s alternative culture, is nowadays evident in the lack of perspective informed by the effects of Yugoslav's class stratification – perspective that would wager the reform of self-managed socialism on the issue of emerging post-Fordist forms of labour and the analysis of class composition instead of demands for human rights without the inclusion of economic rights. It makes little sense to declare citizens as equal – as is characteristic of the notion of human rights in liberal democracies – if they are socially and economically unequal and if the conditions for such inequality are not eliminated.[82] It is true that in Slovenia the unions managed to protect a part of the public sector, and they continued to fight incessantly to preserve the premises of the welfare state.[83] However, what has gone unnoticed in this undoubtedly important victory is that unions found no equitable solutions for the precarious workers, including art workers – in this respect, there was very little social solidarity between the art workers employed in the public sector and freelance art workers. One of the fundamental problems in this constellation was precisely the notion of the civil society, because it obscured the class stratification of people who live in unequal material conditions.

A typical example of such naïveté can also be found in the cultural policy of late socialism. To be exact, it can be found in the laws for independent artists and cultural workers, which institutionalized the independent cultural worker and enabled them to organize themselves in the format of long-term or temporary working communities. All this could no longer be attributed solely to the cultural and political orientation of "supporting artistic creativity"[84] but to the aim of alleviating "pressure to provide full-time employment in cultural institutions."[85] The laws transferred the responsibility of welfare provisions onto the art workers' shoulders and exacerbated inequality on the artistic labour market. This legacy was relegated to the new independent nation-state of Slovenia after the destruction of Yugoslavia in 1991. For example, the law in Slovenia was subject to several changes during the 1990s and 2000s. Most of the amendments further increased the precarious working conditions of art workers. Symptomatically, the designation in each new version of the regulation changed from "independent cultural workers" (1982) to "freelancers in the field of culture" (1994) and finally to the "self-employed persons in the field of culture" (2002).[86] The laws for independent artists and cultural workers are, on the one hand, a testament to the growing power of neoliberal governmentality and, on the other, a consequence of the crisis of the socialist welfare state that was caused by the "marriage between economic liberalism and social democracy" and was from the 1970s and 1980s onwards no longer "protected by economic success."[87]

The rise of neoliberal policies is connected both to the changes in capitalism and to ideological struggles that were foremost "a systematic, abiding critique of the welfare state."[88] One of the key problems of the welfare state according to its critics was that it tended to "encourage economic agents to prefer leisure to work. This argument, repeated *ad nauseam*, linked the security extended to individuals with the loss of a sense of responsibility ... and love for work."[89] Moreover, the critique of the welfare state was also based on arguments that its apparatuses "are profoundly damaging to creativity, innovation and self-realization."[90] In the case of Yugoslavia, the two central social tendencies of the 1980s were, according to Močnik, the disintegration of the welfare state and the eruption of new critical social and cultural movements. As "the complex of the party-state began to lose its legitimacy because it could not hold the promise of social solidarity in a peripheral welfare state,"[91] the critical social movements also attacked the state, however without a solid reflection of its relation to the economy and changing conditions of labour. The spontaneous absorption of liberalism (the realization of personal freedom) and an exclusive focus on the critique of repressive state apparatuses during the last stage of Yugoslav socialism undermined the mandate of the welfare state's institutions that secured collective social reproduction and security.

It is very common to depict the 1990s as the beginning of the restoration of capitalism in the post-Yugoslav territory. However, this claim disregards the many facts that indicate that the origins of this process began in the mid-1960s while socialist Yugoslavia still existed. In the international context, the destruction of Yugoslavia is mostly known as the bloodshed of the Balkan Wars in the 1990s, which took place in most of the republics. Yugoslavia's breakup tends to be related to the emergence of nationalistic tendencies, an approach which obscures the deeper economic and geopolitical issues that contributed to socialism's demise. Murderous ethnic cleansing and the establishment of the dwarfish nation-states on the post-Yugoslav territory were the final stages of this capitalist restoration rather than its beginning. While the SFRY was entwined in the global political and economic processes of the Cold War and played a role in devising strategies to counter capitalist relations (self-management) and neocolonial politics (Nonaligned Movement), the post-Yugoslav nation-states became pawns on the European Union's chessboard. They were instrumental in the process of "enlargement," which is another name for the neoliberal restructuring of the post-Yugoslav territory.

According to liberal teleology's triumphalism, socialism died along with the fall of the Berlin Wall in 1989, or, in the case of Yugoslavia, perhaps even sooner, with the death of Tito. These symbolic events are always evoked to exemplify the so-called fall of communism. The use of the word "communism" is symptomatic. Communism is an ideological term used to refer indiscriminately to socialist countries, which nominally and factually called themselves socialist and not communist. The global ascendency of liberal democracy after 1989 had also caused a proliferation of other notions, such as "post-socialism," "postcommunism," and "transition (to democracy)," that were not mere temporal designations but rather, as critics rightly point out, ideological constructions.

For example, derived from the concept of postmodernism, the term post-socialism, in some scholarly views, means "the proclamation of the end of socialism from within itself."[92] The question is, who associated the end of socialism with 1989 and the demise of socialist institutional arrangements, that is, the real existing socialist states, and why. More importantly, did Yugoslavia's form of socialism actually collapse by itself, or was its death largely due to the intensification of the World Bank and IMF's imposed "decentralization as a Trojan horse for marketization."[93]

Admittedly, there were internal issues in Yugoslavia related to an unacknowledged class stratification and the rigidity of the party apparatus and its factions, which blocked the development of Yugoslav socialism after 1965. However, the Faustian bargain that Yugoslav leaders had struck with the West, and the relentless "anti-communist" ideological offensive led by the West against socialist ideals, were decidedly greater factors in the demise of the SFRY and its socialist self-management model. The term post-socialism as the proclamation of the death of socialism from within, obscures the struggles of the 1980s' alternative movements for a reform of socialism that was far from pro-capitalist. This view erases the heterogeneity of the political spectrum on the left in general and in particular movements within former socialist countries that fought to modify and reform socialism by integrating individual liberties in the system. Ironically, the outcome of these struggles was the installation of a liberal ideology and the final restoration of a capitalist logic that was instrumental in implementing neoliberal policies after the breakup of Yugoslavia.

The ideology behind the post-socialist transition obscured and suppressed those left political positions that could not be identified with the narrative of the fall of socialism and the unabashed celebration of capitalism and liberal democracy. It overruns positions of those actors and groups of the former alternative culture who wanted to reform socialism from within and to whom the transition to capitalism and liberal democracy appeared ludicrous.

While the art workers of alternative art practices in the 1980s critiqued the socialist institution of art either in an attempt to create parallel new alternative art organizations or in an attempt to occupy the existing structures and transform them from within, the cultural policy regulation of working conditions pulled the rug from beneath their feet. The cultural policy of late socialism redefined independent cultural *workers* into independent cultural *entrepreneurs* by implementing juridical arrangements through which the flexibilization of the artistic labour market took place. The new cultural policy regulation for artistic labour transformed independent art workers into outsourced labour, which was structurally deprived of reliable social security and funding. That new category of independent cultural workers became legally bound to take care of their own welfare provisions, which included health care insurance and contributions to the retirement plan.

As the alternative culture was struggling for new production models of art during the disintegration of the self-management paradigm, greater systemic changes were taking place in the political economy, in which, as Dejan Kršić poetically puts it, "the true director is Capital and History its dramaturge."[94] Instead of waking up in the alternative socialism enhanced by human rights and liberties, the people of the former socialist Yugoslavia awoke to find themselves in independent nation-states weakened by war, neoliberal policies, and the disintegration of social solidarity. The existing inequalities among art workers thus further deteriorated due to the extended economic crisis after the breakup of Yugoslavia. The new post-socialist order managed to politically undermine the former alternative culture and enlarged the contingent of underpaid and impoverished art workers. Consequently, the protagonists of the 1980s alternative art scene became members of the post-socialist precariat of self-employed cultural entrepreneurs who are divorced from social security and economic stability.

The insidious effects of the discourse of this post-socialist transition, which delivered the post-Yugoslav territory into the realm of liberal democracy, was a neoliberal attack on the welfare state and its goals of social redistribution. This reinforced a decoupling of political economy from the realm of culture and art practices. Neoliberalism was also instrumental in reinstating the separation between artistic labour and subsistence as well as the "autonomous" rule of the institution of art with all its historical presuppositions, the central one discussed in this book being the naturalization of artistic labour as an inner calling that obfuscates artistic labour as work. The results of this transitioning of the post-Yugoslavian states into liberal democracies were clearly diagnosed by Boris Buden:

> Instead of settling down in a stable regime of sovereignty, as promised by the teleology of transition, the institutions on the ground face the chaos of an uncontrolled globalization they are no longer able to escape. The conditions of their reproduction undergo a similar sort of precarization as the conditions of individual reproduction, of the reproduction of the globalized labor force, of migration, brutal competition on the market.[95]

Due to the war conflicts of the Balkans in the 1990s, the ascent of neoliberal rationality in the countries that are known as "the post-socialist EU periphery"[96] became less visible. Neoliberalism, which gained power due to a global slowdown of capital accumulation and involved demands for the intensification of capital accumulation – fuelled by the European Union as is its main enforcer, had very concrete and devastating effects on social relations in the post-Yugoslav nation-states: the welfare state mechanisms paid the price with their disintegration.

The logic of capital accumulation dismantled the welfare state through a privatization of the social conditions of production and an implementation of market principles into areas that were previously not managed according to market logic but to social solidarity and welfare. The social conditions of production that used to be people's property (*družbena lastnina/društveno vlasništvo*) in Yugoslavia were not completely privatized during the 1990s; they were often owned and managed by the state in the name of the people (via elected officials chosen by the mechanisms of parliamentary democracy), which in fact means that collective people's property rights and its management were replaced by reinstituting individual property rights and/or control of the state via rule of law.[97] In the post-Yugoslav territory, neoliberalism contributed to a deeply transformed socio-economic landscape of "drastic inequalities between the tiny layer of the newly rich, diminishing middle class and the increasingly populous poor strata," that some fittingly refer to as "the desert of post-socialism."[98] Specifically, the neoliberal governmentality, which refers to the "extension of market rationality to existence in its entirety through the generalization of the enterprise-form" became the defining traits of the post-Yugoslav condition. It is also important to note that neoliberalism is often mistakenly portraited as endorsing the withdrawal of the state rather than a redefinition of the state.[99]

Ironically, the former socialist institutions guaranteeing services, such as education, health, culture, and social security, which secured equitable social reproduction during postwar Yugoslavia, have *not* been privatized. They are under the authority of the government and represent the public sector. They have been financially depleted and, as concerns public cultural institutions, explicitly based on the model and ideology of national culture. However, the process of the neoliberal offensive, the results of which presently unite the cultural entrepreneurs with the large population of self-employed as they inhale the omnipresent entrepreneurial spirit, took a specific turn after the breakdown of SFRY.

The new post-Yugoslav cultural policy entailed an unequal integration of alternative art practices into the system of publicly funded cultural production. Ironically, this was the result of the critique that the alternative art practices were levying against the institution of art under socialism. Because the levels of entrepreneurial logic heightened, they undermined the intellectual, creative, and politically emancipatory potentials of the former alternative art practices by increasing the number of underpaid, impoverished art workers. Any intellectual, creative, and politically emancipatory potential was blocked by precarious working conditions and economic marginalization.

The aftermath of the political struggles at the end of the 1980s led to the breakup of the SFRY in 1991. It was followed by the gradual neoliberalization of the political economy and demonstrates that the alternative art practices' attempts to change the production model were not only instrumentalized but also discarded once they were no longer deemed useful by the emerging nationalist political elites. As Dragan Klaić noted, all political parties in Slovenia "be they of nationalist, liberal or conservative convictions have carefully avoided any kind of reform of the public cultural system, except for implementing nationalist perspectives or market-inspired mantras."[100] The situation was similar in other republics, where nationalist tendencies became even more prominent due to ethno-national wars.[101] The alternative of the 1980s was in essence instrumentalized: first by the local liberal elites that wanted to reinstate capitalist nation-states, and then by the Western liberal ideology that used the critique of the socialist alternative movements as a shovel to dig the grave of a supposedly expired socialism. Despite the ongoing pressures of the former alternative, now called "independent culture," the new local rulers were not interested in any reforms of the cultural production models or cultural policy priorities during the 1990s. Even as the agents of this new independent culture continued to voice critique of the rigid and traditional art organizations, the environment was ripe for hegemonic neocolonial interventions from other European countries, mostly German and Austrian state and private initiatives as well as the philanthropic support of George Soros. A number of European foundations attempted to build entirely new networks with the remnants of what used to be Yugoslav alternative art practices' international relationships and structures in order to standardize and control them in a typical neocolonial style. In this process, as Boris Buden noted, the reformist leftist critique of socialist institutions became "a sort of compradorial critique"[102] whereby the local critique of the unchanged traditionalism of mainstream cultural institutions by the independent culture began to imply an identification with the Western European liberal critique of socialism.

Post-Yugoslav Dispossession and the Contradictions of Artistic Labour after Socialism

North American readers are accustomed to a cultural environment that nurtures animosity towards the state.[1] Small business and notions such as enterprise, entrepreneur, and market environment provide a natural (if not superior) logic of how societies and economies should function. It may sound utterly odd that these important pillars of neoliberal capitalism should be problematic in any way, shape, or form. One may wonder how the removal of "state control" and more freedom could be a negative development. How could processes labelled "democratization" possibly mean a decline or a degradation of the social conditions of production or people's welfare. Moreover, for a Western audience that thinks of an entrepreneur as an independent enterprising individual it may come as a surprise that the enterprise-form and entrepreneurial logic would be considered an issue. Entrepreneurs are generally represented as free innovative or creative individuals, not as some ruthless capitalist; they merely seize the opportunities for profit that are possible in the market environment.

Certainly, Yugoslav self-management could be seen as a version of some kind of socialist entrepreneurship since it encouraged people to be independent, responsible, and participate in the management of economic units as well as units of social reproduction – it was envisioned as a society of producers that managed the process of production and other necessary social services, such as health services, child and elderly care, education, culture, social security and so on. In the final analysis, these producers should have led to the dying-off of the state apparatus. What is missing in the Western understanding of Yugoslav socialism, however, is that the model of the entrepreneur was part of the problem, not the solution. It was not that the enterprise-form or entrepreneur were flawed. The issue was that the idea of entrepreneurship was located in a social vacuum, and obscured the role of the state and the welfare-state mechanisms needed to play in protecting individuals from particular forms of risks. The decline, and therefore the problem, is the withdrawal of state-organized support, or better, the decimation of the welfare system, which no longer guarantees basic social and economic rights. While Americans may cringe at the explicit articulation of such socialist precepts, they nonetheless benefit from them in the form of public schools, free education, Medicaid, etc.

Neoliberalism dismantled the welfare state so that it could install a neoliberal state, which is understood as an enterprise that needs to be as lean as possible. In fact, its first order of business was to encourage and make sure that the market functioned freely and with vitality, including when the neoliberal state invested in profitable ventures.[2] Everyone fends for themselves; the idea of the collective and solidarity is void. In such absence of welfare and social solidarity mechanisms, people can no longer be guaranteed access to basic life necessities, and the entrepreneurial logic becomes a dog-eat-dog world of competition and rivalry – the survival of the fittest – which should not be confused with the most hardworking, and so on.

As we saw in the case of Yugoslav art workers turned socialist entrepreneurs in the 1980s, the welfare system was no longer available to them as workers; it was refined via a merit-based system that in fact entailed competing for basic social security resources. What was implied by the new Westernized system was that some art workers deserved this support, or were entitled to it more than others, and that artwork needed to be excellent in order to merit social security and support. Of course, the question of how one then defined excellence becomes particularly cutting, since the lack of a welfare state and paid labour opened the door to the kind of class-determined and nepotistic endorsements of art and artists we typically see. A paradoxical consequence of this logic was that not everyone was free to choose art as a way of living; it became the privilege of those who could afford it or who did what it took to gain the favours of the state's bureaucracy, or rather the hegemonic art circles. In the last decade of socialist Yugoslavia, the reason for the crumbling of welfare-state mechanisms was of course the increasing presence of economic policies that enforced a market logic and competition in combination with the IMF-imposed austerity measures. This is why the idea of all labour being creative faltered. Indeed, being forced to compete for the basic social rights of housing, healthcare, education, culture etc. is antithetical to creativity.

A more contemporary and increasingly popular idea is the demand for universal basic income, which would help us to have a choice in what we do rather than be slaves of the oppressive compulsion to live to work. In other words, the entrepreneurial spirit and enterprise-form would not be an issue if the welfare system existed and guaranteed that each and every member of society had a place to live, access to universal healthcare, social services, free education, and so on. Otherwise, entrepreneurship is a problematic ideology because it omits the fact that an entrepreneur needs assets and not just good luck and creativity or innovation. Once the welfare mechanisms are removed, and as it happened under the neoliberal rationality, where the market environment and competition set the tone and priorities, we live in a ruthless environment of competing individuals who lose sight of the importance of the collective and mutual solidarity.

The hegemony of post-Fordist neoliberalism led to a transformation that changed the worker into an "enterprising" individual. In the neoliberal utopia, there is no such thing as society, merely individuals, as was infamously proclaimed by the empress of neoliberalism, Margaret Thatcher, in the United Kingdom. "In the new world of 'developed society,' individuals must no longer regard themselves as workers, but as enterprises that sell a service to the market."[3] They are no longer part of a collective, they are free individuals operating in the market place; they are responsible for every aspect of their work and life, including social security.

The wrong-headedness of such a model has been made abundantly clear by the 2020 pandemic and the impending economic crash. All of a sudden, the vulnerability of the "independent" entrepreneurs became obvious. It became clear that people cannot carry the brunt of the responsibility for their welfare when a pandemic occurs, that the government has to step in and redistribute and organize social production so that the individuals are able to survive. This is quite the opposite from what the neoliberal gospel preached: there is such a thing as society and collective solidarity that individuals rely on. Paradoxically, this was also proclaimed by a conservative neoliberal agenda-pushing prime minister in the UK during the 2020 pandemic. Despite this cheap PR stunt by the prime minister acknowledging the existence and importance of the society, however, neoliberal governments and companies banked on this anathema putting lives over profits, and even some groups and individuals themselves proclaimed preferring risking death than letting the economy go down.

While ideas that the welfare-state is oppressive and stifles creativity, innovation, and self-realization were the adage that supported the redefinition of the role of the state and mechanism of social solidarity, the global pandemic made clear that these ideas were falsely employed to convince people that they are responsible for their own fate and that they owe nothing to the collective and vice versa. While the neoliberal policies shifted our collective responsibility to each other and generational solidarity to the shoulders of individuals, the pandemic demonstrates the limits of this logic. Clearly, it is beyond the scope of this book to analyse the extent to which the myriad (more or less) problematic forms of state intervention took place in various countries globally to protect the people in general, and how and if they protected art workers specifically. Numerous studies of neoliberalism have already shown that its policies have a lot to do with the devastation of all kinds of public services, including healthcare. Others will no doubt also elaborate on the extent to which the current healthcare crisis we are facing in the United States is in fact a consequence of decades of neoliberal policies that have crumbled public healthcare systems, if countries even had such systems.

The 2020 pandemic has revealed the ruthless face of neoliberal capitalism in stark contrast to capitalism with a human face engendered by social democracy in the West. Capitalism with a putative human face is what the socialist welfare state of Yugoslavia tried to integrate in its economic policy models. The experiment ended in a disaster for workers, including art workers. There is an important role that a state, geared toward the welfare of the people rather than capital accumulation, can accomplish and secure; it can curb competition and implement laws and policies to ensure decent living conditions and universal healthcare. For a North American reader, the New Deal era may resonate as a precedent.

The state-run welfare mechanisms benefited the artist by protecting art from forms of exploitative invisible labour. Not only in existing socialist countries (as the history of Yugoslavia shows us) but also in the capitalist ones, welfare mechanisms can project a more human face on to capitalist exploitation – it cannot, however, abolish it. In that sense Yugoslav socialism went further than what some current politicians in North America, such as Bernie Sanders, who are advocating for socialism, have been proposing. Yugoslav socialism in principle and philosophically was anti-capitalist, it for example rejected and even legally abolished private property and aimed to emancipate human labour. However, as I discussed in this book, this revolutionary idea could not come to a full realization due to both external pressures and internal issues. Metaphorically speaking, socialist Yugoslavia was an island in the sea controlled by capitalist accumulation. It had little chance of surviving despite its aims to build a non-aligned movement of postcolonial countries that would defy the imperialism of the US and USSR. What we can learn from the legacy of Yugoslav socialism, however, is that hybridity between socialism and capitalism is not a solution – there is no happy marriage between the two.

Yugoslav socialism offered the promise of labour's emancipation. This book has tried to show why that promise did not bear fruit, and why socialism was shortchanged. Capitalism both enacted and needed this collapse in order to assert a capitalist mode of production as the only alternative. Yugoslavia was no panacea, but it did provide a context in which art and labour were remunerated in ways that would never occur in nonsocialist settings. In other words, the problem of invisible labour that we have naturalized in the West is neither about art's essence nor about a uniform history of its "pricelessness." Rather, the Yugoslav case reveals that the transformation of art as something outside of and without labour has a history and political context that needs to be exposed and challenged.

We can also conclude that as long as capitalist and, even worse, the neoliberal capitalist logic is the name of the game, the autonomy of art is a misguided strategy to ensure the economic rights of the artist, who is living under the same compulsion to live to work. The processes that ensued in the field of cultural production in the post-Yugoslavian states during the 1990s unfolded as *the enterprisification of the alternative*, whose effect was to transform the relations of social solidarity into individualism, competition, and rivalry. As I showed in this book, this process started already during the last third stage of self-management and became obvious during the final crash in the 1980s. Competition became the central beat in the score of exploitation, and it orchestrated the horizons of unpaid artistic labour after the collapse of Yugoslavia. This "enterprisification" affected cultural organizations and individuals and went hand in hand with the atomization of and the disintegration of former alliances that existed among the actors of the alternative culture. As much as the Yugoslav alternative scene was transnational, the consequences of 1990s nationalistic wars in the republics of socialist Yugoslavia also caused many irreparable breaks and slowed down the vitality of artistic and cultural exchange among Yugoslav art workers.

In the process that led from the historical avant-garde movements to the postwar alternative art practices, we arrived at a so-called independent culture (*neodvisna/nezavisna kultura*). The cultural production that emerged after the dissolution of socialist Yugoslavia and its "normalization" process appeared standard. Its divisions resembled those operating globally today, where dominant art organizations are backed either by unquestioned government funding or the lucrative generosity of private philanthropists, all the while exploiting art workers and dictating the rules of art. During the 1990s, the notion of "independent culture" replaced the term "alternative art practices" but was relegated to the realm of the non-governmental, private sector. As such, it was privatized and had to compete with the public sector it once belonged to but was now comprised of unreformed socialist art organizations. The bureaucratized system of art institutions remains in place even after the neoliberal restructuring and continues to create further issues.

Even though both non-governmental and public sectors are non-profit, the central difference between them is that public-sector institutions have funding secured by national or local governments, while the independent or non-governmental cultural organizations have to compete for government grants and project funding regardless of the fact that they offer and produce public cultural and art programs. There are, of course, also private for-profit organizations that abide by a strictly commercial model of cultural production. This familiar state of affairs mimics the cultural systems of other European and to an extent also the North American countries. In the post-Yugoslav states, employees of public art organizations are public servants while art workers of the independent scene are self-employed or sole proprietors/entrepreneurs. Inevitably, new generations of art workers, engendered by the free socialist education system and public health system, now live in conditions of precarious employment, either as sole proprietors/entrepreneurs or as self-employed workers who compete with one another on the ruthless market of artistic (or other kinds of precarious) labour.

The central characteristics of this post-Yugoslav independent culture has been stagnation, decrease in public funding, and an incessant flow of highly educated art workers that form a reserve army of exploited artistic labour. What is more, the hierarchical relations in the field of cultural production between the fortresses of traditional national culture and the economically marginalized camps of former alternative art practices continues.[4]

In post-socialist Yugoslavia, independent art workers have become self-employed cultural entrepreneurs who operate in a state of permanent uncertainty and see their human capital exploited, all of which is further incentivized by neoliberal cultural policies. What unites the post-Yugoslav reserve army of the second-generation self-employed/independent workers with the global precariat, as some like to call it,[5] is their "separation from the social conditions of production," that is, public education, public health, public pension systems, labour, and other social rights secured by the welfare state, now undergoing a process of dismantling and depletion.[6]

The aftermath of the political struggles at the end of the 1980s that led to the breakup of the SFRY in 1991 was followed by the gradual neoliberalization of the political economy. That is why the case of socialist Yugoslavia and especially the post-Yugoslav territory can be viewed as the canary in the (neoliberal) coalmine. The breakup of Yugoslavia is a case in point to explain this global trend, which has many different forms but all have the same objective: to turn every aspect of reproduction and realms hitherto managed by non-market principles into a source for capital accumulation by employing the entrepreneurial logic. The post-Yugoslav states exposed the failed processes of the transition to neoliberalism that led to populist, crypto, and neo-fascist societies, a general trend now characteristic especially in the former West, and not just in the post-Yugoslav territory. Maybe a better name than the Balkanization of Europe (a recently coined term[7]) would be the end of Western neoliberalism. Similar trends can be seen in other non-Western countries especially in Latin America and Africa. However, there are differences in how these processes take place.

All these phenomena are evidently the effects of the neoliberal turn in the world's economy and politics. The new stage of primitive accumulation that David Harvey has termed "accumulation by dispossession," has mostly capitalized precisely on the restructuring of the realm of reproduction. Everything has been turned into a competitive market or managed according to a competitive logic that reduced established rights, such as free education, universal healthcare, child and elderly care, worker's rights and so on. As Silvia Federici notes,

"Not only has the state investment in the workforce drastically declined, but reproductive activities have been reorganized as value-producing services that workers must purchase and pay for."[8] The expansion of the service sector and the service economy has in the West always included artistic labour.

Since the breakup of Yugoslavia, the global service economy now also includes the former art workers, redefined as cultural entrepreneurs or self-employed, who supposedly make their living based on their entrepreneurial skills and the power of their human capital, that they wisely (self)invest. In post-Yugoslav states, these self-employed art workers or creative entrepreneurs presently compete for scarce public funds since the majority of the available funding for culture goes to the public cultural organizations and their employees. While the governments of the nation states on the post-Yugoslav territory still define culture as a public good, they organize the working conditions on the "artistic labour market" as a ruthless competition that shapes the arena of the class struggle: self-employed precarious art workers versus the protected employees of the public sector. Let me illustrate, in 2010, *Asociacija – Association of Arts and Culture NGOs and Self-Employed*, an advocacy organization founded during the late 1990s by the organizations and freelancers of the independent art scene in Slovenia, conducted a comparative study between self-employed performing artists and performing artists employed in a public theatre in Ljubljana. The study demonstrated not only stark differences in social protection but also a 40 per cent lower income for the self-employed artists.[9] Another study commissioned by the Ministry of Culture in Slovenia, which specifically researched the working conditions of self-employed visual artists in Slovenia, established, among other things, that the work opportunities for them are fewer since 2008 due to a decrease in public funding and the lowering of artists' fees, which contributed to the intensified social insecurity.[10] The restructuring of reproduction has also been detrimental for the ideal of art as labour globally and wherein the final point in the trajectory of the transformation of art workers in socialist Yugoslavia represents a world standard.

As the state retreated from responsibility for social reproduction, it transferred the burden of social security onto the independent art workers. In that context, the logic of the institution of art and its mystification of artistic labour were its inevitable assistants. The conviction that the value of artistic labour is proportional to artistic talent, as measured by the apparatuses of art history and criticism (autonomous institution of art), became a convenient disciplinary mechanism used to set the cultural policy of post-Yugoslav states. The new regulations organize the social security of art workers with the evaluation of their artistic accomplishments and the importance of their creativity to the health of the national culture. For those art workers who are not full-time employees, artistic labour became a labour of love, essentialized as the artists' natural calling, and socially protected and economically valued accordingly, based on the level of creativity and artistic talent. The post-Yugoslav version of the paradox of art emerged. While the state funds cultural production as a public good, it regulates artistic labour by employing exploitative techniques that manufacture entrepreneurial subjects. The transformation of artistic labour during post-war Yugoslavia has therefore come full circle back to the invisibility of artistic labour. Artistic labour was reintegrated in the logic of the competitive market regulated by the enterprising neoliberal state. While it is deemed a free activity it is nevertheless subject to the conditions imposed on it by the capitalist organization of work and life.

This book started by asking the question: Should artists go on strike? The idea referred to a strategy of direct confrontation with the institution of art that Goran Đorđević chose to demystify the illusory power of artists and creativity. Four decades later, Đorđević's actions appear as a lost battle for economic equity within the institution of art, a battle that was lost along with the deconstruction of the welfare state, the dissolution of socialist Yugoslavia, and the evanescence of relatively just economic redistribution. However, during the early 1990s when this battle did not yet appear as lost to the generations that were born and raised in the socialist Yugoslavia, artist Marko Peljhan organized a provocative performative situation titled *Egorythm III: Dialogue Cons 5 – Businessmen and Artists* (*Egoritem III: Dialog Kons 5 – Poslovneži in artisti*). Making his way into the Ljubljana independent art scene in the early years of the post-socialist transition as a recent graduate of the theatre academy, Peljhan's work reintroduced the utopian aspects of the historical avant-gardes in a series of experimental performances. The subtitle *Dialogue Cons 5 – Businessmen and Artists* alluded to a constructivist poem written by Srečko Kosovel in the early twentieth century, in which the avant-garde poet equated gold with manure as a way to criticize the soulless and absurd practice of profit-making and the banality of capitalist greed.

Manure is gold
and gold is manure.
Both = 0
$0 = \infty$
$\infty = 0$
AB<
1, 2, 3.
Whoever has no soul
doesn't need gold.
Whoever has a soul
doesn't need dung.
EE-AW[11]

The event served as an omen that signalled a transfer of power: from the state-funded and socially protected art of the socialist era, which had just ended, to the power of the new competitive, market-dominated economic order.[12] This episode also demonstrates the contradictions of artistic labour after socialism and the new exploitative relations that now govern the global art world.

Notes

Introduction

1 Katja Praznik, "1% of Artistic Labor, or the Pygmalion-Like Effects of the Institution of Art," in *Jaka Babnik: Pygmalion*, eds. Tevž Logar and Julija Hoda (Ljubljana: Muzej in galerije mesta Ljubljane, 2019), 95–100.

2 Andrew Ross, "The Mental Labor Problem," *Social Text* 18, no. 2 (2000): 1–31.

3 Karl Marx, *Capital: A Critique of Political Economy*, (London: Penguin, 1990), 1: 272.

4 Garry Neil, *Culture and Working Conditions for Artists: Implementing the 1980 Recommendation Concerning the Status of the Artists* (Paris: UNESCO, 2019), 6; Ross, "The Mental Labor Problem," 6.

5 See Boris Arvatov, *Art and Production* (London: Pluto Press, 2017).

6 See Marx, *Capital*, 1: 133.

7 See Corina L. Apostol, "Art Workers between Precarity and Resistance: A Genealogy," *ArtLeaks Gazette*, no. 3 (2015): 7–21; Kristin Ross, *Communal Luxury: The Political Imaginary of the Paris Commune* (New York: Verso, 2015).

8 For various applications of the term see, for instance, Michael Szalay, *New Deal Modernism: American Literature and the Welfare State* (Durham: Duke University Press, 2000); Julia Bryan-Wilson, *Art Workers: Radical Practices in the Vietnam Era* (Berkley: University of California Press, 2009); Apostol, "Art Workers between Precarity and Resistance."

9 Apostol, "Art Workers between Precarity and Resistance," 8.

10 For example, there were 700 freelance artists in Serbia in 1969. By 1979, there were 1,182 freelance artists in the territory of Belgrade alone. Similarly, the number of freelance artists grew in other republics. Stevan Majstorović, *Cultural Policy in Yugoslavia: Self-Management and Culture* (Paris: UNESCO, 1980), 85. In Slovenia, the number of freelance artists grew three times higher between 1979 and 1989. Marjana Bele, *Samostojna poklicna kulturna dejavnost* [Independent Professional Cultural Activity] (Ljubljana: Fakulteta za družbene vede, 1987), 31–4, 62–3.

11 Raša Todosijević, "Edinburgh Statement: Who Makes Profit on Art and Who Gains from It Honestly," in *Theories and Documents of Contemporary Art: A Sourcebook of Artists' Writings*, eds. Kristine Stiles and Peter Selz (Berkley: University of California Press, 2012), 879.

12 Todosijević, "Edinburgh Statement," 879–84.

13 Goran Đorđević, "International Strike of Artists, 25. 2. 1979" in *SKC and the Political Practices of Art*, ed. Prelom Kolektiv (Ljubljana: Galerija ŠKUC, 2008), 29.

14 Đorđević, "International Strike of Artists."

15 Sanja Iveković and Dalibor Martinis, "U galerije s ugovorom!" in *Prvi broj* (Zagreb: RZU Podroom, 1980), 7.

16 UNESCO, *Recommendation Concerning the Status of the Artist* (Belgrade: UNESCO, 1980).

17 UNESCO, *Recommendation*, 147.

18 See, for example, European Institute for Comparative Cultural Research (ERICarts), *The Status of Artists in Europe*, IP/B/CULT/ST/2005_89, PE 375.321 (Brussels: European Parliament, 2006); Garry Neil, *Status of the Artist in Canada: An Update on the 30th Anniversary of the UNESCO Recommendation Concerning the Status of the Artist* (Ottawa: Canadian Conference of the Arts, 2010).

19 Garry Neil, *Full Analytic Report (2015) on the Implementation of the UNESCO 1980 Recommendation Concerning the Status of the Artist* (Paris: UNESCO, 2015); Garry Neil, *Culture and Working Conditions for Artists*, 2019.

20 Paula Karhunen, "Social Security and Employment" in *European Symposium on the Status of the Artist*, ed. Auli Irjala (Helsinki: Finish National Commission for UNESCO, 1992), 274; ERICarts, *The Status of Artists in Europe*, 6. To cite from the conclusions published in the book *European Symposium on the Status of the Artist* held in 1992: "The basic problem seems to be the same in Western and Northern European countries: low income level, especially from the artistic work, and inadequate social security systems." Irjala, *European Symposium on the Status of the Artist*, 20.

21 See, for example, *On Curating.org* – Precarious Labor in the Field of Art, no. 16 (2013); Bojan Piškur and Đorđe Balmazović, *A Short Analysis of Worker's Inquiry Investigation* (Belgrade: Fond B92, 2014); Radical Education Collective and Škart, ed., *Radnička Anketa (Worker's Inquiry)* (Belgrade: Kulturni centar Rex and Fond B92, 2012); Scott Indrisek, "The Precarious, Glamorous Lives of Independent Curators," *Artsy*, February 8, 2018, accessed May 28, 2018, https://www.artsy.net/article/artsy-editorial-precarious-glamorous-lives-independent-curators.

22 Luc Boltanski and Eve Chiapelo, *New Spirit of Capitalism* (London: Verso 2005); Ross, "The Mental Labor Problem"; Brian Holmes, "The Flexible Personality," in *Hieroglyphs of the Future* (Zagreb: What How and For Who/Arkzin, 2001); Andrew Ross, *No Collar* (Philadelphia: Temple University Press, 2003).

23 Tiziana Terranova, "Free Labor: Producing Culture for the New Economy," *Social Text* 18, no. 2 (Summer 2000): 33–58; Erin Duffy, *(Not) Getting Paid to Do What You Love* (New Haven: Yale University Press, 2016).

24 Ross, "The Mental Labor Problem," 11.

25 See for instance Richard Florida, *The Rise of the Creative Class* (New York: Basic Books, 2002) and for an example of a critical assessment of creativity on labour policies in the UK, see Angela McRobbie, *Be Creative* (London: Polity Press, 2016).

26 Due to its break with Stalin and Cominform in 1948, Yugoslavia kept an independent position in the Cold War divisions. It was neither a member of NATO nor of the Warsaw Pact. However, Yugoslavia was heavily dependent on loans from the West, in particular the United States, and had to constantly play a diplomatic game that it was willing to switch from one or the other side. Susan L. Woodward explains it best: "Playing on their independence of Moscow and availability to Western military strategy, signaling to each side their willingness to switch to the other, the Yugoslav leaders came to depend on the domestic means for this diplomatic independence and military strength that gave them special access to Western loans and capital markets and to favorable trade agreements in the nonaligned bloc." Yugoslavia had to ensure military self-reliance in order to pursue its political vision of self-managed socialism and the idea of social (not state) ownership. Woodward called this predicament of Yugoslavia a "Faustian bargain" because Yugoslavia was dependent on the Western market and capital, which negatively affected the social policies and priorities (full employment and "people's power" epitomized by social ownership and no labour and capital markets). Susan L. Woodward, *Socialist Unemployment: The Political Economy of Yugoslavia 1945–1990* (Princeton: Princeton University Press, 1995), 224.

27 For example, see Woodward, *Socialist Unemployment*; Darko Suvin, *Splendour, Misery, and Possibilities: An X-Ray of Socialist Yugoslavia* (Leiden: Brill, 2016); Catherine Sammary, *Komunizem v gibanju: zgodovinski pomen jugoslovanskega samoupravljanja* [Communism in Motion: The Historical Meaning of Yugoslav Self-Management] (Ljubljana: Založba /*Cf., 2017); Vladimir Unkovski-Korica, *The Economic Struggle for Power in Tito's Yugoslavia: From World War II to Non-Alignment* (London: I.B. Tauris, 2016); Bojana Videkanić, *Nonaligned Modernism: Socialist Postcolonial Aesthetics in Yugoslavia, 1945–1990* (Montreal: McGill-Queen's University Press, 2019).

28 Christina Kiaer, *Imagine No Possessions: The Socialist Objects of Russian Constructivism* (Cambridge, MA: MIT Press, 2005). Another example would be the work of Russian historian Galina A. Yankovskaya who also explores the economic dimension of art during the Stalinist period, however her work mostly appears in Russian. A translation of her work in English is published in the *Slavic Review*. See Galina Yankovskaya, "The Economic Dimensions of Art in the Stalinist Era: Artists' Cooperatives in the Grip of Ideology and Plan," *Slavic Review* 65, no. 4 (2006): 769–91.

29 See Dubravka Djurić and Miško Šuvaković, eds., *Impossible Histories: Historical Avant-gardes, Neo-avant-gardes, and Post-avant-gardes in Yugoslavia 1918–1991* (Cambridge, MA: MIT Press, 2003); IRWIN, ed., *East Art Map: Contemporary Art and Eastern Europe* (London: Afterall, 2006). For rare scholarly research on the issues of cultural labour during socialism see Ana Hofman, "Music (as) Labor: Professional Musicianship, Affective Labor and Gender in Socialist Yugoslavia," *Ethnomusicology Forum* 24, no. 1 (2015): 28–50.

1 The Autonomy of Art and the Emancipation of Artistic Labour

1 See, for example, Kim Grant, *All About Process: The Theory and Discourse of Modern Artistic Labor* (Pittsburgh: Penn State University Press, 2017). The book gives a good overview of art historical concerns with artists' labour processes as a means of signification.

2 For instance, Pierre-Michel Menger, "Artists as Workers: Theoretical and Methodological Challenges," in *Poetics* 28, no. 4 (2001): 24–251; David Throsby, "A Work-Preference Model of Artist Behavior" in *Cultural Economics and Cultural Policies*, eds. A Peacock and I. Rizzo (Dordrecht: Kluwer Academic Publishers, 1994).

3 Kate Oakley, *"Art Works" – Cultural Labour Markets: A Literature Review* (London: Creativity, Culture and Education, 2009), 16 (original emphasis).

4 The "institution of art" as defined by German comparative literature theorist Peter Bürger is "the production and distribution apparatus as well as ideas about art, that prevail in a particular time and determine the reception of works of art." Peter Bürger, *Theory of the Avant-Garde* (Minneapolis: Minnesota University Press, 1984), 22.

5 See Peter Bürger, *Theory of the Avant-Garde*; Pierre Bourdieu, *The Rules of Art* (Stanford: Stanford University Press, 1992); Paul Mattick, *Art in Its Time: Theories and Practices of Modern Aesthetics* (London: Routledge, 2003); Paul Oskar Kristeller, *Renaissance Thought and the Arts* (New York: Harper & Row, 1965).

6 Paul Oskar Kristeller, a scholar of the Renaissance, demonstrates that the system of five major arts, which included painting, sculpture, architecture, music, and poetry, is of "comparatively recent origin and did not assume definite shape before the eighteenth century, although it has many ingredients which go back to classical, medieval, and Renaissance thought." Kristeller, *Renaissance Thought and the Arts*, 165.

7 Bürger, *Theory of the Avant-Garde*, lii.

8 Theodor Adorno, *Aesthetic Theory* (Minneapolis: University of Minnesota Press, 1997); Herbert Marcuse, "On the Affirmative Character of Culture" in *Negations: Essays in Critical Theory* (Boston: Beacon Pres, 1968); Jürgen Habermas, *The Structural Transformation of the Public Sphere: An Inquiry into a Category of Bourgeois Society* (Cambridge, MA: MIT Press, 1989). For more contemporary considerations of autonomy see Paul Mattick, *Art in Its Time*; John Roberts, *The Intangibilities of Form: Skilling and Deskilling in Art after the Readymade* (London: Verso, 2007); Kerstin Stakemeier and Marina Vishmidt, *Reproducing Autonomy: Work, Money, Crisis, and Contemporary Art* (London: Mute, 2016); Nicholas Brown, *Autonomy: The Social Ontology of Art under Capitalism* (Durham: Duke University Press, 2019).

9 See Olinde Rodrigues, "L'Artiste, le savant et l'industriel: Dialogue" in *Oeuvre de Saint Simone et d'Enfantin (1865–1879)*, vol. 39 (Aalen: O Zeller, 1964);

Peter Bürger, "Avant-Garde," *Encyclopedia of Aesthetics* (2nd edition), ed. Michael Kelly (Oxford: Oxford University Press, 2014), https://www.oxfordreference.com /view/10.1093/acref/9780199747108.001.0001/acref-9780199747108.

10 Bürger, "Avant-Garde."

11 For theories of the avant-garde see for example Renato Poggioli, *The Theory of the Avant-Garde* (New York: Harper & Row, 1971); Bürger, *Theory of the Avant-Garde*; Peter Aleksandar Flaker, *Poetika osporavanja: Avantgarda i književna ljevica* (Zagreb: Liber-Globus, 1984); Lev Kreft, *Spopad na umetniški levici (med vojnama)* [A Confrontation on the Left (between the Wars)] (Ljubljana: Državna založba Slovenije, 1989); Hal Foster, *The Return of the Real: The Avant-Garde at the End of the Century* (Cambridge, MA: MIT Press, 1996); Aleš Erjavec, *Aesthetic Revolutions and Twentieth-Century Avant-Garde Movements* (Durham: Duke University Press, 2015).

12 Bürger, *Theory of the Avant-Garde*, 35–54.

13 Bürger, "Avant-Garde."

14 Geoffrey Wall, "Translator's Note," in Pierre Macherey, *A Theory of Literary Production* (London: Routledge & Kegan Paul, 1978), vii.

15 Peter Bürger, "Avant-Garde and Neo-Avant-Garde: An Attempt to Answer Certain Critics of *Theory of the Avant-Garde*," *New Literary History* 41, no. 4 (2010): 696.

16 Bürger, "Avant-Garde and Neo-Avant-Garde," 696.

17 Louis Althusser, *Lenin and Philosophy, and Other Essays* (New York: Monthly Press, 1972); Louis Althusser, *For Marx* (London: Verso, 2005); Rastko Močnik "Sistem družboslovja in njegovi učinki" [The System of Social Sciences and Its Effects], *Spisi iz humanistitke* [Essays in the Humanities] (Ljubljana: Založba /*cf., 2009), 441–510.

18 Andrea Komlosy, *Work: The Last 1,000 Years* (London: Verso, 2018), 12–15.

19 Bürger, *Theory of the Avant-Garde*, 32.

20 On emergence of artistic genius and its links to creativity see, for example, Andreas Reckwitz, *The Invention of Creativity* (London: Polity Press, 2017).

21 Komlosy, *Work*, 10–13.

22 Adolfo Sánchez Vásquez, *Art and Society: Essays in Marxist Aesthetics* (New York: Monthly Press, 1973), 67.

23 Friedrich Schiller, *On the Aesthetic Education of Man* (Mineola, NY: Dover Publications, 2012).

24 Immanuel Kant, *Critique of Judgment*, trans. Werner S. Pluhar (Indianapolis/ Cambridge: Hackett Publishing Company, 1987). For a critique, see Bürger, *Theory of the Avant-Garde*, 42–4; Martha Woodmansee, *The Author, Art, and the Market: Rereading the History of Aesthetics* (New York: Columbia University Press, 1994).

25 Immanuel Kant, *Critique of Judgment*, 190.

26 Compare the passage in the German original: "[…] denn schöne Kunst muß in doppelter Bedeutung freie Kunst sein: sowohl daß sie nicht als *Lohngeschäft, eine Arbeit sei*, deren Größe sich nach einem bestimmten Maßstabe beurteilen, erzwingen oder bezahlen läßt; sondern auch, daß das Gemüt sich zwar

beschäftigt, aber dabei doch, ohne auf einen andern Zweck hinauszusehen (*unabhängig vom Lohne*) befriedigt und erweckt fühlt." Immanuel Kant, *Kritik der Urteilskraft, Werke in zwölf Bänden*, Band 10 (Suhrkamp Verlag: Frankfurt am Main, 1977), 258.

27 Bürger, *Theory of the Avant-Garde*, 43.

28 Peter Bürger, "Critique of Autonomy," *Encyclopedia of Aesthetics*, ed. Michael Kelly (Oxford: Oxford University Press, 1998), 175.

29 Bürger, *Theory of the Avant-Garde*, 14.

30 Bürger, "Critique of Autonomy," 175–7.

31 Bürger, "Critique of Autonomy," 176.

32 Bürger, *Theory of the Avant-Garde*, 51–4; Bürger, "Avant-Garde and Neo-Avant-Garde," 696–7.

33 See Kiaer, *Imagine No Possessions*.

34 Bürger, *Theory of the Avant-Garde*, 57.

35 A collective of avant-garde artists, among them Daniil Kharms. OBEIRU stands for Union of Real Art.

36 See, for example, Boris Groys, *The Total Art of Stalinism: Avant-Garde, Aesthetic Dictatorship and Beyond* (New Jersey: Princeton University Press, 1992); Igor Golomstock, *Totalitarian Art: In the Soviet Union, the Third Reich, Fascist Italy and the People's Republic of China* (New York: Icon Editions, 1990); Hans Günther, *The Culture of the Stalin Period* (New York: St. Martin's Press, 1990); Kiaer, *Imagine No Possessions*; Evgeny Dobrenko, *Aesthetics of Alienation: Reassessment of Early Soviet Cultural Theories* (Evanston, IL: Northwestern University Press, 2005).

37 John Berger, *Art and Revolution: Ernst Neizvestny and the Role of the Artist in the U.S.S.R.* (London: Writers and Readers Publishing Cooperative, 1969), 50.

38 Inke Arns, *Avantgarda v vzvratnem ogledalu: sprememba paradigem recepcije avantgarde v (nekdanji) Jugoslaviji in Rusiji od 80. let do danes* [The Avant-Garde in the Rearview Mirror: The Changes of the Paradigms in the Reception of the Avant-Garde in (former) Yugoslavia and Russia from the 1980s to the Present] (Ljubljana: Maska, 2006).

39 Szalay, *New Deal Modernism*, 68.

40 Specifically, Szalay points out that New Deal modernism recognized art as "a self-sufficient, regulated activity that produced no outcome by which it might be judged" while simultaneously guaranteeing an artist a salary. Even more, the New Deal's attitude to art aimed toward "a fusion that elided audience members as consumers of art by enshrining them as producers of the very same art." Szalay, *New Deal Modernism*, 68.

41 Szalay, *New Deal Modernism*, 270.

42 Artistic avant-garde movements appeared on the territory of interwar Yugoslavia. "Between the two world wars, while Yugoslavia was a bourgeois, multinational state, avant-gardes were treated as the far-left fringe, thereby excluded from the corpus of national literature and art." Miško Šuvaković, "Impossible Histories," in Djurić and Šuvaković, *Impossible Histories*, 5. See also, Janez Vrečko, "Labodovci,

pilotovci, konstrukteristi in tankisti," in Ilich Klančnik and Zabel, *TANK! Slovenska Zgodovinska avantgarda/Revue international d'art vivant* [TANK! Slovene Historical Avant-Garde/International Journal of Living Art] (Ljubljana: Moderna galerija, 1998), 34–8.

43 Šuvaković, "Impossible Histories," 24.

44 Avant-garde movements often published and anchored themselves around magazines, for instance *Svetokret, Zenit, Dada Tank, Dada Jazz, Rdeči pilot, Novi oder*, and *Tank*. They represented various avant-garde movements, such as zenitism, constructivism, surrealism, and dadaism. See, for example, Ilich Klančnik and Zabel, *TANK! Slovenska Zgodovinska avantgarda/Revue international d'art vivant*; Šuvaković, "Impossible Histories," 12–25; Aleš Erjavec, "The Three Avant-gardes and Their Context: The Early, the Neo, and the Postmodern," in Djurić and Šuvaković, *Impossible Histories*, 37–51.

45 Majstorović, *Cultural Policy in Yugoslavia*, 1980, 21. (Majstorović's book had a second adapted edition, published in 1980, eight years after the first edition. Since both editions have the same title, I added the year of publication to distinguish the editions.)

46 Majstorović, *Cultural Policy in Yugoslavia*, 1980, 21.

47 Rastko Močnik, "East!" in IRWIN, *East Art Map*, 345–7.

48 Močnik, "East!" 346–7.

49 Kreft, *Spopad na umetniški levici*, 161.

50 This why Bürger's theory of the avant-garde distinguishes between historical avant-garde and neo-avant-garde. The distinction therefore pertains to the fact that the historical avant-garde's impulse to transform social relationships – the elementary postulates of the institution of art – did not occur due to the art institutional "resistance to the attack of the avant-gardes"; the means that the historical avant-gardes used in attempts to alter social reality were eventually accepted by the institution of art as aesthetic procedures. Bürger, "Avant-Grade and Neo-Avant-Garde," 707.

51 Kreft, *Spopad na umetniški levici*, 126.

52 The avant-garde in the West became synonymous with the American apolitical modernist avant-garde that was appropriated by the political establishment for the promotion of liberal ideology of freedom and individualism. See Serge Guilbaut, *How New York Stole the Idea of Modern Art: Abstract Expressionism, Freedom and the Cold War* (Chicago: The University of Chicago Press, 1983); Eda Čufer, "Enjoy Me, Abuse Me, I am Your Artist: Cultural Politics, Their Monuments, Their Ruins" in IRWIN, *East Art Map*, 362–78.

53 Arns, *Avantgarda v vzvratnem ogledalu*, 16.

54 Hans Günther and Karla Hielscher, "Zur Rezeption der sowjetischen linen Avantgarde" in *Ästhetik und Kommunikation* 19 (1975): 31–6. As cited in Arns, *Avantgarda v vzvratnem ogledalu*, 16.

55 Arns, *Avantgarda v vzvratnem ogledalu*, 16.

56 Bürger, *The Theory of the Avant-Garde*, 83–92.

57 Guilbaut, *How New York Stole the Idea of Modern Art*.

58 For examples in other Eastern European countries, see IRWIN, *East Art Map*, 21–338.

59 Ješa Denegri, "Inside or Outside 'Socialist Modernism'? Radical Views on the Yugoslav Art Scene 1950–1970," in Djurić and Šuvaković, eds. *Impossible Histories*, 177–8.

60 Ješa Denegri, "Teze za drugu liniju," in *Razlozi za drugu liniju* (Novi Sad: Muzej suvremene umetnosti Vojvodine, 2007), 102.

61 Denegri, "Inside or Outside," 178.

62 See, for instance, Djurić and Šuvaković, *Impossible Histories*; Armin Medosch, *New Tendencies: Art at the Threshold of the Information Revolution (1961–1978)* (Cambridge, MA: MIT Press, 2016); Marijan Susovski, ed., *The New Art Practice in Yugoslavia 1966–1978* (Zagreb: Gallery of Contemporary Art, 1978); Primož Jesenko, *Rob v središču: izbrana poglavja o eksperimentalnem gledališču v Sloveniji 1955–1967* [*The Edge in the Centre: Selected Chapters from the History of the Experimental Theatre in Slovenia 1955–1967*] (Ljubljana: Slovenski gledališki institute, 2015); Ilich Klančnik and Zabel, *TANK! Slovenska zgodovinska avantgarda/Revue international d'art vivant*; Nena Dimitrijević, *Gorgona – umjetnost kao način postojanja* (Zagreb: Galerija suvrenemen umjetnosti, 1977).

63 As far as art practices of socialist Yugoslavia are concerned, the alternative art had numerous beginnings and a long history related not only to the historical avant-garde movements but also to the activities and the milieu of the experimental art of the 1950s, 1960s, and 1970s; the Yugoslav student movement and culture produced within the framework of student cultural centres (such as Novi Sad, Belgrade, Zagreb, and Ljubljana); and the emergence of numerous communes of alternative lifestyles. See, for example, Neven Korda, "Alternative Dawns," in *FV: Alternativa osemdesetih/Alternative Scene of the Eighties* ed. Breda Škrjanec (Ljubljana: Mednarodni grafični likovni center, 2008), 354.

64 See Jelena Stojanović, "Internationaleries: Collectivism, the Grotesque, and Cold War Functionalism," in *Colletivism after Modernism: The Art of Social Imagination after 1945*, eds. Gregory Sholette and Blake Stimson (Minneapolis: University of Minnesota Press, 2007), 17–43.

65 Bürger, *Theory of the Avant-Garde*, 56–9; Bürger, "Avant-Garde and Neo-Avant-Garde," 704–14.

66 Močnik, "East!" 346–7.

67 Močnik, "East!" 347.

68 Bürger, *The Theory of the Avant-Garde*, 86.

69 See Adorno, *Aesthetic Theory*; Georg Lukács, *The Meaning of Contemporary Realism* (London: Merlin Press, 1963). For critique, see Bürger, *The Theory of the Avant-Garde*, 83–92.

70 Bürger, *The Theory of the Avant-Garde*, 86.

71 Bürger, *The Theory of the Avant-Garde*, 86.

72 Bürger, *The Theory of the Avant-Garde*, lii.
73 See Adorno, *Aesthetic Theory*.
74 Theodor Adorno, *In Search of Wagner* (London: NLB, 1981), 83.
75 Bürger, *The Theory of the Avant-Garde*, 96.
76 Bürger, *The Theory of the Avant-Garde*, 86.
77 This other invisible work too is vital for the reproduction of capitalist social relations and deeply imbricated with capitalist accumulation, however it is often not understood as work in an economic sense because it is separated in the private sphere of work. This separation of public and private spheres of work, which is a process linked to the rise of capitalism and division of labour, also affects the sphere of art and contributes to the issues with autonomy of art on a structural level. I discuss this issue in the following chapter (chapter 2).
78 Adorno, *In Search of Wagner*, 83.

2 A Feminist Approach to the Disavowed Economy of Art

1 Angela Davis, "Uprising & Abolition: Angela Davis on Movement Building, 'Defund the Police' & Where We Go from Here," *Democracy Now!* June 12, 2020, https://www.democracynow.org/2020/6/12/angela_davis_historic_moment.
2 See, for example, Linda Nochlin, "Why Have There Been No Great Women Artists?" in *Art and Sexual Politics: Why Have There Been No Great Women Artists?* eds. Thomas B. Hess and Elizabeth C. Baker (New York: MacMillan, 1971); Woodmansee, *The Author, Art, and the Market*, 103–9.
3 Teresa L. Ebert, "Rematerializing Feminism," *Science & Society* 69, no. 1 (2005): 33–4.
4 See Mariarosa Dalla Costa and Selma James, *The Power of Women and the Subversion of the Community* (Bristol: Falling Wall Press, 1972); Silvia Federici, *Wages against Housework* (Bristol: Falling Wall Press, 1975); Maria Mies, *Patriarchy and Accumulation on a World Scale* (London: Zed Books, 1986); Maria Mies, "Housewifisation – Globalisation – Subsistence – Perspective" in *Beyond Marx: Theorizing the Global Labour Relations of the Twenty-First Century*, ed. Marcel van der Linden and Karl Heinz Roth (Leiden: Brill, 2013).
5 Mary Inman, *In Woman's Defense* (Los Angeles: Committee to Organize Advancement of Women, 1940); Margaret Benston, "The Political Economy of Women's Liberation," *Monthly Review* 21, no. 4 (1969): 13–27; Dalla Costa and James, *The Power of Women and the Subversion of the Community*; Federici, *Wages against Housework*; Mies, *Patriarchy and Accumulation on a World Scale*; Silvia Federici, *Caliban and the Witch: Women, the Body and Primitive Accummulation* (Brooklyn: Autonomedia, 2009); Mies, "Housewifisation – Globalisation – Subsistence – Perspective" in *Beyond Marx: Theorizing the Global Labour Relations of the Twenty-First Century*, 218–23.
6 See Anne Oakley, *Women's Work: The Housewife, Past and Present* (New York: Vintage Books, 1976), retitled version of *Housewife* (London: Penguin, 1974); Arlene Kaplan

Daniels, "Invisible Work," *Social Problems* 34, no. 5 (1987): 403–15; Majda Hrženjak, *Invisible Work /Nevidno delo* (Ljubljana: Mirovni inštitut, 2007); Erin Hatton, "Mechanisms of Invisibility: Rethinking the Concept of Invisible Work," *Work, Employment and Society* 31, no. 2 (2017): 336–51. Related to the efforts of feminist interventions, philosopher Ivan Illich devised the term "shadow work" to describe the travail that is not rewarded by wage by explicitly referring to the housewife as the prime example, see Ivan D. Illich, *Shadow Work* (London: Marion Boyars, 1981).

7 Andrea Komlosy, "Transitions in Global Labor History, 1250–2010 Entanglements, Synchronicities, and Combinations on a Local and a Global Scale," *Review (Ferdinand Braudel Center)* 36, no. 2 (2013): 162.

8 Mariarosa Dalla Costa, "Women and the Subversion of the Community" in Dalla Costa and James, *The Power of Women and the Subversion of the Community*, 25–6.

9 Silvia Federici (with Nicole Cox), "Counterplanning from the Kitchen," in Silvia Federici, *Revolution at Point Zero: Housework, Reproduction, and Feminist Struggle* (Oakland: PM Press, 2012), 28.

10 Federici, *Wages against Housework*, 2.

11 Federici, *Wages against Housework*, 2

12 Federici, *Wages against Housework*, 2.

13 See, for example, Kathi Weeks, *The Problem with Work: Feminism, Marxism, Antiwork Politics and Postwork Imaginaries* (Durham: Duke University Press, 2011) for a critical examiniation of the political implications of the Wages for Housework campaign.

14 Silvia Federici, "The Reproduction of Labor Power in the Global Economy and the Unfinished Feminist Revolution," in *Revolution at Point Zero*, 91–111.

15 Mary Poovey, *Uneven Developments: The Ideological Work of Gender in Mid-Victorian England* (Chicago: University of Chicago Press, 1988), 13–14.

16 Poovey, *Uneven Developments*, 122.

17 Poovey, *Uneven Developments*, 123.

18 Weeks, *The Problem with Work*, 3.

19 Weeks, *The Problem with Work*, 4.

20 Dieter Lesage, "A Portrait of the Artist as a Worker," *Maska* 20, no. 94–5 (2005): 93.

21 Weeks, *The Problem with Work*, 7.

22 Teresa L. Ebert and Mas'ud Zavarzadeh, "ABC of Class," *Nature, Society, and Thought* 17, no. 2 (2004): 133.

23 Sergio Bologna, "Workerism beyond Fordism: On the Lineage of Italian Workerism," *Viewpoint Magazine*, December 15, 2014, accessed on May 28, 2018, https://www.viewpointmag.com/2014/12/15/workerism-beyond-fordism-on-the -lineage-of-italian-workerism/.

24 Bologna, "Workerism."

25 Bologna, "Workerism."

26 Weeks, *The Problem with Work*, 8.

27 Federici, *Wages against Housework*, 2.

28 Federici, *Wages against Housework*, 6.

29 See for example David Graeber, "From Managerial Feudalism to the Revolt of the Caring Class," (presentation, 36th Chaos Communication Congress, December 12, 2019) *Open Transcripts.org*, accessed June 19, 2020, http://opentranscripts.org /transcript/managerial-feudalism-revolt-caring-classes/.

30 Lepoldina Fortunati, *Arcane of Reproduction: Housework, Prostitution, Labor and Capital* (Brooklyn: Autonomedia, 1995); Federici, *Caliban and the Witch*; Marta E. Giménez, *Marx, Women, and Capitalist Social Reproduction* (Leiden: Brill, 2018), 131–310.

31 Federici, *Wages against Housework*, 2.

32 This imperative is turned into a "mantra" for every kind of work today. See Miya Tokumitsu, "In the Name of Love," *Jacobin*, no. 13 (2014), accessed on May 28, 2018, https://www.jacobinmag.com/2014/01/in-the-name-of-love/.

33 Reckwitz, *The Invention of Creativity*; Woodmansee, *The Author, Art, and the Market*.

34 Reckwitz, *The Invention of Creativity*.

35 Reckwitz, *The Invention of Creativity*, 47.

36 Reckwitz, *The Invention of Creativity*, 47.

37 Woodmansee, *The Author, Art, and the Market*, 37.

38 For example, Reckwitz, while analysing some representatives of American abstract expressionism, notes that in certain aspects an artist displaying or performing the labour of creation paradoxically became "an aesthetic object in its own right." Reckwitz, *The Invention of Creativity*, 69. Even more, "the philosophical and culture critical discourse of the universality of aesthetic creativity began to be absorbed into psychological and pedagogical models of the 'creative self' where they exerted influence on the educated middle class. Inversely, the bohemian lifestyle was quoted, continued and finally anchored by youth and counter-culture as one of the preconditions for 'aesthetic capitalism.'" Reckwitz, *The Invention of Creativity*, 171.

39 One of the central issues in this respect is an assumption that artistic labour as exceptional or atypical work cannot be standardized while art schools and other creative programs appear to know the secret of how to nurture and train creativity and artistic subjects. Nonetheless, art schools and academies have for decades standardized, trained, and produced artistic subjectivities. See Howard Singerman, *Art Subjects: Making Artists in the American University* (Berkley: University of California Press, 1999).

40 Reckwitz, *The Invention of Creativity*, 47.

41 Eliot Friedson, "Labors of Love in Theory and Practice: A Prospectus," in *The Nature of Work: Sociological Perspectives*, eds. Kai Erikson and Steven Peter Vallas (New Haven: Yale University Press, 1990), 151.

42 Ross, "The Mental Labor Problem," 1–31.

43 Ross, "The Mental Labor Problem," 22. Ross relates the pervasiveness of sacrificial labour in the arts and academic circles to a patronizing "left-leaning integrity" that turns "material self-denial and voluntary poverty" into a monastic signature trait. Ross, "The Mental Labor Problem," 15.

44 For discussions about artistic labour and issues of class divisions see, for example, Kate Oakley and Dave O'Brien, "Learning to Labour Unequally: Understanding the Relationship between Cultural Production, Cultural Consumption and Inequality," *Social Identities* 22, no. 5 (2016): 471–86; Mark Taylor and Dave O'Brien, "'Culture is a Meritocracy': Why Creative Workers' Attitudes May Reinforce Social Inequality," *Sociological Research Online* 22, no. 4 (2017): 27–47; Dave O'Brien and Kate Oakley, *Cultural Value and Inequality: A Critical Literature Review* (Wiltshire: Arts and Humanities Research Council, 2015), https://ahrc .ukri.org/documents/project-reports-and-reviews/cultural-value-and-inequality-a -critical-literature-review/.

45 Regarding art students' debts, see for example BfAMfAPhD, *Artists Report Back: A National Study on the Lives of Arts Graduates and Working Artists*, BfAMfAPhD, 2014, http://bfamfaphd.com/#topic-reports; Caroline Woolard and Susan Jahoda, "BFAMFAPHD: On the Cultural Value Debate and Artists Report Back," *Cultural Policy Yearbook 2016: Independent Republic of Culture*, ed. Serhan Ada (Istanbul: Istanbul University Press, 2017), 37–40.

46 See for example, Dave Beech, *Art and Value* (Leiden: Brill, 2015); Leigh Claire La Berge, *Wages against Artwork* (Durham: Duke University Press, 2019).

47 Ebert and Zavarzadeh, "ABC of Class," 133.

48 Ross, "The Mental Labor Problem," 14.

49 Bourdieu, *The Rules of Art*, 141–73.

3 The Making of Yugoslav Art Workers

1 Before Socialist Federative Republic of Yugoslavia was declared the country's official name by the constitution of 1963, it had two other names. During the Second World War, in 1943, the Antifascist Council of National Liberation of Yugoslavia (AVNOJ) declared the new country as Democratic Federative Yugoslavia (*Demokratska federativna Jugoslavija – DFJ*). After the war, from 1945 to 1963, the country was called Federative People's Republic Yugoslavia (*Federativna narodna republika Jugoslavija – FNRJ*).

2 See chapter 1 (to this book), and Bürger, *Theory of the Avant-Garde*; Bürger, "Critique of Autonomy," 175–8.

3 See for instance Mihailo Marković, "Socialism and Self-Management," *Praxis* 1, no. 2–3 (1965): 178–95.

4 Kreft, *Spopad na umetniški levici*, 119.

5 Despite differences in scholarly periodization of stages in Yugoslav socialism, various periodizations discern the mid-sixties (1963–5) as the turning point when

the economic reform introduced market elements into the previously planned political economy of Yugoslavia. See Samary, *Komunizem v gibanju*, 77–83; Marko Kržan, "Jugoslovansko samoupravljanje in prihodnost socializma" [Yugoslav Self/ Management and the Future of Socialism] in Samary, *Komunizem v gibanju*, 221–33; Suvin, *Splendour, Misery, and Possibilities*, 33–4, 84–5; Vladmir Unkovski-Korica, "Self-Management, Development, and Debt: The Rise and Fall of the 'Yugoslav Experiment,'" in *Welcome to the Desert of Post-Socialism: Radical Politics after Yugoslavia*, eds. Igor Štiks and Srečko Horvat (London: Verso, 2015), 21–43.

6 See Aleš Gabrič, *Slovenska agitpropovska kulturna politika 1945–1952* [Slovene Agitprop Cultural Policy 1945–1952] (Ljubljana: Mladika, 1991).

7 It is important to note that this goal was fully realized only in one of the six republics that comprised Yugoslavia, that is in Slovenia, where full employment reined until the mid 1980s.

8 Woodward, *Socialist Unemployment*, 16.

9 Woodward, *Socialist Unemployment*, 16.

10 Suvin, *Splendour, Misery, and Possibilities*, 36.

11 Rastko Močnik, "Workers' Self-Management in Yugoslavia – Possible Lessons for the Present" (Ljubljana 2012, unpublished paper), 3.

12 Vesna Čopič and Gregor Tomc, "Nacionalno poročilo o kulturni politiki Slovenije [National Report on Cultural Policy of Slovenia]" in *Kulturna politika v Sloveniji* [Cultural Policy in Slovenia] (Ljubljana: Fakulteta za družbene vede, 1997), 53.

13 Uputstvo o kupovini radova likovne i primenjene umetnosti, *Službeni list FNRJ*, no. 6 (January 31, 1951); Uputstvo o kupovini radova likovne i primenjene umetnosti, *Službeni list FNRJ*, no. 39 (August 29, 1951).

14 For instance, a document titled "Podaci o materijalnom položaju likovnih umetnika" (Data on the material condition of visual artists) reported that there were 646 visual artists in Yugoslavia in 1951, out of which 402 were employed and 244 were freelancers. "Podaci o materijalnom položaju likovnih umetnika," 1951, Fond 317, Folder 78, Archive of Yugoslavia, Belgrade. While 38 per cent were freelancers in 1951, the percentage was 12 per cent lower in 1953. According to the report of the Alliance of Visual Artists of Yugoslavia (*Udruženje likovnih umjetnika Jugoslavije*), in 1953 there were 610 visual artists. However, only 26 per cent of artists worked freelance, while the rest (450) were employed. Marko Člebonović, "Problem materijalnog obezbeđenja likovnih umetnika Jugoslavije," 1953, Fond 318, Folder 147, Archive of Yugoslavia, Belgrade.

15 Opća uputstva o visini autorskih honorara za književno-umjetnička djela i naučne radove; Opća uputstva o naknadama nosiocima autorskih prava za izvođenje i prikazivanje književnih i umjetničkih djela, *Službeni list FNRJ*, no. 106 (December 31, 1946): 1448–50. In 1950 authorities passed a more general regulation for fees for literary, artistic, and scientific work: Opšte uputstvo o visini autorskih honorara za objavljivanje književnih, umetničkih i naučnih dela i radova, *Službeni list FNRJ*, no. 38 (May 31, 1950): 704–7.

16 Pravilnik o sudjelovanju i gostovanju umjetnika u nar. kazalištima, 7. 7. 1947, Fond 317, Folder 81, Archive of Yugoslavia, Belgrade.

17 "Ugovor o socialnom osiguranju književnika, zaključen 24. 10. 1952 godine izmedu Saveta za narodno zdravlje i socijalnu politiku Vlade FNRJ i Saveza književnika Jugoslavije" cited in Uredba o socijalnom osiguranju umetnika, *Službeni list FNRJ*, no. 32 (July 13, 1955): 539; Rešenje o socijalnom osiguranju lica zaposlenih na poslovima snjimanja i izrade filmova (filmskih dela), *Službeni list FNRJ*, no. 60 (December 17, 1952): 954–6.

18 Uredba o socijalnom osiguranju umetnika, *Službeni list FNRJ*, no. 32 (July 13, 1955), 536–9.

19 Bojana Videkanić, "Yugoslav Postwar Art and Socialist Realism: An Uncomfortable Relationship," *Artmargins* 5, no. 2 (2016): 21. One way in which the specific geopolitical position of Yugoslavia during the Cold War came to the fore was through the political idea of nonalignment, which also had an important impact on cultural life in the country. In 1961 Yugoslavia, along with India, Egypt, Ghana, Guinea, Ethiopia, Indonesia, Mali, and Sudan (formerly The Sudan) became the initiator of the Nonaligned Movement, which on the international level developed a political project in support of national self-determination against all forms of colonialism and imperialism. As such, these countries refused to align and aimed to resist neocolonial dominance of the two power blocks. Yugoslavia's involvement in the Nonaligned Movement amplified its position as a geopolitical alternative that resulted in a different model of international cultural relations (which Videkanić defines as "nonaligned modernism") and are exemplified by the International Biennial of Graphic Arts in Ljubljana and numerous cultural exchange programs between Yugoslavia and other nations of this political alliance. See Videkanić, *Nonaligned Modernism*.

20 Videkanić, "Yugoslav Postwar Art and Socialist Realism," 23.

21 Videkanić, "Yugoslav Postwar Art and Socialist Realism," 3–26.

22 Exat 51, "Manifesto," in Djurić and Šuvaković, eds. *Impossible Histories*, 539; Denegri, "Inside or Outside," 182–3; Dejan Kršić, "Grafički dizajn i viuzalne komunikacije 1950.–1975." [Graphic Design and Visual Communications, 1950–1975], in *Socializam i modernost: umjetnost, kultura i politika 1950.–1974.* [Socialism and Modernity: Art, Culture, and Politics 1950–1974], ed. Liljana Kolešnik (Zagreb: Institut za povjest umjetnosti and Muzej suvremene umjetnosti), 228–32.

23 Exat 51, "Manifesto," 539.

24 Kršić, "Grafički dizajn i vizualne komunikacije," 229, 232.

25 Kršić, "Grafički dizajn i vizualne komunikacije," 232. See also Branislav Jakovljević, *Alienation Effects: Performance and Self-Management in Yugoslavia, 1945–1991* (Ann Arbor: University of Michigan Press, 2016), 97–8.

26 Močnik, "East!" 348.

27 Videkanić, "Yugoslav Postwar Art and Socialist Realism," 26.

28 Susan L. Woodward, "The Political Economy of Ethno-Nationalism in Yugoslavia," in *Socialist Register 2003: Fighting Identities – Race, Religion and Ethno-Nationalism*, eds. Leo Panitch and Colin Leys (London: The Merlin Press, 2003), 75.

29 Woodward, *Socialist Unemployment*, 222–59.

30 Majstorović, *Cultural Policy in Yugoslavia*, 1972, 17.

31 Majstorović, *Cultural Policy in Yugoslavia*, 1972, 15.

32 In contrast to the Dutch model where artists were understood as commercial agents and could have businesses to sell art. See Mattick, *Art in Its Time*, 24–45; John Berger, *Ways of Seeing* (London: British Broadcasting Corp, 1977), 83–112; Raymonde Moulin, *The French Art Market: A Sociological View* (New Brunswick: Rutgers University Press, 1987).

33 Položaj likovih umetnika u zemlji [Circumstances of Visual Artists in the Country], 1962, Fond 318, Folder 153, Archive of Yugoslavia, Belgrade.

34 Denegri, "Inside or Outside," 177.

35 The notion is meant to be ironic to relativize both articles of this pleonasm since tolerance would be pluralistic. In other words, aesthetic pluralism was an appearance affected by the LCY doctrine of separation of aesthetics and politics. I am indebted to discussions with Rastko Močnik for developing his term.

36 Sveta Lukić, "Socijalistički estetizam," *Umetnost na mostu* (Belgrade: Ideje, 1975), 225–43.

37 Lazar Trifunović cited in Denegri, "Inside or Outside," 178.

38 Trifunović in Denegri, "Inside or Outside," 178.

39 Trifunović in Denegri, "Inside or Outside," 178.

40 Darko Suvin, "On the Class Relationships in Yugoslavia 1945–1974, with a Hypothesis on the Ruling Class," *Debatte: Journal of Contemporary Central and Eastern Europe* 20, no. 1 (2012): 37–71. See also Suvin, *Splendour, Misery, and Possibilities*, 43–80.

41 See Milovan Djilas, *The New Class: An Analysis of the Communist System* (New York: Praeger, 1963). As Darko Suvin emphasizes, Djilas gained international renown after he was dismissed from the LCY and due to the publications of *The New Class*, which was "rewritten by CIA specialists" (Suvin, *Splendour, Misery, and Possibilities*, 351).

42 Suvin, *Splendour, Misery, and Possibilities*, 76–7 et passim.

43 Woodward, *Socialist Unemployment*; Catherine Samary, *The Fragmentation of Yugoslavia: An Overview* (Amsterdam: International Institute for Research and Education, 1993); Suvin, *Splendour, Misery, and Possibilities*.

44 Samary, *Komunizem v gibanju*, 91–107; Kržan, "Jugoslovansko samoupravljanje," 214–21; Johanna Bockman, *Markets in the Name of Socialism: The Left-Wing Origins of Neoliberalism* (Berkley: Stanford University Press, 2011), 76–103.

45 Kržan, "Jugoslovansko samoupravljanje," 213–14.

46 Suvin, *Splendour, Misery, and Possibilties*, 34.

47 From 1948 to 1981 the peasant population decreased from 67 to 20 per cent, while
the percentage of urban population growth was reversed, from 21 per cent in 1947 to
47 per cent in 1981. In the period from 1953 to 1985, the socialist authorities built 3.5
million apartments. In 1984 82 per cent of the population had public health coverage
as compared to 1952 when only 25 per cent were covered. In terms of education,
12 per cent of the population over the age of ten was without education, while in
the early 1950s the percentage was 82. Among the educated population, in 1981 23
per cent finished high school and 5 per cent obtained a post-secondary education.
Dušan Miljković, ed., *Jugoslavia 1945–1985: statistički prikaz* [Yugoslavia 1945–1985:
Statistical Presentation] (Belgrade: Savezni zavod za statistiku, 1986), 12, 18, 25–6.

48 Kreft, *Spopad na umetniški levici*, 133.

49 Bojana Videkanić, "Non-aligned Modernism: Yugoslavian Art and Culture from
1945–1990" (PhD diss., York University, 2013), 98.

50 Marcuse, "On the Affirmative Character of Culture."

51 For instance, many renowned Yugoslav film directors, such as Želimir Žilnik,
gained their film experience in the cinema clubs. Another case in point is artist
Tomislav Gotovac who also created many of his early films as a member of a
cinema club. See Hrvoje Turković, "It's All a Movie: A Conversation with Tomislav
Gotovac," *Magazine FILM*, no. 10–11 (1977): 39–66. See also Bojana Piškur and
Tamara Soban, eds., *This Is All Film: Experimental Film in Yugoslavia 1951–1991*
(Ljubljana: Moderna galerija, 2011).

52 Katja Praznik, "Between the Avant-Grade, Modernism and Amateurism: A
Fragmentary History of Contemporary Dance in Ljubljana in the 1960s and 1970s,"
Maska 24, no. 123–4 (Summer 2009): 68–85.

53 The LSYY was previously known as the League of Yugoslav Youth and People's
Youth of Yugoslavia (*Narodna omladina Jugoslavije*). Its history is connected to the
Youth Communist League of Yugoslavia (the youth wing of the CPY founded in
Zagreb in 1919) and to the antifascist movement (United Alliance of Antifascist
Youth of Yugoslavia, founded in Bihać in 1942). The LSYY, whose members
were from fourteen to twenty-five, was an important element in the postwar
reconstruction of the country. It organized mass youth labour campaigns during
the first postwar decade as well as other social, educational, and cultural activities.
The students were part of the LSYY after a forced merger in 1974 and operated as
the University Conference of LSYY.

54 Before 1974 students were organized in the SAY (*Savez studenta Jugoslavije*),
established in 1951 in Belgrade. Associations of SAY were formed at universities
across Yugoslavia. Before the forced merger with the LSYY, SAY endorsed the
program of the LCY as well as the general principles of the League of Yugoslav
Youth but it operated independently and had its own statutes. SAY also organized
various political, sports, and cultural activities, among them publishing. SAY
was engaged in broader social and political issues. For example, in Slovenia,
it published several newspapers that represented critical political and cultural

platforms of intellectual debate, such as *Tribuna*, *Revija 57*, and *Perspektive*. SAY was an important element of the student movement that began in 1968. The achievements of the student movement – though socialist authorities inevitably reined it in – included newly opened student cultural centres (in Belgrade) as well as Radio Študent, one of the first independent radio stations operated by students.

55 I discuss it at length in chapters 5 and 6.

56 Woodward, *Socialist Unemployment*, 262.

57 For example, a cultural institution was run by a council, which comprised one-third internal members (i.e., its employees/workers) and two-thirds external members representing the interest of a community. The unions and Socialist Alliance of Working People appointed external members, through which the Party's influence was maintained on cultural affairs rather than strictly representing the interests of a particular community.

58 After 1953 the role of the Council for Science and Culture was subsumed under the federal Executive Council (*Savezno izvršno veće/Zvezni izvršni svet*), under which a federal Secretariat for Education and Culture (*Savezni sekretarijat za obrazovanje i kulturu*) existed until 1967. The federal Council for Education and Culture (*Savezni savet za obrazovanje i kulturu*) succeeded it from 1967–71. Finally, a federal Committee for Science and Culture (*Savezni komitet za nauku i kulturu*), as the last federal organ that oversaw culture, was established in 1971 and operated until 1978.

59 Čopič and Tomc, "Nacionalno poročilo," 62–3.

60 Čopič and Tomc, "Nacionalno poročilo," 30.

61 See Majstorović, *Cultural Policy in Yugoslavia* (1972), 34. The situation was similar in other republics. See Majstorović, *Cultural Policy in Yugoslavia* (1980), 24.

62 See, for example, Mira Liehm and Antonin J. Liehm, *The Most Important Art: Soviet and Eastern European Film after 1945* (Berkley: University of California Press, 1977).

63 Ljerka Vidić Rasmussen, *The Newly Composed Folk Music of Yugoslavia* (New York: Routledge, 2002), 80.

64 Sergio Bologna, "Nove oblike dela," [New Forms of Labor] in *Postfordizem: razprave o sodobnem kapitalizmu*, ed. Gal Kirn (Ljubljana: Mirovni inštitut, 2010), 135–6. See also Sabine Grimm and Klaus Ronnerberger, "An Invisible History of Work: An Interview with Sergio Bologna," *Springerin* 10, no. 1 (2007), accessed August 7, 2017, https://www.springerin.at/en/2007/1/eine-unsichtbare-geschichte -der-arbeit/.

65 Independent freelance work in socialist Yugoslavia was performed by lawyers, priests and religious workers, film workers, professional athletes, geodesists, artists and newspaper deliverers. Sklep o pokojninskih osnovah oseb, ki opravljajo samostojno dejavnost, po katerih se določajo pravice iz socialnega zavarovanja, prevedejo pokojninske in plačujejo prispevki za socialno zavarovanje, *Uradni list SFRJ*, no. 5 (February 5, 1965): 103.

66 In 1955 the SFRY passed a decree on social insurance of artists: Uredba o
     socialnom osiguranju umetnika, *Službeni list FNRJ*, no. 32 (July 13, 1955), 536–9,
     and three separate decrees for translators, music and film workers: Odluka o
     socijalnom osiguranju muzičkih umetnika; Odluka o socijalnom osiguranju
     prevodilaca naučnih i književnih dela; Odluka o socijalnom osiguranju filmskih
     radnika, *Službeni list FNRJ*, no. 32 (July 13, 1955), 541–3.

67 Zakon o porezu na prihode od autorskih prava i o Fondu za unapređivanje
     kulturnih delatnosti, *Službeni list FNRJ*, no. 31 (July 28, 1954); Uredba o
     finansiranju socijalnog osiguranja, *Službeni list FNRJ*, no. 12 (March 23, 1955).

68 Uredba o socialnom osiguranju umetnika, *Službeni list FNRJ*, no. 32 (July 13,
     1955), 536–9; Odluka o socijalnom osiguranju muzičkih umetnika; Odluka o
     socijalnom osiguranju prevodilaca naučnih i književnih dela; Odluka o socijalnom
     osiguranju filmskih radnika, *Službeni list FNRJ*, no. 32 (July 13, 1955), 541–3.

69 Pogoba o izvajanju socialnega zavarovanja umetnikov; Pogodba o izvajanju
     socialnega zavarovanja filmskih umetnikov in filmskih delavcev, *Uradni List
     Socialistične republike Slovenije*, no. 26 (August 4, 1966): 229–34; Zakon o
     sredstvima za financiranje socijalnog osiguranja umjetnika i o organiziranju za
     utvrđivanje u posebni staž vremena koje je osiguranik proveo u svojstvu kulturnog
     radnika, *Narodne novine: službeni list socijalističke republike Hrvatske* 23, no. 30
     (July 17, 1967): 213.

70 For example, in Slovenia, Zakon o prispevku SR Slovenije za socialno zavarovanje
     samostojnih umetnikov, *Uradni list SRS*, no. 6 (February 24, 1967): 110; in
     Croatia, Zakon o sredstvima za financiranje socijalnog osiguranja umjetnika i o
     organiziranju za utvrđivanje u posebni staž vremena koje je osiguranik proveo u
     svojstvu kulturnog radnika, *Narodne novine: službeni list socijalističke republike
     Hrvatske* 23, no. 30 (July 17, 1967).

71 Majstorović, *Cultural Policy in Yugoslavia* (1972), 58.

72 See Majstorović, *Cultural Policy in Yugoslavia* (1972), 59–61.

73 Majstorović, *Cultural Policy in Yugoslavia* (1972), 28.

74 Majstorović, *Cultural Policy in Yugoslavia* (1972), 26.

75 Medosch, *New Tendencies*, 7.

76 Emphasis mine; Medosch, *New Tendencies*, 7.

77 Medosch, *New Tendencies*, 7.

78 Rather than opposing the force of technological innovation, artists involved in
     New Tendencies saw a utopian possibility to use technology as a way to surpass
     alienation and oppression. Defined by Medosch as cybernetic socialism, "this
     movement and network suggested a claim by the artistic left on an optimistic
     technological civilization." Medosch, *New Tendencies*, 5.

79 Zagorka Golubović, "Culture as a Bridge between Utopia and Reality," in *Praxis:
     Yugoslav Essays in the Philosophy and Methodology of the Social Sciences*, eds.
     Mihailo Marković and Gajo Petrović (Dordrecht: D. Reidel Publishing Company,

1979), 178. While employed art workers lived off creative work, the freelance art workers' economic conditions began to deteriorate with the economic instability of Yugoslavia after 1965.

80 Golubović, "Culture as a Bridge between Utopia and Reality," 184.

81 Golubović, "Culture as a Bridge between Utopia and Reality," 184.

82 Golubović, "Culture as a Bridge between Utopia and Reality," 171–2.

83 Golubović, "Culture as a Bridge between Utopia and Reality," 172.

84 The difference is visible in the allocation of public funding for the two types of art production. During the 1980s 0.2 to 5 per cent of the entire budget of the Cultural Community of Slovenia (*Kulturna skupnost Slovenije*) was spent on art produced outside of cultural institutions. Čopič and Tomc, "Nacionalno poročilo," 207–8.

85 Rastko Močnik, "Excess Memory," *Transeuropéennes: Revue internationale de pensée critique*, March 3 (2010): 5.

86 Suvin, *Splendour, Misery, and Possibilities*, 78.

87 Suvin, *Splendour, Misery, and Possibilites*, 295.

88 Branislav Dimitrijević, *Potrošeni socijalizam: kultura, konzumerizam i društvena imaginacija u Jugoslaviji (1950–1974)* [Consumable Socialism: Culture, Consumerism and Social Imagination in Yugoslavia (1950–1974)] (Belgrade: Peščanik, 2016), 9.

89 Mihailo Marković, "Marxist Philosophy in Yugoslavia: The *Praxis* Group," in *Marxism and Religion in Eastern Europe*, eds. R.T. De George and Robert H. Scanlan (Dordrecht: D. Reidel Publishing Company, 1976), 76.

90 Primož Jesenko, "Pathwalker as a Ritual Fragment of Theatre Neo-Avant-Garde in Slovenia (First Fragment on Theatre Pekarna)," *Maska* 24, no. 123–4 (2009): 20–49.

91 Marković, "Marxist Philosophy in Yugoslavia," 76.

92 Lev Kreft, *Zjeban od absolutnega – perspketivovci in perspektivaši: portert skupine* [Fucked Up by the Absolute – Perspektivists and Perspectivians: A Group Portrait] (Ljubljana: Znanstveno in publicistično središče, 1998), 108.

93 Suvin, *Splendour, Misery, and Possibilities*, 79.

94 Suvin, *Splendour, Misery, and Possibilities*, 40.

95 Suvin, *Splendour, Misery, and Possibilities*, 40.

96 Woodward, *Socialist Unemployment*; Catherine Samary, *Plan, Market and Democracy* (Amsterdam: International Institute for Research and Education, 1988); Močnik, "Excess Memory," 1–11; Rastko Močnik, "Nismo krivi ali smo odgovorni; razgovarao Ozren Pupovac" [We Are Not Guilty, But We Are Responsible: A Conversation with Ozren Pupovac]," *Up & Underground*, no. 17–18 (Spring 2010): 140–53.

97 See for example, Ljupče Đokić, Dragutin Fletar, and Zlatko Sudović, eds., *Kultura u udruženom radu* [Culture in the Associated Labour] (Zagreb: Zavod za kulturu Hrvatske, 1981).

4 The Mystification of Artistic Labour under Socialism

1 Woodward, "The Political Economy of Ethno-Nationalism in Yugoslavia," 77–8.

2 For example, the federal Council for Education and Culture commissioned a study "Culture as activity and creativity under the conditions of commodity production," conducted by the Yugoslav Institute for Economic Research in Belgrade in 1968. Reviews of the study point to the problem of commodification of culture. Kultura kao delatnost i stvaralaštvo u uslovima robne proizvodnje; Pero Djetelić, Recenzija materijala "Kultura kao delatnost i stvaralaštvo u uslovima robne proizvodnje;" Miladin Vujošević, Recenzija na studiju "Kultura kao delatnost i stvaralaštvo u uslovima robne proizvodnje;" Branko Horvat, Mišljenje Naučnog kolktiva Instituta o studiji "Kultura kao delatnost i stvaralaštvo u uslovima robne proizvodnje;" 1968, Fond 319, Folder 5, Archive of Yugoslavia, Belgrade.

3 Woodward, *Socialist Unemployment*, 171.

4 See Bockman, *Markets in the Name of Socialism*.

5 Močnik, "Worker's Self-Management," 5.

6 For instance, in addition to the SCC of Slovenia (on the level of Slovenian republic), there were sixty municipal SCCs, one regional (for the Slovenian coast towns), and one city SCC for the capital of Ljubljana.

7 Majstorović, *Cultural Policy in Yugoslavia*, 1980, 29.

8 Majstorović, *Cultural Policy in Yugoslavia*, 1980, 29.

9 However, these types of working communities existed even before the new 1974 constitution; they were especially common in film production.

10 "Zakon o svobodni menjavi dela na področju kulturne dejavnosti (Law on Free Exchange of Labour in the Area of Cultural Activity)," *Uradni list SRS*, no. 1–2 (Jan 13, 1981) in *Predpisi s področja kulture* (Legistlation in the Area of Culture) (Ljubljana: Časopisni zavod Uradni list SR Slovenije, 1985), 13.

11 Močnik, "Excess Memory," 5; Suvin, *Splendour, Misery, and Possibilities*, 190–3.

12 Dunja Blažević, "Art as a Form of Ownership Awareness," in *SKC and Political Practices of Art*, ed. by Prelom Kolektiv (Ljubljana: Galerija ŠKUC, 2008), 7.

13 Raša Todosijević, "Art and Revolution," in *SKC and Political Practices of Art*, 9.

14 Todosijević, "Art and Revolution," 9.

15 Todosijević, "Art and Revolution," 9.

16 Todosijević, "Art and Revolution," 9–10.

17 Todosijević, "Art and Revolution," 9.

18 Majstorović, *Cultural Policy in Yugoslavia*, 1980, 30.

19 See Branislav Jakovljević, "Human Resources: June 1968, 'Hair,' and the Beginning of Yugoslavia's End," *Grey Room* 30, no. 30 (2008): 38–53.

20 Goran Đorđević, "Postoji samo istraživanje" [There Is Only Research], *Novi Svet*, no. 24–5 (1972): 11.

21 Former artists Goran Đorđević, interviewed by author, August 3, 2018 (email correspondence). See also Đorđević, "On the Class Character of Art," *The Fox*, no.

3 (1976): 163 where he cites a passage from Marx's *A Contribution to the Critique of Hegel's Philosophy of Right* in which we find the passage on "religion as opium of people" and "sigh of the oppressed creature."

22 Jan Rehmann, *Theories of Ideology: The Power of Alienation and Subjection* (Leiden: Brill, 2013), 27.

23 Rehmann, *Theories of Ideology*, 27.

24 Former artists Goran Đorđević, interviewed by author, August 3, 2018 (email correspondence).

25 Former artists Goran Đorđević, interviewed by author, August 3, 2018 (email correspondence).

26 Đorđević, "On the Class Character of Art," 163. The 1976 text "On the Class Character of Art" was initially published in Serbo-Croatian as "Umjetnost kao oblik religiozne svesti" [Art as a Form of Religious Consciousness] in a 1975 publication that was part of the exhibition *Oktober* in the gallery of the Belgrade SKC. The English translation was reprinted in *SKC and Political Practices of Art*.

27 Đorđević, "On the Class Character of Art," 164 (original emphasis).

28 Former artists Goran Đorđević, interviewed by author, August 3, 2018 (email correspondence).

29 Former artists Goran Đorđević, interviewed by author, August 3, 2018 (email correspondence).

30 Susovski, *The New Art Practice in Yugoslavia 1966–1978*.

31 Goran Đorđević, "Nova tradicija" [The New Tradition], *Kultura*, no. 45–6 (1979): 250–2.

32 Former artists Goran Đorđević, interviewed by author, August 3, 2018 (email correspondence).

33 Goran Đorđević, "Subjekt i pseudosubjekt umetničke prakse" [The Subject and the Pseudo Subject of Artistic Practice], *Vidici* 23, no. 3 (September 1977): 2.

34 Đorđević, "Subjekt i pseudosubjekt," 2 (added emphasis).

35 Đorđević, "Subjekt i pseudosubjekt," 2.

36 Đorđević, "Subjekt i pseudosubjekt," 2.

37 See Branislav Dimitrijevič, "Neke napomene o radu Gorana Đorđevića," *Prelom*, no. 5 (2003): 150 and ff.

38 See Dimitrijevič, "Neke napomene o radu Gorana Đorđevića," 150.

39 Đorđević, "On the Class Character," 164.

40 Đorđević, "On the Class Character," 164.

41 Đorđević, "The International Strike of Artists," 30–9.

42 Goran Đorđević, "Marginalni položaj (razgovarao Jovan Despotović)" [A Marginal Position (A Conversation with Jovan Despotović)], *Kulturne novine*, no. 630 (1981): 38.

43 Đorđević, "Marginalni položaj," 38.

44 Đorđević, "On the Class Character of Art," 164.

45 Đorđević, "On the Class Character of Art," 164.

46 Golubobvić, "Culture as a Bridge between Utopia and Reality," 179 (original emphasis).

47 Golubović, "Culture as a Bridge between Utopia and Reality," 183 (original emphasis).

48 Stipe Šuvar, "Kulturna politika: vizije i stvarnost (1975)," in *Kultura i politika* (Zagreb: Globus, 1980), 139.

49 Predrag Matvejević, *Prema novom kulturnom stvaralaštvu* [Toward a New Cultural Creativity], (Zagreb: Naprijed, 1975), 98.

50 Šuvar, "Kulturna politika," 140.

51 Golubović, "Culture as a Bridge between Utopia and Reality," 183.

52 Golubović, "Culture as a Bridge between Utopia and Reality," 182–3.

53 Golubović, "Culture as a Bridge between Utopia and Reality," 182.

54 Golubović, "Culture as a Bridge between Utopia and Reality," 183.

55 Golubović, "Culture as a Bridge between Utopia and Reality," 181.

56 Golubović, "Culture as a Bridge between Utopia and Reality," 181.

57 Golubović, "Culture as a Bridge between Utopia and Reality," 184.

58 Golubović, "Culture as a Bridge between Utopia and Reality," 183 (original emphasis).

59 Woodward, "The Political Economy of Ethno-Nationalism in Yugoslavia," 78.

60 Woodward, "The Political Economy of Ethno-Nationalism in Yugoslavia," 76. Moreover, "the leader's goal of a technologically advanced, highly productive, administratively lean, full-employment economy within the context of the country's international position came to be realized in only a small part of Yugoslav territory – above all in Slovenia." Woodward, *Socialist Unemployment*, 263.

61 Woodward, "The Political Economy of Ethno-Nationalism in Yugoslavia," 76.

62 Woodward, "The Political Economy of Ethno-Nationalism in Yugoslavia," 76.

63 Some of the founding members included Boris Demur, Ivan Dorogi, Antun Maračić, Vlado Martek, Goran Petercol, Mladen Stilinović, and Goran Trbuljak.

64 Mladen Stilinović, *Prvi broj* (Zagreb: RZU Podroom, 1980), 4.

65 The entire issue of *Prvi broj* and other documents related to the groups are available in the digital archive Digitizing Ideas: http://digitizing-ideas.org/en /entry/19682, accessed August 15, 2018.

66 Boris Demur, *Prvi broj* (Zagreb: RZU Podroom, 1980), 2.

67 Dalibro Martinis, *Prvi broj* (Zagreb: RZU Podroom, 1980), 2.

68 Iveković and Martinis, "Ugovor," *Prvi broj* (Zagreb: RZU Podroom, 1980), 8–9.

69 Sanja Iveković, *Prvi broj* (Zagreb: RZU Podroom, 1980), 16.

70 Iveković, *Prvi broj*, 16.

71 Martinis, *Prvi broj*, 16.

72 Later, during the 1990s Dalibor Martinis successfully used this contract with the Croatian Ministry of Culture for his participation in the 1997 Venice Biennale. He also credits the curator and selector Berislav Valušek from the modern art gallery in Rijeka who supported the use of the contract. Dalibor Martinis, interviewed by author, August 11, 2018 (email correspondence).

73 Dalibor Martinis, interviewed by author, August 11, 2018 (email correspondence).

74 Iveković and Martinis, "Ugovor," *Prvi broj*, 8–9.

75 Dalibor Martinis, interviewed by author, August 10, 2018 (email correspondence).

76 Iveković and Martinis, "U galerije s ugovorom!" 7.

77 Iveković and Martinis, "U galerije s ugovorom!" 7.

78 Iveković and Martinis, "U galerije s ugovorom!" 7.

79 Iveković and Martinis, "U galerije s ugovorom!" 7.

80 See Zakon o svobodni menjavi dela na področju kulture [The Law on Free Exchange of Labour in the field of Culture], *Uradni list SR Slovnije*, no. 1–2 (1981).

81 Iveković and Martinis, "U galerije s ugovorom!" 7.

82 Iveković and Martinis, "U galerije s ugovorom!" 7.

83 Iveković and Martinis, "U galerije s ugovorom!" 7.

84 Iveković and Martinis, "U galerije s ugovorom!" 7.

85 Iveković and Martinis, "U galerije s ugovorom!" 7.

86 *Prvi broj*, 3.

87 Zakon o samostalnim umjetnicima, *Narodne novine* 35, no. 48 (November 20, 1979): 708.

88 Iveković and Martinis, "Pokazatelj odnosa između prihoda samostalnog likovnog umjetnika i njegovog stvarnog osobnog dohotka kao i osobnog dohotka radnika u kulturi" [An Indicator of the Relationship between the Income of an Independent Visual Artist and Their Actual Personal Income as well as the Personal Income of a Worker in the Field of Culture], *Prvi broj*, 6.

89 Iveković and Martinis, "Pokazatelji odnosa," 6.

90 Sanja Iveković, interviewed by author, July 18, 2018 (email correspondence).

91 Primož Krašovec, "Še enkrat o neoliberalizmu II: politika" *Andragoška spoznanja* 22, no. 1 (2016): 81.

92 Katja Praznik, "Producing a Reserve Army of Cultural Labor, or, the Surpluses of Slovene Cultural Policy 2005–2015," in *Crises and New Beginnings: Art in Slovenia 2005–2015* (Ljubljana: Moderna galerija, 2016), 57–69; Katja Praznik, "Women, Art and Labor, or on the Limits of Representational Politics," in *City of Women Reflecting 2019/2020*, ed. Tea Hvala (Ljubljana: Mesto žensk – društvo za promocijo žensk v kulturi, 2020), 27–34.

5 Art Workers and the Hidden Class Conflict of Late Socialism

1 Samary, *The Fragmentation of Yugoslavia*, 12.

2 For example, in Slovenia, the first urban communes of artists and intellectuals appeared in the first half of the 1970s in Tacen, Brod, Rokavci, Kamberško and elsewhere. See Korda, "Alternative Dawns," 53; Goranka Kreačič, "Pogled na študentsko gibanje v Sloveniji 1968–1972 z današnje perspektive: pogovor z dr. Franetom Adamom" [Views on Student Movement in Slovenia 1968–1972 from Today's Perspective: A Conversation with Dr. Frane Adam], *Zgodovina v šoli,*

Zgodovinska priloga 17, no. 3–4 (2008): 22. The Šempas Family, a commune in Šempas, was founded by the members of the renowned art collective OHO.

3 Krašovec, "Vrnitev neodpisanega: Foucault," in Michel Foucault, *Družbo je treba braniti: predavanja na Collège de France (1975–1976)* (Ljubljana: Studia Humanitatis, 2015), 308.

4 See also Bockmann, *Markets in the Name of Socialism*, where the author develops an argument that neoliberalism was a parasitic structure that existed within socialist economies.

5 Particularly after 1965, a socialist market began to take hold in Yugoslavia and public services began to be perceived as "social spending." Močnik, "Workers' Self-Management," 4.

6 Eric Hobsbawm, *Age of Extremes: The Short Twentieth Century 1914–1991* (London: Abacus, 1995), 473.

7 Hobsbawm, *Age of Extremes*, 473.

8 Dominic Boyer and Alexei Yurchak, "American Stiob Or, What Late-Socialist Aesthetics of Parody Reveal about Contemporary Political Culture in the West," *Cultural Anthropology* 25, no 2. (2010): 179.

9 See for example Bockmann, *Markets in the Name of Socialism*; Videkanić, *Nonaligned Modernism*.

10 Amin Ash, ed., *Post-Fordism: A Reader* (Oxford: Blackwell, 1995); Bologna, "Workerism."

11 Pierre Dardot and Christian Laval, *The New Way of the World: On Neoliberal Society* (New York: Verso, 2013). The authors explain that neoliberalism as *governmental rationality* is not simply a response to the crisis of accumulation, but foremost to the crisis of governmentality (11). Neoliberalism is therefore not simply a "heteroclite doctrine" – what is more characteristic of it is "the deployment of the logic of the market as a generalized normative logic, from the state to innermost subjectivity" of individuals (18).

12 Rastko Močnik, "Delovni razredi v kapitalizmu" [Working Classes in Capitalism], in *Postfordizem: razprave o sodobnem kapitalizmu*, ed. Gal Kirn (Ljubljana: Mirovni inštitut, 2010), 164.

13 Močnik, "Delovni razredi v kapitalizmu," 167. According to Močnik, the consumerist nature of Fordism is precisely where we should search for reasons why the labour movement was politically blocked. Social stability depended on "whether it was possible to maintain the legal regulation of the welfare state (social rights, labour rights connected to employment etc.) in the status of 'social wage.'"

14 Michael Heinrich, *An Introduction to the Three Volumes of Karl Marx's* Capital (New York: Monthly Review Press, 2012), 170.

15 Heinrich, *An Introduction to the Three Volumes*, 170.

16 Woodward, *Socialist Unemployment*, 194, 319.

17 Woodward, *Socialist Unemployment*, 333.

18 The only exception in terms of investment was the building of a new cultural and congress centre in Ljubljana, Slovenia called Cankarjev dom. I discuss it at length in chapter 6.

19 Igor Vidmar, "Sedaj gre zares" [Now It's for Real], *Punk pod Slovenci* [Punk under Slovenians], eds. Tomaž Mastnak, Nela Malečkar (Ljubljana: Republiška konferenca ZSMS and Univerzitetna konferenca ZSMS, 1985), 226.

20 Darko Štrajn, "Kako razumeti študentska gibanja" [How to Understand Student Movements], *Zgodovina v šoli, Zgodovinska priloga* 17, no. 3–4 (2008): 3.

21 Dardot and Laval, *The New Way of the World*, 3. What authors term neoliberal rationality has produced a particular form of social relations, way of life, and subjectivity that "enjoins everyone in the world of generalized competition.… It calls upon wage-earning classes and populations to engage in economic struggle against one another; it aligns social relations with the model of the market; it promotes the justification of ever greater inequalities; it even transforms the individual, now called on to conceive and conduct him- or herself as an enterprise."

22 Tomaž Mastnak, *Vzhodno od raja: civilna družba pod komunizmom in po njem* [East of Eden: Civil Society before Communism and After] (Ljubljana: Državna založba Slovenije, 1992).

23 Tomaž Mastnak, "Civil Society and Fascism," in *NSK from* Kapital *to Capital*, eds. Zdenka Badovinac, Eda Čufer, Anthony Gardner (Ljubljana/Cambridge, MA: Moderna galerija/MIT Press, 2015), 285.

24 Rastko Močnik, "Kaj vse je pomenil izraz 'civilna družba'" [All the Meanings of the Notion "Civil Society"], *Medijska preža*, no. 43 (2012): 13. An expanded version of the text is available under the title "Kaj vse je pomenil izraz 'civilna družba': jugoslovanska alternativa" at: http://www.internationaleonline.org/research /real_democracy/2_kaj_vse_je_pomenil_izraz_civilna_dru_ba_jugoslovanska _alternativa, accessed on May 28, 2018.

25 Mastnak, "Civil Society and Fascism," 285.

26 Močnik, "Kaj vse je pomenil izraz 'civilna družba,'" 13.

27 Močnik, "Kaj vse je pomenil izraz 'civilna družba,'" 13.

28 Tomaž Mastnak, "Za anarholiberalizem" [For Anarcho-Liberalism], *Problemi* 22, no. 239–41 (1984): 206.

29 Štrajn, "Kako razumeti študentska gibanja," 2.

30 Mastnak, "Civil Society and Fascism," 285–6. In his sobering words: "Anarchism played no role, whereas liberalism we absorbed spontaneously, like sponges, without any thought whatsoever, from the broader world marked by the ideological defeat of communism even before the walls of the system came tumbling down."

31 Rastko Močnik, "Political Practices at the End of Capitalism," in *Postfordism and Its Discontents*, ed. Gal Kirn (Maastricht/Ljubljana: Jan van Eyck Academie/Mirovni inštitut, 2010), 227.

32 Woodward, *Socialist Unemployment*, 312–27.

33 Woodward, *Socialist Unemployment*, 312.

34 Woodward, *Socialist Unemployment*, 312.

35 Woodward, *Socialist Unemployment*, 313.

36 Woodward, *Socialist Unemployment*, 313.

37 Woodward, *Socialist Unemployment*, 314.

38 Woodward, *Socialist Unemployment*, 317.

39 Čopič and Tomc, "Nacionalno poročilo," 130.

40 Čopič and Tomc, "Nacionalno poročilo," 234–5.

41 Mastnak, "Civil Society and Fascism," 287.

42 Stipe Ćurković, "Civilnom scenom do restavracije kapitalizma," *Portal Novosti*, no. 613 (September 17, 2011), http://arhiva.portalnovosti.com/2011/09/civilnom -scenom-do-restauracije-kapitalizma/. I am grateful to Primož Krašovec for bringing Ćurković's text to my attention.

43 Woodward, *Socialist Unemployment*, 313.

44 Woodward, *Socialist Unemployment*, 313.

45 In Slovenia, the case point was the circle of intellectuals around a journal called *Nova revija* that in 1987 published a special issue entitled "Contributions towards the Slovene National Program." "Prispevki za slovenski nacionalni program," *Nova revija* 6, no. 57 (1987).

46 Močnik, "Nismo krivi," 141.

47 Nikolai Jeffs, "FV and the 'Third Scene,' 1980–1990," in *FV: The Alternative Scene of the Eighties*, ed. Breda Škrjanec (Ljubljana: Mednarodni grafični likovni center, 2008), 349.

48 Močnik, "Delovni razredi v kapitalizmu," 184.

49 Franco Berardi (Bifo), "What Does Cognitariat Mean? Work, Desire and Depression," in *Cultural Studies Review* 11, no. 2 (2005): 59.

50 "Zakon o samostalnim umjetnicima (Law for Independent Artists)," *Narodne novine – službeni list SR Hrvatske* 35, no. 48 (November 20, 1979): 709; "Zakon o samostojnih kulturnih delavcih (Law for Independent Cultural Workers)," *Uradni list Socialistične republike Slovenije*, no. 9 (March 19, 1982): 505–7; "Zakon za samostojnite umetnici" (Law for Independent Artists), *Služben vesnik na socialistička republika Makedonija* (*Official Gazette of Socialist Republic Macedonia*) 38, no. 46 (1982): 828–30.

51 "Zakon o samostalnim umjetnicima"; "Zakon o samostojnih kulturnih delavcih"; "Zakon za samostojnite umetnici."

52 Bele, *Samostojna poklicna kulturna dejavnost*, 10–11.

53 Bologna, "Nove oblike dela," 136.

54 "Zakon o samstojnih kulturnih delavcih," 505; "Zakon o samostalnim umjetnicima," 708; "Zakon za samostojnite umetnici," 828.

55 Bele, *Samostojna poklicna kulturna dejavnost*, 18.

56 Bologna, "Nove oblike dela," 138.

57 Bologna, "Nove oblike dela," 138.

58 Primož Krašovec, "Še enkrat o neoliberalizmu III: psihoafektivni učinki neoliberalizma in neoliberalna subjektivnost," *Andragoška spoznanja* 22, no. 2 (2016): 71.

59 "Zakon o samostalnim umjetnicima," 709.

60 Dardot and Laval, *The New Way of the World*, 7.

61 Dardot and Laval, *The New Way of the World*, 7 (original emphasis).

62 Korda, "Alternative Dawns," 312.

63 Jeffs, "FV and the 'Third Scene,'" 351.

64 Barbara Borčić, "The ŠKUC Gallery, Alternative Culture, and Neue Slowenische Kunst in the 1980s," in Badovinac, Čufer, and Gardner, *NSK from* Kapital, 299.

65 That is, at the time when the conflict with the Yugoslav People's Army escalated after the magazine *Mladina* reported on illegal arms trade and the establishment of the committee on human rights.

66 David Harvey, *The New Imperialism* (Oxford: Oxford University Press, 2003).

67 Mastnak, "Civil Society and Fascism," 286.

6 The Contradictions of 1980s Alternative Art

1 Golubović, "Culture as a Bridge," 183.

2 Đorđević, "Nova Tradicija," 250–2.

3 Golubović, "Culture as a Bridge," 183.

4 The name FV 112/15 is a code: it's a reference to the dictionary of foreign terms by Franc Verbinc (FV), page 112, entry 15 (112/15), which reads "C'est la guerre," meaning "This is war." The group's members were Zemira Alajbegović, Goran Devide, Aldo Ivančić, Neven Korda, Dario Seraval, Dragan Čolaković - Šilja, Sergej Hrvatin, Nerina Kocjančič, Anita Lopojda, Mirela Miklavčič, and Bojana Vajt. Škrjanec, ed., *FV: Alternativa osemdesetih / The Alternative Scene of the Eighties*, 233–40)

5 Korda, "Alternative Dawns," 323.

6 Korda, "Alternative Dawns," 321.

7 Korda, "Alternative Dawns," 327.

8 Zemira Alajbegović, "Alternativni spektakli: FV 112/15," *Problemi* 20, no. 226 (12) (1982): 45.

9 Alajbegović, "Alternativni spektakli: FV 112/15," 48.

10 A detailed history of FV's activities can be found in the catalog published on the occasion of a comprehensive exhibition about the FV collective organized in the Centre for Graphic Arts in Ljubljana in 2008. See Škrjanec, ed., *FV: Alternativa osemdesetih / The Alternative Scene of the Eighties*.

11 Jeffs, "FV and the 'Third Scene,'" 394.

12 Saša Šavel, "Videodokumenti skupine Borghesia," in *Do roba in naprej: slovenska umetnost 1975–1985*, eds. Igor Španjol and Igor Zabel (Ljubljana: Moderna galerija, 2003), 223.

13 Korda, "Alternative Dawns," 326.

14 Korda, "Alternative Dawns," 331 (ft. 128).

15 Jeffs, "FV and the 'Third Scene,'" 365.

16 Korda, "Alternative Dawns," 327.

17 Korda, "Alternative Dawns," 330 (ft. 127).

18 Korda, "Alternative Dawns," 328.

19 Bratko Bibič, *Hrup z Metelkove* [The Noise from Metelkova] (Ljubljana: Mirovni inštitut, 2003), 15–16.

20 Jeffs, "FV and the 'Third Scene,'" 354.

21 Korda, "Alternative Dawns," 334, see also 331–5.

22 Alajbegović, "Alternativni spektakli: FV 112/15," 44.

23 For example, Marina Gržinić, "Neue Slowenische Kunst (NSK): The Art Groups Laibach, IRWIN, and Noordung Cosmocinetic Theatre Cabinet – New Strategies in the Nineties," *Slovene Studies* 15, no. 1–2 (1993): 5–16.

24 Badovinac, Čufer, and Gardner, "Introduction," in *NSK from* Kapital, 14.

25 Močnik, "Workers' Self-Management in Yugoslavia."

26 The group's name is coded and not coincidental. It was inspired by a reference to the Roman consul Publius Cornelius Scipio Nasica Corculum in Antonin Artaud's essay, "The Theatre and the Plague." Antonin Artaud, *Theatre and Its Double* (New York: Groove Press, 1983), 15–32. Scipio Nasica supposedly ordered all Roman theatres to be destroyed in order to preserve public morality. SNST members co-founded the broader collective Neue Slowenische Kunst (NSK) in 1984.

27 SNST, "The Founding Act," in Badovinac, Čufer, and Gardner, *NSK from* Kapital, 474.

28 Badovinac, Čufer, and Gardner, "Introduction," in *NSK from* Kapital, 16.

29 Badovinac, Čufer, and Gardner, "Introduction," in *NSK from* Kapital, 16.

30 Jelka Šutej and Goran Schmidt, "Vzpon in padec gledališke dejavnosti" [The Rise and Fall of Theatre Activities], *Delo*, January 17, 1986.

31 Prešeren Day, which has now become a national holiday in Slovenia, marks the death of France Prešeren, the greatest Slovenian poet, on February 8. Celebrations became a tradition during World War II in 1941, when Prešeren Day was a holiday of Slavic unity and was celebrated on the preceding day, February 7. The Slovenian cultural holiday has been celebrated on February 8 since 1945. Prešeren's significance in nation-building is telling since a stanza from his poem is the national anthem of Slovenia.

32 Eda Čufer, "Athletics of the Eye: *Baptism* and the Problem of Writing and Reading Contemporary Performance," *Maska* 17, no. 74–5 (2002): 81.

33 See Jaša Zlobec, "Sterilni Krst v votlem hramu [A Sterile Baptism in a Hollow Chamber]," *Mladina* 21, no. 6 (February 14, 1986): 37; Igor Likar, "Gledališče ikon in emblemov [The Theatre of Icons and Emblems]," *Maske* 2, no. 2 (1986): 85–9.

34 Alenka Zupančič, "Umetnikov mladostni portret," transcript of the radio show "Bricolages Krstu," aired on Radio Študent Ljubljana, March 2, 1986, 6–7.

35 SNST, "First Sisters Letter," in *Impossible Histories*, eds. Djurić and Šuvaković, 575.

36 Badovinac, Čufer, and Gardner, "Introduction," in *NSK from* Kapital, 15.

37 The name of the institution in English would be Cankar's House (or even Cankar's Home); named after the greatest Slovenian writer Ivan Cankar (1876–1918).

38 Cited in Aleš Erjavec and Marina Gržinić, *Ljubljana, Ljubljana: osemdeseta leta v umetnosti in kulturi* [Ljubljana, Ljubljana: The Eighties in the Arts and Culture] (Ljubljana: Mladinska knjiga, 1991), 26.

39 Erjavec and Gržinić, *Ljubljana, Ljubljana*, 27.

40 Goran Schmidt is a Slovenian theatre studies scholar, dramaturge, editor, and literary historian. Between 1977 and 1981, he was the dramaturge and artistic director of the Viba Film production company, established by the Association of Slovenian Film Workers in 1956. Before coming to CD, from 1981 to 1984 Schmidt was also artistic director of the Slovenian People's Theatre Celje (SLG Celje). Since 1988 he has worked as a researcher and editor for Slovenian National Radio (Radio Slovenia).

41 Erjavec and Gržinić, *Ljubljana, Ljubljana*, 27.

42 Čufer, "The Athletics of the Eye," 82.

43 The director of the project, producer and film organizer Igor Pobegajlo, produced the performance by adopting the "methodology of film production." Čufer, "Athletics of the Eye."

44 CD should have managed the show's guest appearances elsewhere, but despite invitations from abroad, *Baptism under Triglav* never made it past Belgrade, where it was featured as part of the central program at the BITEF in 1986. The performance was also invited abroad, for instance to the London International Festival of Theatre (LIFT) (see B.S., "Izjemna priložnost za 'Krst' v Londonu," *Delo* [December 30, 1986], 4.), but CD did not support any future tours abroad. For instance, in order to raise the necessary funds for a guest appearance in London, CD organized a tender (!) that was published under the culture section of the newspaper *Dnevnik. Dnevnik* (30 December 1986), 12.

45 Another event that was made possible by CD from 1983 to 1989 was the video biennale *Video CD*. Erjavec and Gržinić, *Ljubljana, Ljubljana*, 28.

46 Šutej and Schmidt, "Vzpon in padec gledališke dejavnosti," n.p.

47 "Zakon o samostojnih kulturnih deleavcih," Article 1, 505.

48 Čopič and Tomc, "Nacionalno poročilo," 79.

49 Bele, *Samostojna poklicna kulturna dejavnost*, 20.

50 Bele, *Samostojna poklicna kulturna dejavnost*, 27.

51 Dardot and Laval, *The New Way of the World*, 7.

52 "Independent cultural workers must cover the costs of social insurance by themselves ever since the adoption of the Law for Independent Cultural Workers (Article 21) – some have been entitled to a refund from the Cultural Community of Slovenia." Bele, *Samostojna poklicna kulturna dejavnost*, 31.

53 Michel Foucault, *The Birth of Biopolitics: Lectures at Collège de France 1978–79* (Basingstoke: Palgrave Macmillan, 2008), 215–37. Foucault goes on to explain

that in this way, the *homo oeconomicus*, regarded in classical economic theory as a partner in an exchange based on a problematic of needs, is transformed into "an entrepreneur, an entrepreneur of himself. This is true to the extent that, in practice, the stake in all neoliberal analyses is the replacement every time of *homo oeconomicus* as [a] partner of exchange with a *homo oeconomicus* as entrepreneur of himself, being for himself his own capital, being for himself his own producer, being for himself the source of [his] earnings" (225–6).

54	Bologna, "Nove oblike dela," 138–9.

55	Bologna, "Nove oblike dela," 139.

56	Bologna, "Nove oblike dela," 139.

57	Dardot and Laval, *The New Way of the World*, 266.

58	Dardot and Laval, *The New Way of the World*, 266.

59	Bele, *Samostojna poklicna kulturna dejavnost*, 87.

60	Dardot and Laval, *The New Way of the World*, 180.

61	Dardot and Laval, *The New Way of the World*, 180.

62	Dardot and Laval, *The New Way of the World*, 150–5.

63	Krašovec, "Še o neoliberalizmu II," 76.

64	Dardot and Laval, *The New Way of the World*, 261.

65	Dardot and Laval, *The New Way of the World*, 262.

66	Bele, *Samostojna poklicna kulturna dejavnost*, 1.

67	Independent cultural workers were obliged to pay a 6 per cent tax on royalties after 1983, which was 70 per cent less than other cultural workers. Bele, *Samostojna poklicna kulturna dejavnost*, 32.

68	In 1984, there were 749 independent cultural workers, of which 485 were entitled to subsidized social contributions. Čopič and Tomc, "Nacionalno poročilo," 79.

69	Bele, *Samostojna poklicna kulturna dejavnost*, 26–7.

70	Močnik, "Political Practices at the End of Capitalism," 227.

71	Woodward, *Socialist Unemployment*, 192; Boris Buden, "Gastarbajteri, glasnici bodućnosti" in *Zarez* 14, no. 338–9 (2012), 36.

72	Korda, "Alternative Dawns," 321.

73	Boris Buden, *Cona prehoda: o koncu postkomunizma* [The Transit Zone: On the End of Communism] (Ljubljana: Založba Krtina, 2014), 31.

74	Buden, *Cona prehoda*, 32.

75	Viktor Misiano, "On Critique Declared but Not Realized or, Realized but Not Declared (or, On the Love of Power)," in *Atlas of Transformation*, 2011, accessed May 28, 2019, http://monumenttotransformation.org/atlas-of-transformation /html/i/impossibility-of-criticism/on-critique-declared-but-not-realized-or -realized-but-not-declared-or-on-the-love-of-power-viktor-misiano.html.

76	Buden, *Cona prehoda*, 34.

77	Luciano Canfora, *Democracy in Europe: A History of an Ideology* (Oxford: Blackwell Publishing, 2006).

78	Močnik, "Kaj vse je pomenil izraz 'civilna družba,'" 13.

79 Rastko Močnik, *3 teorije: ideologija, nacija, institucija* [3 Theories: Ideology, Nation, Institution] (Ljubljana: Založba /*cf., 1999).

80 Buden, *Cona prehoda*, 34.

81 In "On the Jewish Question," Marx claimed that the state is based on idealism, because it moves political decision-making into a special sphere that is based on the abstract individual separated from his economic (or class) situation. The abstract equal citizen thereby becomes the central foundation of the state, which provides and recognizes his so-called human rights and ultimately allows him the freedom to pursue his individual interests and the freedom of private property. "Nevertheless, the political annulment of private property not only fails to abolish private property but even presupposes it. The state abolishes, in its own way, distinctions of birth, social rank, education, occupation, when it declares that birth, social rank, education, occupation, are non-political distinctions, when it proclaims, without regard to these distinctions, that every member of the nation is an equal participant in national sovereignty, when it treats all elements of the real life of the nation from the standpoint of the state. Nevertheless, the state allows private property, education, occupation, to act in their way – i.e., as private property, as education, as occupation, and to exert the influence of their special nature. Far from abolishing these real distinctions, the state only exists on the presupposition of their existence; it feels itself to be a political state and asserts its universality only in opposition to these elements of its being." Karl Marx, "On the Jewish Question," (*Deutsch-Französische Jahrbücher*, February 1844), accessed May 1, 2019, https://www.marxists.org/archive/marx/works/1844/jewish-question/.

82 Goran Lukić and Rastko Močnik, eds., *Sindikalno gibanje odpira nove poglede* (Ljubljana: Zveza svobodnih sindikatov Slovenije, 2008).

83 Čopič and Tomc, "Nacionalno poročilo," 61.

84 Čopič and Tomc, "Nacionalno poročilo," 78.

85 Similar is the situation with the "Law for Independent Artists" in Croatia, which was renamed and changed in 1996 to the "Law on Artists' Rights and the Support of Cultural and Artistic Creation" (*Narodne novine*, no. 43/96 [1996]) along with a special decree that then further regulated the conditions and access to social security provision, i.e., "Regulations about the procedures and conditions for the recognition of the rights of artists to have their retirement, disability and medical insurance paid out of the national budget of the Republic of Croatia."

86 Hobsbawm, *Age of Extremes*, 271.

87 Dardot and Laval, *The New Way of the World*, 150.

88 Dardot and Laval, *The New Way of the World*, 165.

89 Dardot and Laval, *The New Way of the World*, 166.

90 Močnik, "Nismo krivi," 140.

91 Močnik, "Nismo krivi," 140.

92 Aleš Erjavec, "Introduction," in *Postmodernism and the Postsocialist Condition: Politicized Art under Late Socialism*, ed. Aleš Erjavec (Durham: Duke University Press, 2003), 7.

93 Woodward, *Socialist Unemployment*, 171.

94 Dejan Kršić, "Krst pod Triglavom" [Baptism under Triglav], *Maska* 1, no. 1 (1991): 24–5.

95 Boris Buden, "The Post-Yugoslavian Condition of Institutional Critique: An Introduction," *Transversal* 02/08 (2007), accessed on May 30, 2019, https://transversal.at/transversal/0208/buden/en.

96 Ana Podvršič, "From a Success Story to the EU Periphery: Spatialization Strategies of Capitalist Accumulation in Slovenia's Post-Yugoslav Development," *Wirtschaft und Management* 22 (2015): 79–94.

97 Dardot and Laval, *The New Way of the World*, 11.

98 Igor Štiks and Srečko Horvat, "Introduction," in Štiks and Horvat, *Welcome to the Desert of Post-Socialism*, 3.

99 Dardot and Laval, *The New Way of the World*, 216.

100 Dragan Klaić, "Komentar" [Commentary], in Maja Breznik, *Posebni skepticizem v umetnosti* (Ljubljana: Založba Sophia, 2011), 96.

101 See for example, Teodor Celakoski et al., eds., *Open Institutions: Institutional Imagination and Cultural Public Sphere* (Zagreb: Aliance Operation City, 2011).

102 Buden, "The Post-Yugoslavian Condition of Institutional Critique."

Conclusion

1 Alberto Alesina and Edward L. Glaeser, *Fighting Poverty and Inequality in the US and Europe: A World of Difference* (Oxford: Oxford University Press, 2004).

2 Dardot and Laval, *The New Way of the World*, 216–54.

3 Dardot and Laval, *The New Way of the World*, 266.

4 See for example Milica Pekić and Katarina Pavić, eds., *Exit Europe: New Geographies of Culture* (Zagreb: Clubture Network, 2011).

5 The term "precariat" has been largely popularized by Guy Standing's *The Precariat: The New Dangerous Class* (London: Bloomsbury, 2011). The book is based on Standing's academic research on the effects of neoliberalism on labour relations. The term is an allusion to the word "proletariat"; Standing uses it as a concept defining, per negationem, a new social class comprising a very wide variety of workers (student work, temporary work, contract work, internships, migrant labour, domestic work, prison labour etc.), united by shared uncertainties (of employment, of work, of income, of social security etc.). The concept of the precariat as a social class immediately raised numerous valid objections, stressing that the definition of the precariat as suggested by Standing depends, first, on the definition of the proletariat, and, second, on the interpretation of Marx's concept of class. Hence, rather than speaking of a social class (the precariat), it makes better sense to speak of a condition of precarity, of a precarization of labour relations, which have, however, existed since the first emergence of the capitalist mode of production.

6 Močnik, "Political Practices at the End of Capitalism," 242.

7 See for example, Dorian Jano, "From 'Balkanization' to 'Europeanization': The Stages of Western Balkans Complex Transformations," *L'Europe en Formation* 349–50, no. 3 (2008): 55–69. For the proliferation of the term "Balkanization" see, for example, David Keating, "Will China Balkanize Europe?" *Berlin Policy Journal* (April 15, 2019), accessed June 4, 2019, https://berlinpolicyjournal.com/will-china -balkanize-europe/; Robert H. Hamilton, "Rethoric, Violence, and Civil War: The Balkanization of America?" *Geopoliticus* (November 9, 2018), accessed June 4, 2019, https://www.fpri.org/article/2018/11/rhetoric-violence-and-civil-war-the -balkanization-of-america/.

8 Silvia Federici, "The Reproduction of Labor Power in the Global Economy and the Unfinished Feminist Revolution," in *Revolution at Point Zero*, 100.

9 Irena Pivka et al., *Ocena stroškov dela za samozaposlene v kulturi* [An Estimation of the Labour Costs for Self-Employed Persons in Culture] (Ljubljana: Asociacija, 2010).

10 Vidmar Horvat et al., *Socialni položaj samozaposlenih v kulturi in predlogi za njegovo izboljšanje s poudarkom na temi preživetvene strategije na področju vizualnih umetnosti* [The Social Conditions of Self-employed Persons in Culture and Recommendations for Improvements with an Emphasis on the Topic of Survival Strategies in the Field of Visual Arts] (Ljubljana: Filozofska fakulteta, 2012), 113, 143–4.

11 Srečko Kosovel, *Cons 5* (modified translation), in *Look Back, Look Ahead: The Selected Poems of Srečko Kosovel*, trans. Ana Jelnikar and Barbara Siegel Carlson (Brooklyn, NY: Ugly Duckling Presse, 2010).

12 Peljhan's reference to the poem was a logical decision since *Egorythm III* was in fact a panel discussion between three transition-era businessmen (a banker, a director of marketing at a PR agency, and a CEO of a foreign car company) and three artists (theatre directors), including Peljhan. As the overture into the discussion, Peljhan, who served as the moderator, shattered a big piece of glass with the words "Power Religion" written on it. The capital letters alluded to a well-know abbreviation designating public relations, an emerging business that swelled along with the proliferation of marketing experts during 1990s Slovenia. Public relations was also the subject of the panel discussion in which the artists confronted the potential patrons of contemporary art.

Bibliography

Primary Sources

Archives

Archive of Yugoslavia, Belgrade:
Fond 317 "Savet za nauku i kulturu Vlade FNRJ" 1945–53.
Fond 318 "Savezni sekretarijat za obrazovanje i kulturo" 1954–67.
Fond 319 "Savezni savet za obrazovanje i kulturu" 1967–71.

Laws and Decrees

In SFRY, all legislation was published in the Official Gazette (*Uradni list/Službeni list*) in three official languages, Serbo-Croatian, Slovenian, and Macedonian, respectively; however republic-specific laws were published in the official language of that republic only.

1946

Splošna navodila o višini honorarjev za književna, umetniška in znanstvena dela/Opća uputstva o visini autorskih honorara za književno-umjetnička djela i naučne radove, *Uradni list/Službeni list FLRJ*, no. 106 (December 31, 1946): 1448–9.

Splošna navodila o povračilih imetnikom avtorskih pravic za izvajanja in predvajanje književnih in umetniških del/Opća uputstva o naknadama nosiocima autorskih prava za izvođenje i prikazivanje književnih i umjetničkih djela, *Uradni list/Službeni list FNRJ*, no. 106 (December 31, 1946): 1449–50.

1950

Splošno navodilo o višini honorarjev za objavo književnih, umetniških, in znanstvenih del/Opšte uputstvo o visini autorskih honorara za objavljivanje književnih, umetničkih i naučnih dela i radova, *Uradni list FLRJ/Službeni list FNRJ*, no 38. (May 31, 1950): 704–7.

1951

Navodilo o kupovanju del upodabljajoče umetnosti in umetne obrti/Uputstvo o kupovini radova likovne i primenjene umetnosti, *Uradni list FNRJ/Službeni list FNRJ*, no. 6 (January 31, 1951): 106–7.

Navodilo o kupovanju del upodabljajoče umetnosti in umetne obrti/Uputstvo o kupovini radova likovne i primenjene umetnosti, *Uradni list FNRJ/Službeni list FNRJ*, no. 39 (August 29, 1951): 485–6.

1952

Splošno navodilo o avtorskih honorarjih za objavo književnih del/Opšte uputstvo o autroskim honorarima za objavljivanje književnih dela, *Uradni list FLRJ/Službeni list FNRJ*, no. 22 (April 19, 1952): 446–8.

Splošno navodilo o avtorskih honorarjih za uprizoritev in izvajanje književnih in umetniških del/Opšte uputstvo o autroskim honorarima za prikazivanje i izvođenje književnih i umetničkih dela, *Uradni list FLRJ/Službeni list FNRJ*, no. 23 (April 23, 1952): 462–3.

Splošno navodilo o avtorskih honorarjih za objavo glasbenih del/ Opšte uputstvo o autroskim honorarima za objavljjivanje muzičkih dela, *Uradni list FLRJ/Službeni list FNRJ*, no. 23 (April 23, 1952): 463–4.

Odločba o socialnem zavarovanju oseb, ki sodelujejo pri snemanju in izdelavi filmov (filmskih del)/Rešenje o socijalnom osiguranju lica zaposlenih na poslovima snjimanja i izrade filmova (filmskih dela), *Uradni list FLRJ/Službeni list FNRJ*, no. 60 (December 17, 1952): 95–156.

1953

Splošno navodilo o honorarjih izvajalcev glasbenih in književnih del za reproduciranje njihovih posnetih izvedb/Opšte uputstvo o honorarima izvođača muzičkih I književnih dela za reproduktovanje njihovih snimljenih izvođenja, *Uradni list FLRJ/Službeni list FNRJ*, 19 (May 6, 1953): 186–7.

1954

Zakon o davku od dohodkov od avtorskih pravic in o skladu za pospševanje kulturnih dejavnosti/Zakon o porezu na prihode od autorskih prava i o Fondu za unapređivanje kulturnih delatnosti, *Uradni list FLRJ/Službeni list FNRJ*, no. 31 (July 28, 1954): 538–40.

1955

Uredba o finansiranju socialnega zavarovanja/Uredba o finansiranju socijalnog osiguranja, *Uradni list FLRJ/Službeni list FNRJ*, no. 12 (March 23, 1955): 149–61.

Odlok o socialnem zavarovanju filmskih delavcev/Odluka o socijalnom osiguranju filmskih radnika, *Uradni list FLRJ/Službeni list FNRJ*, no. 32 (July 13, 1955): 542–3.

Odlok o socialnem zavarovanju glasbenih umetnikov/Odluka o socijalnom osiguranju muzičkih umetnika, *Uradni list FLRJ/Službeni list FNRJ*, no. 32 (July 13, 1955): 543.

Odlok o socialnem zavarovanju prevajalcev znanstvenih in književnih del/Odluka o socijalnom osiguranju prevodilaca naučnih i književnih dela, *Uradni list FLRJ/Službeni list FNRJ*, no. 32 (July 13, 1955): 543–4.

Uredba o socialnem zavarovanju umetnikov/Uredba o socijalnom osiguranju umetnika, *Uradni list FLRJ/Službeni list FNRJ*, no. 32 (July 13, 1955): 536–9.

1965

Sklep o pokojninskih osnovah oseb, ki opravljajo samostojno dejavnost, po katerih se določajo pravice iz socialnega zavarovanja, prevedejo pokojninske in plačujejo prispevki za socialno zavarovanje, *Uradni list SFRJ*, no. 5 (February 5, 1965): 103.

1966

Pogoba o izvajanju socialnega zavarovanja umetnikov, *Uradni List Socialistične republike Slovenije*, no. 26 (August 4, 1966): 229–31.

Pogodba o izvajanju socialnega zavarovanja filmskih umetnikov in filmskih delavcev, *Uradni List Socialistične republike Slovenije*, no. 26 (August 4, 1966): 231–4.

1967

Zakon o sredstvima za financiranje socijalnog osiguranja umjetnika i o organiziranju za utvrđivanje u posebni staž vremena koje je osiguranik proveo u svojstvu kulturnog radnika, *Narodne novine: službeni list socijalističke republike Hrvatske* 23, no. 30 (July 17, 1967).

Zakon o prispevku SR Slovenije za socialno zavarovanje samostojnih umetnikov, *Uradni list Socialistične republike Slovenije*, no. 6 (February 24, 1967): 110

1979

Zakon o samostalnim umjetnicima, *Narodne novine: službeni list socijastičke republike Hrvatske* 35, no. 48 (November 20, 1979): 705–11.

1982

Zakon o samostojnih kulturnih delavcih, *Uradni list Socialistične republike Slovenije*, no. 9 (March 19, 1982): 505–7.

Zakon za samostojnite umetnici, *Služben vesnik na socialistička republika Makedonija*, no. 46 (December 17, 1982): 828–30.

1994

Zakon o uresničevanju javnega interesa na področju kulture (ZUJIPK), *Uradni list Republike Slovenije*, no. 75 (November 30, 1994).

1996

Zakon o pravima samostalnih umjetnika i poticanju kulturnog i umjetničkog stvaralaštva, *Narodne novine Republike Hrvatske*, no. 43 (May 17, 1996).

2002

Zakon o uresničevanju javnega interesa za kulturo (ZUJIK), *Uradni list Republike Slovenije*, no. 96 (November 14, 2002).

Other Publications

Prvi broj. Zagreb: RZU Podroom, 1980. Accessed June 15, 2016. http://digitizing-ideas.org/en/entry/19682.

Interviews

Former artist Goran Đorđević, August 1–3, 2018 (email correspondence)
Sanja Iveković, July 18, 2018 (email correspondence)
Dalibor Martinis, August 10–11, 2018 (email correspondence)

Secondary Sources

Adorno, Theodor. *In Search of Wagner.* London: NLB, 1981.
– *Aesthetic Theory.* Minneapolis: University of Minnesota Press, 1997.
Alajbegović, Zemira. "Alternativni spektakli: FV 112/15," *Problemi* 20, no. 226 (12) (1982): 42–8.
Alesina, Alberto and Edward L. Glaeser. *Fighting Poverty and Inequality in the US and Europe: A World of Difference.* Oxford: Oxford University Press, 2004.
Althusser, Louis. *Lenin and Philosophy, and Other Essays.* New York: Monthly Press, 1972.
– *For Marx.* London: Verso, 2005.
Apostol, Corina L. "Art Workers between Precarity and Resistance: A Genealogy." *ArtLeaks Gazette*, no. 3 (2015): 7–21.
Arns, Inke. *Avantgarda v vzvratnem ogledalu: sprememba paradigem recepcije avantgarde v (nekdanji) Jugoslaviji in Rusiji od 80. let do danes* [The Avant-Garde in the Rearview Mirror: The Changes of the Paradigms in the Reception of the Avant-Garde in (former) Yugoslavia and Russia from the 1980s to the Present]. Ljubljana: Maska, 2006.
Artaud, Antonin. *Theatre and Its Double.* New York: Groove Press, 1983.
Arvatov, Boris. *Art and Production.* London: Pluto Press, 2017.
Ash, Amin, ed. *Post-Fordism: A Reader.* Oxford: Blackwell, 1995.
Badovinac, Zdenka, Eda Čufer, and Anthony Gardner. "Introduction: Neue Slowenische Kunst from *Kapital* to Capital." In *NSK from* Kapital *to Capital*, edited

by Zdenka Badovinac, Eda Čufer, and Anthony Gardner. Ljubljana/Cambridge, MA: Moderna galerija/MIT Press, 2015.

Beech, Dave. *Art and Value.* Leiden: Brill, 2015.

Bele, Marjana. *Samostojna poklicna kulturna dejavnost* [Independent Professional Cultural Activity]. Ljubljana: Fakulteta za sociologijo, politične vede in novinarstvo [Faculty for sociology, political science, and journalism], 1987.

Benston, Margaret. "The Political Economy of Women's Liberation." *Monthly Review* 21, no. 4 (1969): 13–27.

Berardi (Bifo), Franco. "What Does Cognitariat Mean? Work, Desire and Depression." *Cultural Studies Review* 11, no. 2 (2005): 57–63.

Berger, John. *Art and Revolution: Ernst Neizvestny and the Role of the Artist in the U.S.S.R.* London: Writers and Readers Publishing Cooperative, 1969.

– *Ways of Seeing.* London: British Broadcasting Corp, 1977.

BfAMfAPhD. *Artists Report Back: A National Study on the Lives of Arts Graduates and Working Artists.* BfAMfAPhD, 2014. http://bfamfaphd.com/#topic-reports.

Bibič, Bratko. *Hrup z Metelkove* [The Noise from Metelkova]. Ljubljana: Mirovni inštitut, 2003.

Blažević, Dunja. "Art as a Form of Ownership Awareness." In *SKC and Political Practices of Art*, edited by Prelom Kolektiv. Ljubljana: Galerija ŠKUC, 2008.

Bockman, Johanna. *Markets in the Name of Socialism: The Left-Wing Origins of Neoliberalism.* Berkley: Stanford University Press, 2011.

Bologna, Sergio. "Nove oblike dela" [New Forms of Labour]. In *Postfordizem: razprave o sodobnem kapitalizmu*, edited by Gal Kirn. Ljubljana: Mirovni inštitut, 2010.

– "Workerism Beyond Fordism: On the Lineage of Italian Workerism." *Viewpoint Magazine*, December 15, 2014. Accessed July 25, 2016. https://viewpointmag .com/2014/12/15/workerism-beyond-fordism-on-the-lineage-of-italian-workerism /#rf2-3822.

Boltanski, Luc and Eve Chiapelo. *New Spirit of Capitalism.* London: Verso 2005.

Borčić, Barbara. "The ŠKUC Gallery, Alternative Culture, and Neue Slowenische Kunst in the 1980s." In *NSK from* Kapital *to Capital*, edited by Zdenka Badovinac, Eda Čufer, and Anthony Gardner. Ljubljana/Cambridge, MA: Moderna galerija/MIT Press, 2015.

Bourdieu, Pierre. *The Rules of Art: Genesis and Structure of the Literary Field.* Stanford: Stanford University Press, 1992.

Boyer, Dominic and Alexei Yurchak. "American Stiob Or, What Late-Socialist Aesthetics of Parody Reveal about Contemporary Political Culture in the West." *Cultural Anthropology* 25, no 2. (2010): 179.

Brown, Nicholas. *Autonomy: The Social Ontology of Art under Capitalism.* Durham: Duke University Press, 2019.

Bryan-Wilson, Julia. *Art Workers: Radical Practices in the Vietnam Era.* Berkley: University of California Press, 2009.

B.S. "Izjemna priložnost za 'Krst' v Londonu." *Delo* (December 30, 1986): 3.

Buden, Boris. "The post-Yugoslavian Condition of Institutional Critique: An Introduction." *Transversal* 02/08 (2008). Accessed May 30, 2019. https://transversal.at/transversal/0208/buden/en.

– "Gastarbajteri, glasnici bodućnosti" [Guest Workers the Harbingers of the Future]. *Zarez* 14, no. 338–9 (2012): 36.

– *Cona prehoda: o koncu postkomunizma* [The Transit Zone: On the End of Communism]. Ljubljana: Založba Krtina, 2014.

Bürger, Peter. *Theory of the Avant-Garde.* Minneapolis: University of Minnesota Press, 1984.

– "Critique of Autonomy." In *Encyclopedia of Aesthetics.* Edited by Michael Kelly. New York: Oxford University Press, 1998.

– "Avant-Garde and Neo-Avant-Grade: An Attempt to Answer Certain Critics of Theory of the Avant-Garde." *New Literary History* 41, no. 4 (2010): 695–715.

– "Avant-Garde." In *Encyclopedia of Aesthetics.* 2nd ed., edited by Michael Kelly. Oxford: Oxford University Press, 2014. https://www.oxfordreference.com/view/10.1093/acref/9780199747108.001.0001/acref-9780199747108.

Canfora, Luciano. *Democracy in Europe: A History of an Ideology.* Oxford: Blackwell Publishing, 2006.

Celakoski, Teodor, Miljenka Buljević, Tomislav Medak, and Emina Višnić, eds. *Open Institutions: Institutional Imagination and Cultural Public Sphere.* Zagreb: Alliance Operation City, 2011.

Čopič, Vesna and Gregor Tomc. "Nacionalno poročilo o kulturni politiki Slovenije" [National Report on Cultural Policy of Slovenia]. In *Kulturna politika v Sloveniji* [Cultural Policy in Slovenia]. Ljubljana: Fakulteta za družbene vede, 1997.

Čufer, Eda. "Athletics of the Eye: *Baptism* and the Problem of Writing and Reading Contemporary Performance." *Maska* 17, no. 74–5 (2002): 81–8.

– "Enjoy Me, Abuse Me, I am Your Artist: Cultural Politics, Their Monuments, Their Ruins." In *East Art Map: Contemporary Art and Eastern Europe*, edited by IRWIN. London: Afterall, 2006.

Ćurković, Stipe. "Civilnom scenom do restavracije kapitalizma." *Portal Novosti*, no. 613 (September 17, 2011). Accessed August 28, 2015. http://arhiva.portalnovosti.com/2011/09/civilnom-scenom-do-restauracije-kapitalizma/.

Dalla Costa, Mariarosa and Selma James. *The Power of Women and the Subversion of the Community.* Bristol: Falling Wall Press, 1973.

Dalla Costa, Mariarosa. "Women and the Subversion of the Community." In Mariarosa Dalla Costa and Selma James, *The Power of Women and the Subversion of the Community.* Bristol: Falling Wall Press, 1973.

Daniels, Arlene Kaplan. "Invisible Work." *Social Problems* 34, no. 5 (1987): 403–15.

Dardot, Pierre and Christian Laval. *The New Way of the World: On Neoliberal Society.* New York: Verso, 2013.

Davis, Angela. "Uprising & Abolition: Angela Davis on Movement Building, 'Defund the Police' & Where We Go from Here." *Democracy Now!* June 12, 2020. https://www.democracynow.org/2020/6/12/angela_davis_historic_moment.

Denegri, Ješa. "Inside or Outside 'Socialist Modernism'? Radical Views on the Yugoslav Art Scene 1950–1970." In *Impossible Histories: Historical Avant-Gardes, Neo-avant-gardes and Post-avant-gardes in Yugoslavia 1918–1991*, edited by Dubravka Djurić and Miško Šuvaković. Cambridge, MA: MIT Press, 2003.

Denegri, Ješa. "Teze za drugu liniju" [Theses for the Alternative Route]. In *Razlozi za drugu liniju* [Reasons for the Alternative Route]. Novi Sad: Muzej suvremene umetnosti Vojvodine, 2007.

Dimitrijevič, Branislav. "Neke napomene o radu Gorana Đorđevića." *Prelom*, no. 5 (2003): 148–55.

– *Potrošeni socijalizam: kultura, konzumerizam i društvena imaginacija u Jugoslaviji (1950–1974)* [Consumable Socialism: Culture, Consumerism and Social Imagination in Yugoslavia (1950–1974)]. Belgrade: Peščanik, 2016.

Dimitrijević, Nena. *Gorgona – umjetnost kao način postojanja* [Gorgona – Art as a Way of Being]. Zagreb: Galerija suvremene umjetnosti, 1977.

Djilas, Milovan. *The New Class: An Analysis of the Communist System*. New York: Praeger, 1963.

Djurić, Dubravka and Miško Šuvaković, eds. *Impossible Histories: Historical Avant-Gardes, Neo-avant-gardes and Post-avant-gardes in Yugoslavia 1918–1991*. Cambridge, MA: MIT Press, 2003.

Dobrenko, Evgeny. *Aesthetics of Alienation: Reassessment of Early Soviet Cultural Theories*. Evanston, IL: Northwestern University Press, 2005.

Đokić, Ljupče, Dragutin Fletar, and Zlatko Sudović, eds. *Kultura u udruženom radu* [Culture in the Associated Labour]. Zagreb: Zavod za kulturu Hrvatske, 1981.

Đorđević, Goran. "Postoji samo istraživanje" [There is Only Research]. *Novi Svet*, no. 24–5 (1972): 11.

– "On the Class Character of Art." *The Fox*, no. 3 (1976): 163–5.

– "Subjekt i pseudosubjekt umetničke prakse" [The Subject and the Pseudo Subject of Artistic Practice]. *Vidici* 23, no. 3 (September 1977): 2.

– "Nova tradicija" [The New Tradition]. *Kultura*, no. 45–6 (1979): 250–2.

– "Marginalni položaj (razgovarao Jovan Despotović)" [A Marginal Position (A Conversation with Jovan Despotović)]. *Kulturne novine*, no. 630 (1981): 38–9.

– "Art as a Form of Religious Consciousness." In *SKC and Political Practices of Art*, ed. Prelom Kolektiv. Ljubljana: Galerija ŠKUC, 2008.

– "International Strike of Artists, 25. 2. 1979." In *SKC and the Political Practices of Art*, edited by Prelom Kolektiv. Ljubljana: Galerija ŠKUC, 2008.

Duffy, Erin. *(Not) Getting Paid to Do What You Love*. New Haven: Yale University Press, 2016.

Ebert, Teresa L. "Rematerializing Feminism." *Science & Society* 69, no. 1 (2005): 33–4.

Ebert, Teresa L. and Mas'ud Zavarzadeh. "ABC of Class." *Nature, Society, and Thought* 17, no. 2 (2004): 133.

Erjavec, Aleš, ed. *Postmodernism and the Postsocialist Condition: Politicized Art under Late Socialism*. Durham: Duke University Press, 2003.

– "The Three Avant-Gardes and Their Context: The Early, the Neo, and the Postmodern." In *Impossible Histories: Historical Avant-Gardes, Neo-avant-gardes and Post-avant-gardes in Yugoslavia 1918–1991*. Edited by Dubravka Djurić and Miško Šuvaković. Cambridge, MA: MIT Press, 2003.

– *Aesthetic Revolutions and Twentieth-Century Avant-Garde Movements*. Durham: Duke University Press, 2015.

Erjavec, Aleš and Marina Gržinić. *Ljubljana, Ljubljana: osemdeseta leta v umetnosti in kulturi* [Ljubljana, Ljubljana: The Eighties in the Arts and Culture]. Ljubljana: Mladinska knjiga, 1991.

ERICarts (European Institute for Comparative Cultural Research). *The Status of Artists in Europe (A Study)*. IP/B/CULT/ST/2005_89, PE 375.321. Brussels: European Parliament, 2006.

Exat 51. "Manifesto." In *Impossible Histories: Historical Avant-Gardes, Neo-avant-gardes and Post-avant-gardes in Yugoslavia 1918–1991*. Edited by Dubravka Djurić and Miško Šuvaković. Cambridge, MA: MIT Press, 2003.

Federici, Silvia. *Wages against Housework*. Bristol: Falling Wall Press, 1975.

– *Caliban and the Witch: Women, the Body and Primitive Accumulation*. Brooklyn: Autonomedia, 2009.

– *Revolution at Point Zero: Housework, Reproduction and Feminist Struggle*. Oakland: PM Press, 2012.

Flaker, Aleksander. *Poetika osporavanja: avantgarda i književna ljevica*. Zagreb: Liber-Globus, 1984.

Florida, Richard. *The Rise of the Creative Class*. New York: Basic Books, 2002.

Fortunati, Leopoldina. *Arcane of Reproduction: Housework, Prostitution, Labor and Capital*. Brooklyn: Autonomedia, 1995.

Foster, Hal. *The Return of the Real: The Avant-Garde at the End of the Century*. Cambridge, MA: MIT Press, 1996.

Foucault, Michel. *The Birth of Biopolitics: Lectures at Collège de France 1978–79*. Basingstoke: Palgrave Macmillan, 2008.

Friedson, Eliot. "Labors of Love in Theory and Practice: A Prospectus." In *The Nature of Work: Sociological Perspectives*, edited by Kai Erikson and Steven Peter Vallas. New Haven: Yale University Press, 1990.

Gabrič, Aleš. *Slovenska agitpropovska kulturna politika 1945–1952* [Slovene Agitprop Cultural Policy 1945–1952]. Ljubljana: Mladika, 1991.

Giménez, Marta E. *Marx, Women, and Capitalist Social Reproduction*. Leiden: Brill, 2018.

Golomstock, Igor. *Totalitarian Art: In the Soviet Union, the Third Reich, Fascist Italy and the People's Republic of China*. New York: Icon Editions, 1990.

Golubović, Zagorka. "Culture as a Bridge between Utopia and Reality." In *Praxis: Yugoslav Essays in the Philosophy and Methodology of the Social Sciences*. Edited by Mihailo Marković and Gajo Petrović. Dordrecht: D. Reidel Publishing Company, 1979.

Graeber, David. "From Managerial Feudalism to the Revolt of the Caring Class, a talk presented at 36th Chaos Communication Congress, Dec 12, 2019." *Open Transcirtpts.org*. Accessed June 19, 2020. http://opentranscripts.org/transcript /managerial-feudalism-revolt-caring-classes/.

Grant, Kim. *All About Process: The Theory and Discourse of Modern Artistic Labor.* Pittsburgh: Penn State University Press, 2017.

Grimm, Sabine and Klaus Ronnerberger. "An Invisible History of Work. An Interview with Sergio Bologna." *Springerin* 10, no. 1 (2007). Accessed August 7, 2017. https:// www.springerin.at/en/2007/1/eine-unsichtbare-geschichte-der-arbeit/.

Groys, Boris. *The Total Art of Stalinism: Avant-Garde, Aesthetic Dictatorship and Beyond.* New Jersey: Princeton University Press, 1992.

Gržinić, Marina. "Neue Slowenische Kunst (NSK): The Art Groups Laibach, IRWIN, and Noordung Cosmocinetic Theatre Cabinet – New Strategies in the Nineties." *Slovene Studies* 15, no. 1–2 (1993): 5–16.

Guilbaut, Serge. *How New York Stole the Idea of Modern Art: Abstract Expressionism, Freedom and the Cold War.* Chicago: University of Chicago Press, 1983.

Günther, Hans. *The Culture of the Stalin Period.* New York: St. Martin's Press, 1990.

Günther, Hans and Karla Hielscher. "Zur Rezeption der sowjetischen linen Avantgarde." *Ästhetik und Kommunikation* 19 (1975): 31–6.

Habermas, Jürgen. *The Structural Transformation of the Public Sphere: An Inquiry into a Category of Bourgeois Society.* Cambridge, MA: MIT Press, 1989.

Hamilton, Robert H. "Rhetoric, Violence, and Civil War: The Balkanization of America?" *Geopoliticus*, November 9, 2018. Accessed June 4, 2019. https://www.fpri .org/article/2018/11/rhetoric-violence-and-civil-war-the-balkanization-of-america/.

Harvey, David. *The New Imperialism.* Oxford: Oxford University Press, 2003.

Hatton, Erin. "Mechanisms of Invisibility: Rethinking the Concept of Invisible Work." *Work, Employment and Society* 31, no. 2 (2017): 336–51.

Heinrich, Michael. *An Introduction to the Three Volumes of Karl Marx's* Capital. New York: Monthly Review Press, 2012.

Hobsbawm, Eric. *Age of Extremes: The Short Twentieth Century 1914–1991.* London: Abacus, 1995.

Hofman, Ana. "Music (as) Labor: Professional Musicianship, Affective Labor and Gender in Socialist Yugoslavia." *Ethnomusicology Forum* 24, no. 1 (2015): 28–50.

Holmes, Brian. "The Flexible Personality." *Hieroglyphs of the Future.* Zagreb: What How and For Who/Arkzin, 2001.

Hrženjak, Majda. *Nevidno delo/Invisible Labor.* Ljubljana: Mirovni inštitut, 2007.

Illich, Ivan D. *Shadow Work.* London: Marion Boyars, 1981.

Indrisek, Scott. "The Precarious, Glamorous Lives of Independent Curators." *Artsy*, February 8, 2018. Accessed May 28, 2018. https://www.artsy.net/article/artsy -editorial-precarious-glamorous-lives-independent-curators.

Inman, Mary. *In Woman's Defense.* Los Angeles: Committee to Organize Advancement of Women, 1940.

IRWIN, ed. *East Art Map: Contemporary Art and Eastern Europe*. London: Afterall, 2006.

Iveković, Sanja and Dalibor Martinis. "Pokazatelj odnosa između prihoda samostalnog likovnog umjetnika i njegovog stvarnog osobnog dohotka kao i osobnog dohotka radnika u kulturi" [An Indicator of the Relationship between the Income of an Independent Visual Artist and Their Actual Personal Income as well as the Personal Income of a Worker in the Field of Culture]. In *Prvi broj*. Zagreb: RZU Podroom, 1980.

– "U galerije sa ugovorom!" In *Prvi broj*. Zagreb: RZU Podroom, 1980.

– "Ugovor." In *Prvi broj*. Zagreb: RZU Podroom, 1980.

Jakovljević, Branislav. "Human Resources: June 1968, 'Hair,' and the Beginning of Yugoslavia's End." *Grey Room* 30, no. 30 (2008): 38–53.

– *Alienation Effects: Performance and Self-Management in Yugoslavia, 1945–1991*. Ann Arbor: University of Michigan Press, 2016.

Jano, Dorian. "From 'Balkanization' to 'Europeanization': The Stages of Western Balkans Complex Transformations." *L'Europe en Formation* 349–50, no. 3 (2008): 55–69.

Jeffs, Nikolai. "FV and the 'Third Scene,' 1980–1990." In *FV: Alternativa osemdesetih/ The Alternative Scene of the Eighties*. Edited by Breda Škrjanec. Ljubljana: Mednarodni grafični likovni center, 2008.

Jesenko, Primož. *Rob v središču: izbrana poglavja o eksperimentalnem gledališču v Sloveniji 1955–1967* [The Edge in the Centre: Selected Chapters from the History of Experimental Theatre in Slovenia 1955–1967]. Ljubljana: Slovenski gledališki inštitut, 2015.

– "Pathwalker as a Ritual Fragment of Theatre Neo-Avant-Garde in Slovenia (First Fragment on Theatre Pekarna." *Maska* 24, no. 123–4 (2009): 20–49.

Kant, Immanuel. *Kritik der Urteilskraft, Werke in zwölf Bänden*, Band 10. Suhrkamp Verlag: Frankfurt am Main, 1977.

– *Critique of Judgment*. Translated by Werner S. Pluhar. Indianapolis/Cambridge: Hackett Publishing Company, 1987.

Karhunen, Paula. "Social Security and Employment." In *European Symposium on the Status of the Artist*. Edited by Auli Irjala. Helsinki: Finish National Commission for UNESCO, 1992.

Keating, David. "Will China Balkanize Europe?" *Berlin Policy Journal*, April 15, 2019. Accessed June 4, 2019. https://berlinpolicyjournal.com/will-china-balkanize-europe/.

Kiaer, Christina. *Imagine No Possessions: The Socialist Objects of Russian Constructivism*. Cambridge, MA: MIT Press, 2005.

Klaić, Dragan. "Komentar" [Commentary]. In Maja Breznik, *Posebni skepticizem v umetnosti* [The Distinctive Scepticism in Art]. Ljubljana: Založba Sophia, 2011.

Komlosy, Andrea. "Transitions in Global Labor History, 1250–2010 Entanglements, Synchronicities, and Combinations on a Local and a Global Scale." *Review (Ferdinand Braudel Center)* 36, no. 2 (2013): 155–90.

– *Work: The Last 1000 Years*. London: Verso, 2018.

Korda, Neven. "Alternative Dawns." In *FV: Alternativa osemdesetih/Alternative Scene of the Eighties*. Edited by Breda Škrjanec. Ljubljana: Mednarodni grafični likovni center, 2008.

Kosovel, Srečko. *Look Back, Look Ahead: The Selected Poems of Srečko Kosovel*. Translated by Ana Jelnikar and Barbara Siegel Carlson. Brooklyn, NY: Ugly Duckling Presse, 2010.

Krašovec, Primož. "Vrnitev neodpisanega: Foucault." In Michel Foucault, *"Družbo je treba braniti": predavanja na Collège de France (1975–1976)*. Ljubljana: Studia humanitatis, 2015.

– "Še enkrat o neoliberalizmu II: politika." *Andragoška spoznanja* 22, no. 1 (2016): 71–84.

– "Še enkrat o neoliberalizmu III: psihoafektivni učinki neoliberalizma in neoliberalna subjektivnost." *Andragoška spoznanja* 22, no. 2 (2016): 67–79.

Kreačič, Goranka. "Pogled na študentsko gibanje v Sloveniji 1968–1972 z današnje perspektive: pogovor z dr. Franetom Adamom" [A View on the Student Movement in Slovenia 1968–1972 from Today's Perspective: A Conversation with Dr. Frane Adam]. *Zgodovina v šoli, Zgodovinska priloga* 17, no. 3–4 (2008): 21–2.

Kreft, Lev. *Spopad na umetniški levici (med vojnama)* [A Confrontation on the Left (between the Wars)]. Ljubljana: Državna založba Slovenije, 1989.

– *Zjeban od absolutnega – perspektivovci in perspektivaši: portret skupine*. [Fucked Up by the Absolute – Perspectivists and Perspectivians: A Group Portrait]. Ljubljana: Znanstveno in publicistično središče, 1998.

Kristeller, Paul Oskar. *Renaissance Thought and the Arts*. New York: Harper & Row, 1965.

Kršić, Dejan. "Krst pod Triglavom" [Baptism under Triglav]. *Maska* 1, no. 1 (1991): 24–5.

– "Grafički dizajn i viuzalne komunikacije, 1950.–1975." [Graphic Design and Visual Communications, 1950–1975]. In *Socializam i modernost: umjetnost, kultura i politika 1950.–1974*. [Socialism and Modernity: Art, Culture, and Politics 1950–1974]. Edited by Liljana Kolešnik. Zagreb: Institut za povjest umjetnosti and Muzej suvremene umjetnosti, 2012.

Kržan, Marko. "Jugoslovansko samoupravljanje in prihodnost socializma" [Yugoslav Self-Management and the Future of Socialism]. In Catherine Samary, *Komunizem v gibanju: zgodovinski pomen jugoslovanskega samoupravljanja* [Communism in Motion: The Historical Meaning of Yugoslav Self-Management]. Ljubljana: Založba /*Cf., 2017.

La Berge, Leigh Claire. *Wages against Artwork*. Durham: Duke University Press, 2019.

Lesage, Dieter. "A Portrait of the Artist as a Worker." *Maska* 20, no. 94–5 (2005): 93–4.

Liehm, Mira and Antonon J. Liehhm. *The Most Important Art: Soviet and Eastern European Film after 1945*. Berkley: University of California Press.

Likar, Igor. "Gledališče ikon in emblemov" [The Theatre of Icons and Emblems]. *Maske* 2, no. 2 (1986): 85–9.

Lukács, Georg. *The Meaning of Contemporary Realism*. London: Merlin Press, 1963.

Lukić, Goran and Rastko Močnik, eds. *Sindikalno gibanje odpira nove poglede*. Ljubljana: Zveza svobodnih sindikatov Slovenije, 2008.

Lukić, Sveta. *Umetnost na mostu*. Belgrade: Ideje, 1975.

Majstorović, Stevan. *Cultural Policy in Yugoslavia*. Paris: UNESCO, 1972.

– *Cultural Policy in Yugoslavia: Self-Management and Culture*. Paris: UNESCO, 1980.

Marcuse, Herbert. *Negations: Essays in Critical Theory*. Boston: Beacon Press, 1958.

Marković, Mihailo. "Socialism and Self-Management." *Praxis* 1, no. 2–3 (1965): 178–95.

– "Marxist Philosophy in Yugoslavia: The *Praxis* Group." In *Marxism and Religion in Eastern Europe*. Edited by R.T. De George and Robert H. Scanlan. Dordrecht: D. Reidel Publishing Company, 1976.

Marx, Karl. *Capital: A Critique of Political Economy*, Vol. I. London: Penguin, 1990.

– "On the Jewish Question." *Deutsch-Französische Jahrbücher*, February 1844. Accessed May 1, 2019, https://www.marxists.org/archive/marx/works/1844/jewish-question/.

Mastnak, Tomaž. "Za anarholiberalizem" [For Anarcho-Liberalism]. *Problemi* 22, no. 239–41 (1984): 206.

– *Vzhodno od raja: civilna družba pod komunizmom in po njem* [East of Eden: Civil Society before Communism and After]. Ljubljana: Državna založba Slovenije, 1992.

– "Civil Society and Fascism." In *NSK from* Kapital *to Capital*. Edited by Zdenka Badovinac, Eda Čufer, and Anthony Gardner. Ljubljana/Cambridge, MA: Moderna galerija/MIT Press, 2015.

Mattick, Paul. *Art in Its Time: Theories and Practices of Modern Aesthetics*. London: Routledge, 2003.

Matvejević, Predrag. *Prema novom kulturnom stvaralaštvu* [Toward a New Cultural Creativity]. Zagreb: Naprijed, 1975.

McRobbie, Angela. *Be Creative*. London: Polity Press, 2016.

Medosch, Armin. *New Tendencies: Art at the Threshold of the Information Revolution (1961–1978)*. Cambridge, MA: MIT Press, 2016.

Menger, Pierre-Michel. "Artists as Workers: Theoretical and Methodological Challenges." *Poetics* 28, no. 4 (2001): 241–54.

Mies, Maria. *Patriarchy and Accumulation on a World Scale*. London: Zed Books, 1986.

– "Housewifisation – Globalisation – Subsistence – Perspective." In *Beyond Marx: Theorizing the Global Labour Relations of the Twenty-First Century*. Edited by Marcel van der Linden and Karl Heinz Roth. Leiden: Brill, 2013.

Miljković, Dušan (ed.), *Jugoslavija 1945–1985: statistički prikaz* [Yugoslavia 1945–1985: Statistical Presentation]. Belgrade: Savezni zavod za statistiku, 1986.

Misiano, Viktor. "On Critique Declared but Not Realized or, Realized but Not Declared (or, On the Love of Power)." *Atlas of Transformation*, 2011. Accessed May 28, 2019. http://monumenttotransformation.org/atlas-of-transformation/html/i/impossibility

-of-criticism/on-critique-declared-but-not-realized-or-realized-but-not-declared
-or-on-the-love-of-power-viktor-misiano.html.

Močnik, Rastko. *3 teorije: ideologija, nacija, institucija* [3 Theories: Ideology, Nation, Institution]. Ljubljana: Založba /*cf., 1999.

– "East!" In *East Art Map: Contemporary Art and Eastern Europe*. Edited by IRWIN. London: Afterall, 2006.

– "Sistem družboslovja in njegovi učinki" [The System of Social Sciences and Its Effects]. In *Spisi iz humanistitke* [Essays in the Humanities]. Ljubljana: Založba /*cf., 2009.

– "Delovni razredi v kapitalizmu [Working Classes in Capitalism]." In *Postfordizem: razprave o sodobnem kapitalizmu*. Edited by Gal Kirn. Ljubljana: Mirovni inštitut, 2010.

– "Excess Memory." *Transeuropéennes: Revue internationale de pensée critique* (March 3, 2010): 1–11.

– "Nismo krivi ali smo odgovorni; razgovarao Ozren Pupovac" [We Are Not Guilty, But We Are Responsible. A Conversation with Ozren Pupovac]. *Up & Underground*, no. 17–18 (Spring 2010): 140–53.

– "Political Practices at the End of Capitalism." In *Postfordism and Its Discontents*. Edited by Gal Kirn. Maastricht/Ljubljana Jan van Eyck Academie/Mirovni inštitut, 2010.

– "Kaj vse je pomenil izraz 'civilna družba'" [All the Meanings of the Notion "Civil Society"]. *Medijska preža*, no. 43 (2012): 13.

– "Workers' Self-management in Yugoslavia – Possible Lessons for the Present." Unpublished manuscript. Ljubljana, 2012.

Moulin, Raymonde. *The French Art Market: A Sociological View*. New Brunswick: Rutgers University Press, 1987.

Neil, Garry. *Status of the Artist in Canada: An Update on the 30th Anniversary of the UNESCO Recommendation concerning the Status of the Artist*. Ottawa: Canadian Conference of the Arts, 2010.

– *Full Analytic Report (2015) on the Implementation of the UNESCO 1980 Recommendation Concerning the Status of the Artist*. Paris: UNESCO, 2015.

– *Culture and Working Conditions for Artists: Implementing the 1980 Recommendation Concerning the Status of the Artists*. Paris: UNESCO, 2019.

Nochlin, Linda. "Why Have There Been No Great Women Artists?" In *Art and Sexual Politics: Why Have There Been No Great Women Artists?* Edited by Thomas B. Hess and Elizabeth C. Baker. New York: MacMillan, 1971.

Nova revija 6, no. 57 (Prispevki za slovenski nacionalni program) (1987).

Oakley, Anne. *Women's Work: The Housewife, Past and Present*. New York: Vintage Books, 1976. Retitled version of *Housewife*. London: Penguin, 1974.

Oakley, Kate. *"Art Works" – Cultural Labour Markets: A Literature Review*. London: Creativity, Culture and Education, 2009.

Oakley, Kate and Dave O'Brien. "Learning to Labour Unequally: Understanding the Relationship between Cultural Production, Cultural Consumption and Inequality." *Social Identities* 22, no. 5 (2016): 471–86.

O'Brien, Dave and Kate Oakley. *Cultural Value and Inequality: A Critical Literature Review*. Wiltshire: Arts and Humanities Research Council, 2015. https://ahrc.ukri.org/documents/project-reports-and-reviews/cultural-value-and-inequality-a-critical-literature-review/.

On Curating.org – Precarious Labor in the Field of Art, no. 16 (2013). https://www.on-curating.org/files/oc/dateiverwaltung/old%20Issues/ONCURATING_Issue16.pdf

Pekić, Milica and Katarina Pavić, eds. *Exit Europe: New Geographies of Culture*. Zagreb: Clubture Network, 2011.

Piškur, Bojan and Đorđe Balmazović, eds. *A Short Analysis of Worker's Inquiry Investigation*. Belgrade: B92, 2014.

Piškur, Bojana and Tamara Soban, eds. *This Is All Film: Experimental Film in Yugoslavia 1951–1991*. Ljubljana: Moderna galerija, 2010.

Pivka, Irena, Denis Miklavčič, Aldo Milohnić, and Vesna Bukovec. *Ocena stroškov dela za samozaposlene v kulturi* [An Estimation of the Labour Costs for Self-Employed Persons in Culture]. Ljubljana: Društvo Asociacija, 2010.

Podvršič, Ana. "From a Success Story to the EU Periphery: Spatialization Strategies of Capitalist Accumulation in Slovenia's Post-Yugoslav Development," *Wirtschaft und Management* 22 (2015): 79–94.

Poggioli, Renato. *The Theory of Avant-Garde*. New York: Harper & Row, 1971.

Poovey, Mary. *Uneven Developments: The Ideological Work of Gender in Mid-Victorian England*. Chicago: University of Chicago Press, 1988.

Praznik, Katja. "Between the Avant-Garde, Modernism and Amateurism: A Fragmentary History of Contemporary Dance in Ljubljana in the 1960s and 1970s." *Maska* 24, no. 123–4 (Summer 2009): 68–85.

– "Producing a Reserve Army of Cultural Labor, or, the Surpluses of Slovene Cultural Policy 2005–2015." In *Crises and New Beginnings: Art in Slovenia 2005–2015*. Ljubljana: Moderna galerija, 2016.

– "1% of Artistic Labor, or the Pygmalion-Like Effects of the Institution of Art." In *Jaka Babnik: Pygmalion*. Edited by Tevž Logar and Julija Hoda. Ljubljana: Muzej in galerije mesta Ljubljane, 2019.

– "Women, Art and Labor, or on the Limits of Representational Politics." In *City of Women Reflecting 2019/2020*. Edited by Tea Hvala. Ljubljana: Mesto žensk – društvo za promocijo žensk v kulturi, 2020.

Radical Education Collective and Škart, eds. *Radnička Anketa* [Worker's Inquiry]. Belgrade: B92, 2012.

Reckwitz, Andreas. *The Invention of Creativity*. London: Polity Press, 2017.

Rehmann, Jan. *Theories of Ideology: The Powers of Alienation and Subjection*. Leiden: Brill, 2013.

Roberts, John. *The Intangibilities of Form: Skilling and Deskilling in Art after the Readymade*. London: Verso, 2007.

Rodrigues, Olinde. "L'Artiste, le savant et l'industriel: Dialogue." In *Oeuvre de Saint Simone et d'Enfantin (1865–1879)*, Vol. 39. Aalen: O Zeller, 1964.

Ross, Andrew. "The Mental Labor Problem." *Social Text* 18, no. 2 (Summer 2000): 1–31.
– *No Collar*. Philadelphia: Temple University Press, 2003.
Ross, Kristin. *Communal Luxury: The Political Imaginary of the Paris Commune* (New York: Verso, 2015).
Samary, Catherine. *Plan, Market and Democracy*. Amsterdam: International Institute for Research and Education [Notebooks for Study and Research, no. 7–8], 1988.
– *The Fragmentation of Yugoslavia: An Overview*. Amsterdam: International Institute for Research and Education [Notebooks for Study and Research, no. 19–20], 1993.
– *Komunizem v gibanju: zgodovinski pomen jugoslovanskega samoupravljanja* [Communism in Motion: The Historical Meaning of Yugoslav Self-Management]. Ljubljana: Založba /*Cf., 2017.
Šavel, Saša. "Videodokumenti skupine Borghesia." In *Do roba in naprej: slovenska umetnost 1975–1985*. Edited by Igor Španjol and Igor Zabel. Ljubljana: Moderna galerija, 2003.
Schiller, Friedrich. *On the Aesthetic Education of Man*. Mineola, NY: Dover Publications, 2012.
Scipion Nasice Sisters Theatre (SNST). "First Sisters Letter." In *Impossible Histories: Historical Avant-Gardes, Neo-avant-gardes, and Post-avant-gardes in Yugoslavia, 1918–1991*. Edited by Dubravka Djurić and Miško Šuvaković. Cambridge, MA: MIT Press, 2003.
– "The Founding Act." In *NSK from* Kapital *to Capital*. Edited by Zdenka Badovinac, Eda Čufer, and Anthony Gardner. Ljubljana/Cambridge, MA: Moderna galerija and MIT Press, 2015.
Singerman, Howard. *Art Subjects: Making Artists in the American University*. Berkley: University of California Press, 1999.
Stakemeier, Kerstin and Marina Vishmidt. *Reproducing Autonomy: Work, Money, Crisis, and Contemporary Art*. London: Mute, 2016.
Standing, Guy. *The Precariat: The New Dangerous Class*. London: Bloomsbury, 2011.
Štiks, Igor and Srečko Horvat, eds. *Welcome to the Desert of Post-Socialism: Radical Politics After Yugoslavia*. London: Verso, 2015.
Stojanović, Jelena. "Internationaleries: Collectivism, the Grotesque, and Cold War Functionalism." In *Collectivism after Modernism: The Art of Social Imagination after 1945*. Edited by Gregory Sholette and Blake Stimson. Minneapolis: University of Minnesota Press, 2007.
Štrajn, Darko. "Kako razumeti študentska gibanja" [How to Understand Student Movements]. *Zgodovina v šoli, Zgodovinska priloga* 17, no. 3–4 (2008): 1–7.
Susovski, Marijan (ed.). *The New Art Practice in Yugoslavia 1966–1978*. Zagreb: Gallery of Contemporary Art, 1978.
Šutej, Jelka and Goran Schmidt. "Vzpon in padec gledališke dejavnosti" [The Rise and Fall of Theatre Activities]. *Delo* (January 17, 1986).
Šuvaković, Miško. "Impossible Histories." In *Impossible Histories: Historical Avant-Gardes, Neo-avant-gardes and Post-avant-gardes in Yugoslavia 1918–1991*. Edited by Dubravka Djurić and Miško Šuvaković. Cambridge, MA: MIT Press, 2003.

Šuvar, Stipe. *Kultura i politika*. Zagreb: Globus, 1980.

Suvin, Darko. "On the Class Relationships in Yugoslavia 1945–1974, with a Hypothesis on the Ruling Class." *Debatte: Journal of Contemporary Central and Eastern Europe* 20, no. 1 (2012): 37–71.

– *Splendour, Misery, and Possibilities: An X-Ray of Socialist Yugoslavia*. Leiden: Brill, 2016.

Szalay, Michael. *New Deal Modernism: American Literature and the Welfare State*. Durham: Duke University Press, 2000.

TANK! Slovenska Zgodovinska avantgarda/Revue international d'art vivant. Edited by Breda Ilich Klančnik and Igor Zabel. Ljubljana: Moderna galerija, 1998.

Taylor, Mark and Dave O'Brien. "'Culture is a Meritocracy': Why Creative Workers' Attitude May Reinforce Social Inequality." *Sociological Research Online* 22, no. 4 (2017): 27–47.

Terranova, Tiziana. "Free Labor: Producing Culture for the New Economy." *Social Text* 18, no. 2 (Summer 2000): 33–58.

Throsby, David. "A Work-Preference Model of Artist Behavior." In *Cultural Economics and Cultural Policies*. Edited by A. Peacock and I. Rizzo. Dordrecht: Kluwer Academic Publishers, 1994.

Todosijević, Raša. "Art and Revolution." In *SKC and Political Practices of Art*. Edited by Prelom Kolektiv. Ljubljana: Galerija ŠKUC, 2008.

– "Edinburgh Statement: Who Makes Profit on Art and Who Gains from It Honestly." In *Theories and Documents of Contemporary Art: A Sourcebook of Artists' Writings*, edited by Kristine Stiles and Peter Selz. Berkley: University of California Press, 2012.

Tokumitsu, Miya. "In the Name of Love." *Jacobin*, no. 13 (2014). Accessed May 28, 2018. https://www.jacobinmag.com/2014/01/in-the-name-of-love/.

Turković, Hrvoje. "It's All a Movie: A Conversation with Tomislav Gotovac." *Magazine FILM*, no. 10–11 (1977): 39–66.

UNESCO. *Recommendation Concerning the Status of the Artists, Adopted by the General Conference at Its 21st Session), Belgrade, 27 October 1980*. Belgrade: UNESCO, 1980. http://unesdoc.unesco.org/images/0011/001114/111428mo.pdf.

Unkovski-Korica, Vladmir. "Self-Management, Development, and Debt: The Rise and Fall of the 'Yugoslav Experiment.'" In *Welcome to the Desert of Post-Socialism: Radical Politics After Yugoslavia*. Edited by Igor Štiks and Srećko Horvat. London: Verso, 2015.

– *The Economic Struggle for Power in Tito's Yugoslavia: From World War II to Non-Alignment*. London: I.B. Tauris, 2016.

Vásquez, Adolfo Sánchez. *Art and Society: Essays in Marxist Aesthetics*. New York: Monthly Review Press, 1973.

Videkanić, Bojana. "*Non-aligned Modernism: Yugoslavian Art and Culture From 1945–1990*." PhD diss., York University, 2013.

– "Yugoslav Postwar Art and Socialist Realism: An Uncomfortable Relationship." *Artmargins* 5, no. 2 (2016): 3–26.

– *Nonaligned Modernism: Socialist Postcolonial Aesthetics in Yugoslavia, 1945–1990*. Montreal: McGill-Queen's University Press, 2019.

Vidić Rasmussen, Ljerka. *The Newly Composed Folk Music of Yugoslavia*. New York: Routledge, 2002.

Vidmar, Igor. "Sedaj gre zares" [Now It's for Real]. In *Punk pod Slovenci* [Punk under Slovenians]. Edited by Tomaž Mastnak in Nela Malečkar. Ljubljana: Republiška konferenca ZSMS and Univerzitetna konferenca ZSMS, 1985.

Vidmar, Ksenja Horvat, Damjan Mandelc, Ana Ješe, Tjaša Učakar, Irena Ograjenšek, Lejla Perviz, Ivo Lavrač. *Socialni položaj samozaposlenih v kulturi in predlogi za njegovo izboljšanje s poudarkom na temi preživitvene strategije na področju vizualne umetnosti* [The Social Conditions of Self-Employed Persons in Culture and Recommendations for Improvements with an Emphasis on the Topic of Survival Strategies in the Field of Visual Arts]. Ljubljana: Filozofska fakulteta, 2012.

Vrečko, Janez. "Labodovci, pilotovci, konstrukteristi in tankisti." In *TANK! Slovenska Zgodovinska avantgarda/Revue international d'art vivant*. Edited by Breda Ilich Klančnik and Igor Zabel. Ljubljana: Moderna galerija, 1998.

Wall, Geoffrey. "Translator's Note." In *A Theory of Literary Production*, by Pierre Macherey. London: Routledge & Kegan Paul, 1978.

Weeks, Kathi. *The Problem with Work: Feminism, Marxism, Antiwork Politics and Postwork Imaginaries*. Durham: Duke University Press, 2011.

Woodmansee, Martha. *The Author, Art, and the Market: Rereading the History of Aesthetics*. New York: Columbia University Press, 1994.

Woodward, Susan L. *Socialist Unemployment: The Political Economy of Yugoslavia 1945–1990*. Princeton: Princeton University Press, 1995.

– "The Political Economy of Ethno-Nationalism in Yugoslavia." *Socialist Register 2003: Fighting Identities – Race, Religion and Ethno-Nationalism*. Edited by Leo Panitch and Colin Leys. London: The Merlin Press, 2003, 73–92.

Woolard, Caroline and Susan Jahoda. "BFAMFAPHD: On the Cultural Value Debate and Artists Report Back." In *Cultural Policy Yearbook 2016: Independent Republic of Culture*. Edited by Serhan Ada. Istanbul: Istanbul University Press, 2017.

Zlobec, Jaša. "Sterilni Krst v votlem hramu" [A Sterile Baptism in a Hollow Chamber]. *Mladina* 21, no. 6 (February 14, 1986): 37.

Zupančič, Alenka. "Umetnikov mladostni portret" [The Portrait of an Artist as a Young Man]. Transcript of the radio show "Bricolages Krstu," aired on Radio Študent Ljubljana, March 2, 1986, 6–7.

Index

Page numbers in *italics* represent illustrations.

abstract citizen, 181n81

abstraction, 28, 53, 161n38

Adorno, Theodor, 21, 31–2, 34

aesthetic of genius, 41. *See also* artistic
genius

aesthetics: and autonomy of art, 21–2
(*see also* paradox of art); and avant-
garde social relationships, 157n50; as
central to Western art, 30; and merit-
based logic, 90; perpetuating invisible
labour, 44 (*see also* paradox of art);
and policies in SPRY stage two art, 63;
and universality, 22, 161n38

agitprop cultural policy (1945–53). *See*
art in SFRY, stage 1: Artists as Workers

Alajbegović, Zemira, 120

"alternative, the." *See* 1980s alternative, the

alternative art practices: overview,
29–30, 158n63; disillusionment,
74; and Đorđević, 76–87; Exat 51,
52–3; and the new art practice, 78,
91, 92; in 1990s, 127, 138; pluralistic
tolerance, 57; RZU Podroom, 91–6;
SFRY vs. Cominform, 56; vs. social
aestheticism, 56–7, 65; and student
centres, 59; vs. traditional national
culture, 65, 146; as uncritical to

exceptionality and autonomy of
art, 49, 98–9. *See also* avant-garde
movement; "independent culture";
1980s alternative, the

amateur professional associations, 55.
See also associational culture

amateurs, 55, 59, 75, 76

American Abstract Expressionism, 161n38

antifacism, 26, 52, 67

art/culture: affirming reality, 88; art
education, 110; and bourgeois society,
87–9; and class, 77, 87, 88–9; and
consumerism, 26, 88; contradictions
in (*see* paradox of art); defined in
SFRY stage two, 64; demand for, 72;
end of, 20; five major arts, 154n6; and
human personality, 62; as ideology,
80–1; and Marxist superstructure, 64;
as separate and specialized, 21, 38, 64,
87 (*see also* art workers as exceptional
subjects; autonomy of art); and value,
45 (*see also* value)

art and everyday life: and aesthetics,
22; art as anything, 42; and artists
as workers, 51; disconnection and
exploitation, 8; and free associations,
64; in New Deal, 25, 147n40; and

rejecting autonomy of art, 24; SFRY
stage two, 62–3; SFRY stage three, 88.
See also democratization of culture
"Art and Revolution" (Todosijević), 74
"Art as a Form of Religious
Consciousness" (Đorđević), 78
art as institution. *See* institution of art
art in modern day former SFRY
countries, 145–8
art in SFRY (general), 25–6, 29, 30, 48,
49–50, 158n63. *See also* alternative
art practices; "independent culture";
1980s art; 1990s art
art in SFRY, overview, 7–9, 10–11, 47,
49, 68–9, 71. *See also* book overview;
chapter overviews; 1980s alternative,
the; 1980s art; 1990s art
art in SFRY, stage one: Artists as
Workers, 49, 50; overview, 68–9;
affirming status quo, 57; alternative
art practices/avant-garde, 52–3,
56; art workers as employees, 52,
163n14; associational culture,
55–6; avant-garde's alternative vision,
52–3; copying European organization
models, 54–6; cultural engagement,
51; cultural institutions nationalized,
50; funding through federal budget,
51; professional associations, 51, 55–6;
social security/insurance, 52; visual
art cooperatives, 54–5; and Western
influence, 53, 54
art in SFRY, stage two: Testing the
Limits of Art as Labour, 56; overview,
68–9; administration, 60–1,
167nn57–8; aesthetics and labour
policies, 63; affirming status quo, 88;
alternative art practices and socialist
aestheticism, 56–7, 65; alternative art
practices and student centres, 59; art
and everyday life, 62–3; art workers as
employees, 62, 63–4, 65; associational

culture, 59, 65; autonomy of art, 57,
58, 64; class divisions, 65; cultural
exchanges, 62; Đorđević, Goran,
76–7 (*see also* Đorđević, Goran);
festivals, 62; freelancers, 62, 65,
168n65, 169n79; funding, 60–1, 65;
institutions and autonomy, 60; New
Tendencies, 63, 169n78; pluralistic
tolerance, 56–7, 60, 165n35; political
critique, 56–7, 58, 66; professional
associations, 62, 63; and self-
management (socialism), 57–8
art in SFRY, stage three:
Disenfranchisement of Art Workers,
68; overview, 68, 71; administration,
73–4; art workers as vulnerable to
exploitation, 89–90; artists' contracts
with galleries, 92–3; Đorđević, Goran,
76–87, 117, 118, 148; employees
vs. freelancers, 90–1; funding for
culture, 73–4; liberalization of market
principles, 72; 1980s (*see* 1980s art;
1980s alternative, the); social security/
insurance, 98; strikes, 79–81, 83; and
traditional art organizations, 87–8
art schools, 161–2n39
art workers/artists: as adaptable, 11;
and art systems, 79; vs. artisans,
41–2; artist's name, 42, 45;
autonomy, 18, 79; as commercial,
45; conditions deteriorating,
72 (*see also* entrepreneurs/self-
employment; freelancers); Disko
FV, 59, 119–22; Đorđević, 76–87;
Dutch artists, 165n32; forced to sell
art works, 94; and galleries, 3, 91,
92–3, 94; and ideas of autonomy, 55;
marginalization of new generation,
74; during 1980s, 112–14, 119,
127–31, 142 (*see also* 1980s alternative,
the); during 1990s, 138; 1990s to
modern day, 146–8; as one-person

associations, 113; and paradox of art, 34; as part of CPY, 26; as proletarians, 112, 113; as pseudo subjects, 78–9, 81, 117; as public servants, 145; as service providers, 93–4, 103–4, 147; during SFRY stage one, 51–3, 55, 56; during SFRY stage two, 60, 62–3; during SFRY stage three, 74, 75, 89–98, 97 (*see also* Đorđević, Goran); SNST, 122–7, 178n26; and social inclusiveness, 43; strikes, 83; subsistence and labour split, 83; success and financial reward, 45; as term, 3–4, 8; traditional independent work (*see* freelancers); and UNESCO recommendation, 9; visual artists in 1951/3, 163n14; as white men, 5, 22, 35, 43. *See also* entrepreneurs/self-employment; freelancers

art workers and audience: art as anything, 42; and divide of high culture/mass culture, 88; negotiating needs, 93–4; New Deal aspirations, 25, 157n40; public participation, 55; and rejection of autonomy of art, 24; SNST, 124–5. *See also* democratization of culture

art workers as exceptional subjects: overview, 34; and art schools, 161–2; as blind spot of self-management, 87; and class, 77; creativity and genius, 42; and division of labour, 21; domestic labour, 38; 1980s reinforcement, 131; and paradox of art, 42; and rejecting autonomy of art, 24; spiritual superstructure and, 64. *See also* artistic genius

artisans, 41–2

artistic genius: and art as institution, 41; during Cold War, 28; Đorđević's ideas of, 76–7, 78, 89; history of, 23; mystique and value, 45, 147; and New Tendencies, 63, 169n78; as racialized and gendered, 5; renouncing, 24

artistic labour: art as service, 93–4, 103–4, 147; as artistic object, 161n38; and class, 40; definitions, 17; and dictionary definition of artworks, 17; and division of labour, 21; and domestic labour, 37–8, 40–1, 42–4, 45–6; and enjoyment of work, 40, 41, 44; entwined with creativity, 62; essentialized creativity, 89; and expenses, 113; and exploitation (*see* exploitation); as glorified, 43; as invisible (*see* paradox of art); as leisure, 44; as love, 147; as masculine, 5, 22, 35, 41, 43; 1980s undoing, 118, 127–30; as non-work, 40–1, 94; outsourced by institutions, 118–19; as paradox of art, 4 (*see also* paradox of art); and privatization of work, 39; as recognized in SFRY stage one, 51–2, 63; and sacrifice, 44, 162n43; scholarship of, 12–13; 70s vs. 80s, 98; strikes, 79–81; and talent, 147; as therapy, 44; types of tasks, 18; value of, 3, 4, 93, 147 (*see also* paradox of art; unpaid work); as work, 63. *See also* non-work

artworks: acquisitions, 51; commercialization and value, 45; as communications of creativity, 93; consecration, 45; donation of, 94; as non-work, 23; as performed labour, 161n38; as priceless, 18; as term, 8, 17

Asociacija, 147

Association of Arts and Culture NGOs and Self-Employed, 147

associational culture, 55–6, 59, 65, 75, 90, 127–8

austerity, 101, 114

authorship, 30

autonomy, 18, 35

autonomy of art: overview, 144–5; and
aesthetics, 22–3 (*see also* paradox of
art); and art cooperatives, 55; and
avant-garde, 19, 20–1, 23–45, 26–7,
30–3, 53, 58–9, 157n50; and avant-
garde in SFY stage one, 28, 53; and
avant-garde in SFY stage two, 58–9;
definition, 18; and entrepreneurship,
131; and exploitation, 33; as gendered,
22, 35; as historical idea, 22–3, 30–1,
34; ideological aspects, 21–2, 32, 34,
45; and Marxist scholars, 31–2; new
art practice and, 78; in 1980s, 98–9; in
the 1980s alternative, 115; obscuring
class, 64; and paradox of art, 22,
31–2, 33–4; as progressive sign, 58;
rejecting, 24; and revolutionary
situations, 26; as self-management
blind spot, 87; and social change, 23,
24; and spiritual sphere, 64; structural
aspects, 21, 32, 33, 34, 38, 45; and
wages, 22
avant-garde movement: as apolitical,
157n52; appropriation of, 25,
157n50; assimilation in SFRY stage
three, 92; and autonomy of art,
19, 20, 23–4, 26–7, 28, 30–3, 53,
58–9, 157n50; and Cold War, 28–9;
definitions, 20–1, 28; demystification
of creativity/labour, 33, 42, 83;
and impact of exploitation, 31; in
Kingdom of Yugoslavia, 26; and
Marxist scholars, 31–2; neo-avant-
garde, 29, 157n50; New Tendencies,
63, 169n78; and political parties,
27; and revolutionary situations,
25–6, 30; and SFRY stage one, 28,
52–3; and SFRY stage two, 58–60,
63; and SFRY stage three, 74–5, 92
(*see also* alternative art practices;
1980s alternative, the); SNST
appropriation of imagery, 124, 125;

and social change, 23–5, 27–8, 30;
and United States, 25; and USSR, 25;
Western attack of, 112. *See also* 1980s
alternative, the

Babnik, Jaka, *4*
Balkan Wars, 135, 137, 145
"Baptism on the Savica" (Prešeren), 124
Baptism under Triglav (SNST
performance), 124, 125, 126,
179nn43–4
Basic Organization of Associated Labour
(BOAL), 73, 129
Bele, Marjana, 113, 130
Belgrade, Serbia, 151n10
Belgrade Student Cultural Centre (SKC),
76, 78, 80–1
Belgrade Triennial of Yugoslav Art, 78
Berger, John, 25
Berlin Wall, 135, 176n30
Blažević, Dunja, 74
bohemians, 161n38
Bologna, Sergio, 39, 113, 129
book overview, 5–8, 9–10, 11–13, 14–15.
See also chapter overviews
Borčić, Barbara, 115
Bosnia and Herzegovina, 10, 54, 55, 90
Bourdieu, Pierre, 45
bourgeois society: and aesthetics, 22;
copied in SFRY stage one, 54–6; and
elitist culture in SFRY stage three,
87–9; influence ignored in 1980s, 115;
and institutionalization of art, 17–18,
19; mutated in SFRY stage three,
74; rejected in SFRY stage one, 53;
rejection and revolution, 26; in SFRY
stage two art, 67; socialist realism,
75 (*see also* socialist realism); theatre
model, 123
Buden, Boris, 132, 133, 137, 139
Bürger, Peter, 19–24 passim, 30–2
passim, 154n4, 157n50

Canfora, Luciano, 133

Cankarjev dom (CD), 119, 124, 125–7, 179nn44–5

capital accumulation, 137–8, 146

capitalism: as absurd, 148; artists vs. art work, 18; as democracy, 133; division of labour, 21, 36, 48; and enjoyment of work, 40; and entrepreneurship, 141; expectations of, 39; Golden Age, 104; and institution of art, 18–19; late capitalism, 37; and the 1980s alternative, 136; and patriarchy, 37; and private sphere labour, 38; and revised feminist critique, 37; vs. self-management (socialism), 48, 104; and SFRY alternative art, 29–30; vs. socialism, 58; and subjectivism about freedom, 39; transitioning from socialism, 25, 135; work as leisure, 44. *See also* consumerism; market principles; neoliberalism; Western art; Western countries

censorship, 88, 101, 105

centralized state cultural policy (1945–53). *See* art in SFRY, stage one

chapter overviews: chapter 1, 14, 18–19; chapter 2, 25, 45–6; chapter 3, 14–15, 47–8; chapter 4, 15, 47–8, 71, 98; chapter 5, 15, 98, 101–3; chapter 6, 15, 101–3, 117, 136–7

CIA, 165n41

cinema clubs, 59, 166n51

civil society, 106, 107–11, 115–16, 133–4

class: and artists as exceptional, 77; and creativity, 161n38; Djilas's "new class," 57, 165n41; and economic exclusion, 89; and first 20 years of SFRY, 58; and labour of art, 40; obscured by autonomy of art, 64; and paradox of art, 45; and self-management (socialism), 47; stratification in 1980s, 108, 110, 134; stratification in 1990s,

138; stratification in SFRY stage two, 57, 65, 66; stratification in SFRY stage three, 75, 88; and unpaid work, 39, 44; working class precarity, 112, 113, 131, 138, 146, 182–3n5

"Class Character of Art, On the" (Đorđević), 87

classophobia, 57

Cold War: and avant-garde, 28–9; and the 1980s alternative, 106; SFRY as independent, 47, 54, 56, 72, 144, 153n26, 164n15

commodification, 30, 33, 63, 83

communes, 60, 61, 73, 174n1

communism, 135, 136, 176n30

Communist Party of Yugoslavia (CPY), 26, 50, 52. *See also* League of Communists of Yugoslavia; self-management (socialism)

compensation/remuneration: art as service, 93–4; art works sold as forced, 94; artist contracts, 92–3, 173n72; artist vs. exhibition budget, 78, 94, 145; and enjoyment of work, 40, 41, 44; fees during SFRY stage one, 52; freelancers vs. associations, 127–8; freelancers vs. employed art workers, 96, *97*, 98, 128–9, 147; vs. glorification, 43–4; Kant's views, 22; vs. pricelessness of artworks, 18; and social sciences definition of artistic labour, 17; and success, 45; as suspect, 44; traditional vs. associational, 90–1. *See also* funding; social security/insurance; unpaid work

competition, 114, 130, 142–3, 144, 145, 147

conformism, 87, 89, 118

Cons 5 (Kosovel), 148, 183n12

constitution of 1974, 72, 94, 123, 128

constructivism, 24, 42

consumerism, 26, 66–7, 88, 104, 174–5n13

contracts, 10, 92–3, 173n72
co-productions, 126, 127
coronavirus pandemic, 143–4
craftsmen. *See* artisans
creativity: and competition, 142; and
　creative self, 161n38; Đorđević's
　ideas of, 76–7, 78, 89; entwined with
　labour, 62; and genius, 41; as gift to
　humanity, 39; as illusion, 76–7, 78;
　and institution of art, 41; mythical
　power of, 21, 96; as non-work, 42; and
　value, 93; and white male subjects, 22;
　and work, 17
Croatia: economic inequalities in
　republics, 90; full employment, 110;
　funding social security/insurance,
　62; Law for Independent Artists, 96,
　112–13, 114, 181n85; and nationalism,
　72; New Tendencies, 63, 169n78; RZU
　Podroom, 91–6, *97*; student centres,
　59; visual art cooperatives, 54, 55
Čufer, Eda, 123
cultural associations. *See* associational
　culture
cultural institutions. *See* institution of art
cultural policy, decentralized (1954–74).
　See art in SFRY, stage two
cultural policy of centralized state
　(1945–53). *See* art in SFRY, stage one
cultural policy of self-management
　(1974–91). *See* art in SFRY, stage three
culture. *See* art/culture; *various art entries*
Ćurković, Stipe, 110
cybernetic socialism, 169n78

dance, 59
Dardot, Pierre, 114, 129, 175n21
Davis, Angela, 35
debts, 101, 104, 114
decentralization, 67, 72
decentralized cultural policy (1954–74).
　See art in SFRY, stage two

democracy, 133, 135. *See also* liberalism
democratization, 133, 141
democratization of art/culture:
　associational culture for mass
　access, 55, 59; Disko FV, 120; and
　new generation of art workers, 65;
　and presumptions of socialism,
　132–3; producing inequality, 98,
　134; and protection, 63. *See also* art
　and everyday life; art workers and
　audience
Demur, Boris, 91–6
demystification of labour practice, 33,
　42, 83. *See also* mystification of labour
　process
Denegri, Ješa, 29, 56
depoliticization, 27, 38, 39, 40, 80–1,
　89. *See also* autonomy of art; paradox
　of art
Depression, 25
Dimitrijević, Branislav, 66
Disko FV, 119–22, 127
Disko Študent, 59, 119–21
division of labour: overview, 21; and
　art's social function, 75; and class
　in culture, 88–9; public and private,
　36, 37, 38–9; and self-management
　(socialism), 48, 64
Djilas, Milovan, 57, 165n41
domestic labour: and artistic labour,
　37–8, 40–1, 42–3, 45–6; as degraded,
　43; and femininity, 36–7, 40–1; as
　invisible, 36–7, 43; as non-work, 36–7,
　38; and political struggle, 37; and
　secondary jobs, 40
Đorđević, Goran, 76–87, 117, 118, 148
Duchamps, Marcel, 42

Ebert, Teresa L., 35, 44–5
economic crash 2020, 143
economic growth, 58
education, 110, 166n47

Egorythm III (Peljhan), 148
elitism, 87–9, 139
emancipation, 27, 66, 67, 89
enjoyment/self-fulfillment, 40, 41, 44
entrepreneurs/self-employment: 1990s
    to modern day, 146–8; and assets,
    142; and autonomy of art, 131; Disko
    FV, 119–22, 127; as false choice, 114;
    human capital, 129; impoverished art
    workers, 138; Law for Independent
    Cultural Workers, 128–31; myth of
    self-reliance, 127; replacing employed
    art workers, 112; as rivalry, 142; SNST,
    122–7, 178n26; and welfare state,
    141–2; Western ideas of, 141; worker
    as enterprise, 129, 143, 180n53. *See
    also* freelancers; outsourced labour
equality, 181n81
Erjavec, Aleš, 125, 126
essentialization, 37–8, 41, 42–4, 89.
    See also femininity; masculinity
ethnic cleansing, 135
European Free Trade Association
    (EFTA), 54
*European Symposium on the Status of the
    Artist* (Irjala), 152n20
European Union, 135, 137, 139
Exat 51, 52–3
exceptionality. *See* art workers as
    exceptional subjects
exhibition/galleries, 3, 91, 92–3, 94.
    See also institution of art
experimental art, 59
exploitation: art affirming status quo,
    57; and art/artistic labour definitions,
    17, 83, 89–90; artistic labour and
    everyday life, 8; and autonomy of
    art, 33; and competition, 145; due
    to mystification of artistic labour, 5;
    and enjoyment of work, 40, 41, 44; as
    human rights issue, 33; and impact of
    avant-garde critiques, 31; outsourced

labour, 118–19; and prestige of artistic
    work, 34; protection from, 63; and
    religion, 77; and secondary jobs, 40

Faustian bargain, 54, 66, 72, 136
Federici, Silvia, 37, 39–40, 83, 146–7
femininity, 35, 36–7, 38, 40, 42–4
feminism, 33, 35, 36, 37, 44
festivals, 62
film, 59, 61, 112, 121
Fischer, Hervé, 86
Fordism, 63, 104, 105, 112, 174–5n13
Foucault, Michel, 129, 180n53
Founding Act, The (SNST declaration), 123
free associations, 64
free exchange of labour, 73–4, 93–4
freedom, 39, 108, 110, 133, 157n52,
    181n81. *See also* liberalism
freelancers: vs. associations, 127–8;
    increasing in 1980s, 112, 128, 130,
    151n10; jobs of, 168n65; marginalized
    in SFRY stage three, 92–6, 169n79;
    number in 1951/3, 163n14; number
    in 1984, 180n68; during SFRY stage
    one, 52; during SFRY stage two, 62,
    169n79. *See also* entrepreneurs/self-
    employment
freelancers and employed art workers:
    overview, 65, 90–1; compensation,
    96, *97*, 98, 147; and laws, 96, 112–13,
    114, 128–31, 134, 181n85; post-
    Fordism, 112; royalty taxes, 180n67;
    social protection, 52, 62, 128, 130–1,
    152n10; and solidarity, 134
full employment, 51–2, 63, 90, 110,
    163n7. *See also* unemployment
Fund for Cultural Advancement, 61
funding: 1990s–modern day art, 145–6;
    and administration, 60–1; for *Baptism
    under Triglav* (SNST performance),
    126; for CD, 126–7; Disko FV, 122;
    exhibition vs. artist compensation, 3;

the 1980s alternative, 105, 122; and
SFRY stage one art, 51; and SFRY
stage two art, 60–1, 65; traditional
vs. associational, 65, 90–1. *See also*
compensation/remuneration
FV 112/15, 118–19, 177n4. *See also*
Disko FV

galleries, 3, 91, 92–3, 94. *See also*
institution of art
gender, 5, 22, 35, 43. *See also* femininity;
masculinity
General Agreement on Tariffs and Trade
(GATT), 54
genius, 41. *See also* artistic genius
globalization, 137
Golubović, Zagorka, 30, 64, 87–9, 118
Gotovac, Tomislav, 166n51
Gržinić, Marina, 125, 126

Harvey, David, 146
health coverage, 166n47
healthcare crisis, 143–4
heterogeneity of 1980s art workers,
111, 115, 136
Hinkemann (SNST performance),
123–4
Hobsbawm, Eric, 104
housework. *See* domestic labour
human capital, 129
human rights, 109, 110, 111, 133, 134,
177n65

idealism, 181n81
ideology of modernity, 39
ideology vs. economic focus, 49, 105,
106, 108–9, 118. *See also* 1980s
alternative, the
independent art groups (cultural
associations), 55
"independent culture," 145–8

independent entrepreneur. *See*
entrepreneurs/self-employment
"Indicator of the Relationship between
the Income of an Independent
Visual Artist …, An" (Iveković and
Martinis), 96, *97*
individualism, 28, 157n52
industrialization, 50, 58, 104. *See also*
modernization; urbanization
inspiration, 42
institution of art: overview, 17–19;
and art as creation, 77; art systems,
78–9, 81, 83, 87, 92–4; and artistic
genius, 41; assimilating avant-garde,
92; avant-garde attack of, 24, 28,
30–3; capitalist entanglement, 83;
compensation from art workers, 94;
as conservative, 87; and crumbling
welfare state, 127; defined, 154n4;
distinctive elements, 54–5; as
economic system, 129; employment
in SFRY stage three, 110; and
exchange of labour, 94, 96; funding
for exhibitions vs. artists, 3; funding
in SFRY stage two, 61; 1990s–modern
day art, 145; outsourcing labour,
118–19; and radical art, 56; SFRY
copying Europe, 54–6; as social
institution, 20, 23–45 (*see also* Scipion
Nasice Sisters Theatre); social power
of, 79; as unrevolutionary, 58–9, 75.
See also autonomy of art
International Monetary Fund (IMF), 54,
67, 72, 114
International Strike of Artists
(Đorđević), *80–2, 84–6*
intersectionality, 35
invisibility of labour, 36–8. *See also*
paradox of art
Irjala, Auli, 152n20
Iveković, Sanja, 91, 92, 96

Jedinstvo, 76
Jeffs, Nikolai, 111, 115, 121, 122
"Jewish Question, On the" (Marx), 181n81

K4, 121
"*Kaj je alternativa?* (What Is the
    Alternative?)" (Mandić), *107*
Kant, Immanuel, 22
Kiaer, Christina, 13
Klaić, Dragan, 139
Korda, Neven, 114–15, 119, 121, 122
Kosovel, Srečko, 148, 183n12
Kovacs, Adrian. *See* Đorđević, Goran
Kreft, Lev, 66
Kristeller, Paul Oskar, 154n6
Krleža, Miroslav, 52, 53
Kršić, Dejan, 53, 137

labour: emancipation of, 27, 48, 88; and
    Fordist model of productivity, 105; as
    human rights issue, 33; and knowing
    oneself, 39; as leisure, 44; vs. leisure,
    134–5; Marxism vs. neoliberalism,
    129, 180n53; privatization of work,
    39; and welfare state in 1980s, 104–5.
    See also domestic labour
labour of art. *See* artistic labour
labour of art as invisible. *See* paradox
    of art
labour of writing, 38
late capitalism, 37
Laval, Christian, 114, 129, 175n21
Law for Independent Artists, 96, 112–13,
    114, 134, 181n85
Law for Independent Cultural Workers,
    112–13, 114, 128–31, 134
law of property, 30
League of Communists of Yugoslavia
    (LCY): and capitalist West, 54;
    censorship, 88, 101, 105; concessions
    from protests, 76, 115; consolidation
of rule, 68; constitution of 1974, 72,
    94, 123; and decentralization, 67;
    freedom of expression, 56; law vs.
    practice, 94, 96, 128; and nationalism,
    109; as oligarchy, 57, 66, 67; as
    repressive/oppressive, 94, 105, 106,
    108–9, 115; and SFRY stage two, 65–6;
    and Stalin, 67; unemployment (*see*
    unemployment). *See also* Communist
    Party of Yugoslavia; self-management
    (socialism); *all entries with SFRY;
    individual countries*
League of Socialist Youth of Yugoslavia
    (LSYY), 59, 166–7n53
League of Yugoslav Youth, 166–7n53
leisure, 44, 134–5
Lesage, Dieter, 39
LGBTQ+, 103, 120, 121
liberalism, 58, 109, 135–6, 139, 157n52,
    176n30. *See also* democracy
loans, 90, 153n26. *See also* World Bank
lottery tickets, *4*
Lukács, Georg, 31, 32
Lukić, Sveta, 56

Macedonia, 61, 90, 112–13, 114
Majstorović, Stevan, 26, 54, 73
Malevič, Kazimir, 28
Mandić, Dušan, *107*, 121
Marija Nablocka (SNST performance), 124
market principles, 67–8, 72, 83, 101, 138.
    See also neoliberalism
market regulation, 58
Martinis, Dalibor, 91, 92–3, 96, 173n72
Marx, Karl, 3, 8, 77, 181n81
Marxism, 31–2, 33, 36, 52, 63, 64
masculinity, 5, 35, 38, 41
Mastnak, Tomaž, 107, 108, 110, 115–16,
    176n30
Matvejević, Predrag, 87
Medosch, Armin, 169n78

middle class, 38, 108. *See also* bourgeois society

ministry for culture, 51

Misiano, Viktor, 133–4

Močnik, Rastko, 26–7, 30, 50, 53, 66, 72, 108–11 passim, 135, 174–5n13

modern art as antisocial, 23

modernism, 21, 28, 39, 52, 53, 58

modernization, 57. *See also* industrialization; urbanization

Mohar, Miran, 123

Montenegro, 10, 62, 90

mystification of labour process, 5–6, 10, 31. *See also* demystification of labour practice

nationalism: and art workers alliances, 115; Croatia, 72; and economics, 65; and the 1980s alternative, 111, 118; in 1990s, 139; and self-management transformation, 109; Serbia, 72; and SFRY breakup, 72, 123; in SFRY stage three art, 72; Slovenia, 72, 109, 123, 124, 139; and theatre model, 123

nationalization, 50

Nazi Punk Affair, 105

neo-avant-garde, 29, 157n50

neoliberalism: and art as public service, 93–4, 103–4, 147; character of, 142, 174n11, 175n21; critiquing welfare state, 134–5; defined, 104; enjoyment of unpaid work, 40; and entrepreneurial logic, 114, 142–3 (*see also* entrepreneurs/self-employment); increasing inequalities, 131; and independent artist laws, 130; labour as opposite to Marx's ideas, 129, 180n53; and the 1980s alternative, 106; and paradox of art, 40; and self-management (socialism), 71–2, 141–2; and SFRY breakup, 104, 137–8, 146; and welfare state, 134–5, 137–8;

West embracing, 141; and working class, 128, 131. *See also* capitalism; market principles

Neue Slowenische Kunst (NSK), 122–3, 125, 178n26

new art practice, 78, 91, 92

New Deal Art Projects, 25, 157n40

New Left, 108–9

New Tendencies, 63, 169n78

1980s, overview, 101

1980s alternative, the: overview, 136–7; appropriation of imagery, 124, 125; and capitalism, 136; civil society, 106, 107–11, 115–16, 133–4; class analysis, 108; and Cold War, 106; defined, 101–3; Disko FV, 119–22, 127; as diverse, 111, 115, 136; focus on oppressive socialism, 105, 106, 108–9; focus on resisting conformity, 118; funding, 105, 122; lack of spaces, 121–2; legacy of struggles, 138–9; and liberalism, 136; and nationalism, 111, 118; Nazi Punk Affair, 105; and neoliberalism, 106; and paradox of art, 131–2; parallel institutionalization, 118–22; and political orientations, 111; and self-management (socialism), 102, 111–12; SFRY breakup and, 131–5; SNST, 122–7, 178n26; socialism reform through critique, 118, 122–7; state and economy, 110–11; strategies of resistance, 106; struggle for inclusion, 114–15, 118; struggles obscured, 136, 139; working class precarity, 112

1980s art: overview, 136–7, 142; alternative production model, 117, 126–7 (*see also* parallel institutionalization; socialism reform through critique); art workers as protected, 112; art workers as unprotected, 127–30; entrepreneurial

logic, 112–13, 114 (*see also* entrepreneurs/self-employment); laws for creators, 112–13, 114; and nationalism, 109; self-employment replacing employees, 112
1990s, overview, 137–9, 145. *See also* SFRY breakup
1990s art: overview, 127; alternative art practices, 138; entrepreneurial logic, 117; and European interventions, 139; "independent culture," 145–6; lack of spaces, 122; Law for Independent Artists, 181n85; Law for Independent Cultural Workers, 134
Nochlin, Linda, 35
Nonaligned Movement, 72, 106, 144, 164n15
nonconformism, 87, 89, 118
non-work: artistic labour as, 23, 40–1, 94; creativity as, 42; domestic labour as, 36–7, 38; middle class work as, 38
not-for-profit organizations, 145

Oakley, Kate, 17
Oktober exhibitions, 78
"On the Class Character of Art" (Đorđević), 87
"On the Jewish Question" (Marx), 181n81
outsourced labour, 118–19

pandemics, 143–4
paradox of art: and alternative art practices, 49; and artistic genius, 23, 24; artists' ideas of, 34, 76; and autonomy of art, 23, 31–2, 33–4; and class, 45; vs. commissions, 96; and critique of political economy, 35–6; defined, 4; and dictionary definition of artworks, 17; and economic crisis, 98–9; and exceptional subjectivity, 42 (*see also* art workers as exceptional subjects); modern

day, 148; as naturalized in West, 144; and neoliberalism, 40; during 1980s, 127–32; as political, 33; timelessness of autonomy of art concept, 23; types of tasks, 18. *See also* autonomy of art; compensation/remuneration
Paris Commune, 8
patriarchy and capitalism, 37. *See also* domestic labour
Peljhan, Marko, 148, 183n12
planned economy, 58
pluralistic tolerance, 56–7, 60, 106, 165n35
Pobegajlo, Igor, 179n43
political economy, phases of, 49. *See also* neoliberalism; self-management (socialism)
political struggle. *See* social change/political struggle/revolutionary aims
Poovey, Mary, 38
"Portrait of the Artist as a Worker, A" (Lesage), 39
post-Fordism, 104, 105, 112
post-socialism, 136, 137. *See also* SFRY breakup
poverty, 162n43
Praxis group, 30
Precariat: The New Dangerous Class, The (Standing), 182n5
precariats, 146, 182–3n5
Prešeren, France, 124, 178–9n31
Prešeren Day, 178–9n31
prestige, 34. *See also* art workers as exceptional subjects
private property, 144, 181n81
privatization, 138; of work, 39
professional associations, 51, 55–6, 62, 63, 75
professionalization, 21, 87–8
propaganda, 27, 52
protests, 59, 67, 76, 105, 106, 115
Prvi broj (magazine), 92, *95*, 96

public relations, 183n12
publishing, 61
punk movement, 105, 119, 121
Pygmalion (Babnik), 4

Radio Študent, 167n54
radio/television, 61, 167n54
Radna zajednica umjetnika (RZU).
    See RZU Podroom
Ramsden, Mel, 85
Reckwitz, Andreas, 41, 43, 161n38
Recommendation, the (UNESCO), 9
Red Feminism, 35
Rehman, Jan, 77
religion, 76–7
"Reproduction of Labor Power in the
    Global Economy and the Unfinished
    Feminist Revolution, The" (Federici), 37
revolutionary aims. *See* social change/
    political struggle/revolutionary aims
Romantic period, 41–2
Ross, Andrew, 11, 44, 45, 162n43
ruling class, 77
RZU Podroom, 91–6, *97*

Saint-Simonian utopia, 20
SAY (Yugoslav Alliance of Students), 59,
    167n54
Schmidt, Goran, 124, 126, 179n40
scholarship: alternative art practices
    and associations, 65; of artistic
    labour, 12–13; Marx and unwaged
    labour, 33; overlooking autonomy
    of art, 23; overlooking avant-garde
    critiques, 21, 31–2
Scipion Nasice Sisters Theatre (SNST),
    122–7, 178n26
secondary jobs, 40, 41
self-management (socialism): overview,
    49, 50; administration, 60, 167nn57–8;
    as anti-capitalist, 144; and artistic
    labour overview, 9–10; art's role in,

48; and autonomy of art, 87; and CD,
    125; concealing inequality and class
    conflict, 110; and constitution of
    1974, 128; contradiction in, 6; crisis
    of, 101, 135–6, 176n30 (*see also* SFRY
    breakup); cultural policy periods, 49;
    defined, 47, 48; and full employment,
    51–2, 63, 90, 110, 163n7; inequality,
    130, 134; integrated development, 65;
    legacy of, 132, 144; marginalization of,
    66, 67; market regulation and planned
    economy, 58, 67; and nationalism,
    109; and neoliberalism, 71–2,
    141–2; and the 1980s alternative,
    102, 111–12; as oppressive, 94, 105,
    106, 108–9; phases of, 49; reforming,
    106, 109, 118, 122–7, 132, 136; and
    SFRY stage two art, 57–8; and SFRY
    stage three art, 83, 87, 94; social
    self-management, 72–3 (*see also* art
    in SFRY, stage three); as socialist
    entrepreneurship, 141; and the state,
    108; and traditional art organizations,
    76. *See also* League of Communists
    of Yugoslavia; state, the; welfare state;
    various SFRY entries
self-managing communities (SCC),
    73–4
self-managing interest communities
    (SIC), 73–4
self-sacrifice, 44, 162n43
Serbia: Belgrade Student Cultural
    Centre (SKC), 76, 78, 80–1;
    Belgrade Triennial of Yugoslav
    Art, 78; decrees/contracts for art
    workers, 10; and Đorđević, 76–87;
    economic inequalities in republics,
    90; freelancers in, 151n10; and
    nationalism, 72; *Oktober* exhibitions,
    78; student centres, 59; visual art
    cooperatives, 54, 55
Šetinc, Zlatko, 105

SFRY breakup: and art workers alliances, 115; art workers as service providers, 147; democratization, 133; Fordism/post-Fordism, 104; and globalization, 137; "independent culture" and, 145–8; key problems in cultural policy, 119; nationalism and nation states, 72, 123; and neoliberalism, 104, 137–8, 146; and the 1980s alternative, 131–5; 1990s as final stages, 135, 176n30; paradox of art, 148; self-employment replacing employees, 112; value of artistic labour, 147; working class in alternative culture and, 112

Šiška Youth Centre, 121

ŠKD Forum (Student Cultural Association Forum), 119, 122

Slovenia: *Asociacija*, 147; civil society discussions, 108; communes, 174n1 (*see also* communes); democratization, 133; Disko FV/Študent, 119–22; economic inequalities in republics, 90; free exchange of labour, 73–4; freelancers in, 128, 130, 147, 151n10; full employment, 110, 163n7; funding social security/insurance, 62; increase in cultural institutions, 61; *Kaj je alternativa* symposium, 107; Law for Independent Cultural Workers, 112–13, 114, 128–31, 134; nationalism, 72, 109, 123, 124, 139; Nazi Punk Affair, 105; Peljhan, 148; Prešeren, 124, 178–9n31; SAY newspapers, 167n54; and SFRY breakup, 123; student centres, 59; unions, 134; visual art cooperatives, 54, 55

Slovenian Culture Day, 124, 126

social change/political struggle/revolutionary aims: art's role in, 48; and autonomy of art, 23, 24, 26; and avant-garde, 23–6, 29–30, 52–3; and

domestic labour, 37; exclusion from SKC and, 80–1; New Tendencies, 63, 169n78; and oligarchy, 67; in SFRY stage two art, 56–7, 58, 66; in SFRY stage three art, 80–1; of theatre and political economy, 125. *See also* alternative art practices; avant-garde movement; 1980s alternative, the

social contract, 39–40

social inclusiveness, 43

social security/insurance: freelance laws, 113–14, 128–31, 181n85; freelancers and democratization sign, 98; funding for, 62; history for freelancers, 52; modern-day Slovenia, 147; regulations in 1996, 181n85; subsidized, 130, 180n68

social solidarity, 104–5, 143

socialism, 103–4, 108–9, 135–6. *See also* self-management (socialism)

socialist aestheticism, 56–7

Socialist Federative Republic of Yugoslavia (SFRY): economic conflicts, 72; as independent, 47, 54, 56, 72, 144, 153n26, 164n15; market reform of 1965, 65–7; names of country in mid-century, 162–3n1; and oppositional movements, 56; and proletarian socialism, 47; republic economic differences, 66, 67, 90, 109; system as contradictory, 12; and Western economic assistance, 54. *See also* self-management (socialism); state, the; welfare state; *various SFRY entries*

socialist realism, 25, 52, 53, 74–5

socio-economics. *See* compensation/remuneration; funding

sociologists, 44

sole proprietor. *See* entrepreneurs/self-employment

Soros, George, 139

Stalin, Joseph, 25
Standing, Guy, 182–3n5
state, the: and competition, 144; losing
    ability to protect, 141–2; Marx
    on, 181n81; the 1980s alternative's
    opposition to, 110–11, 119, 125, 135;
    Western animosity towards, 141, 142.
    See also welfare state
Stilinović, Mladen, 91
Štrajn, Darko, 106
strikes, 9, 68, 79–81, *80*, 83
students: alliances and cultural centres,
    59, 158n63, 167nn53–4; Disko FV/
    Študent, 59, 119–22, 127; '68 protests,
    76, 105, 106, 115; as workers, 105.
    See also 1980s alternative, the
"Subject and the Pseudo Subject of
    Artistic Practice, The" (Đorđević), 78
superstructure, 64
Šuvar, Stipe, 87
Suvin, Darko, 50, 57, 66, 67, 165n41
symbolic capital, 45
Szalay, Michael, 25, 157n40

talent, 147
taxes: for copyright, 96; funding for
    Fund for Cultural Advancement, 61;
    funding for social security, 62; and
    profit in 1980s, 105; redistributed by
    SICs, 73; on royalties, 130, 180n67;
    and visual art cooperatives, 55
Thatcher, Margaret, 143
theatre, 120, 122. *See also* Disko FV;
    Scipion Nasice Sisters Theatre
Theatre FV 112/154, 118–19, 177n4
theology, 76–7
Tito, Josip, 105, 135
Todosijević, Raša, 74–5
traditional independent work. *See*
    freelancers
Trifunović, Lazar, 56

unemployment, 67, 90, 105, 109–10,
    112, 131
UNESCO, 9
unions, 134, 174–5n13
United States: and avant-garde
    appropriation, 25, 74; and liberal
    modernist ideology, 54, 72; and "new
    class" publications, 165n41; and SFRY
    loans, 153n26. *See also* Western art;
    Western countries
universal basic income, 142
unofficial art, 56
unpaid work: and class, 39; and
    devaluation, 36; enjoyment of, 40, 41,
    44; and exceptionality, 131 (*see also*
    art workers as exceptional subjects);
    and excuses, 39; the 1980s alternative,
    122; reasons for in SFRY stage three
    art, 72; selfless vs. self-fulfilling, 42,
    43, 44, 46; and social contract, 40. *See
    also* domestic labour; paradox of art
urbanization, 58, 104, 166n47
USSR: and avant-garde, 25; SFRY
    independent from, 47, 54, 56, 72, 144,
    153n26, 164n15; and SFRY stage one
    art, 52
utopian socialism, 20

value, 3, 4, 45, 50–1, 93, 94, 147
Valušek, Berislav, 173n72
Vásquez, Adolfo Sánchez, 21
Videkanić, Bojana, 52
Video CD, 179n45
Vidmar, Igor, 105
visual art cooperatives, 54–5

wages, 22, 104, 105. *See also*
    compensation/remuneration; funding;
    unpaid work
Wages against Housework (Federici), 37, 83
Weeks, Kathi, 39

welfare state: overview, 104–5, 112; artists benefiting from, 144; vs. competition, 142–3; and entrepreneurship, 141; maintaining, 175n13; and neoliberalism, 134–5, 137–8; weakening for freelancers, 113–14, 127

Western art: art worker critique, 76; and avant-garde, 23–4, 25, 28, 74, 157n52; creativity and genius, 41; and Đorđević, 76; influence and SFRY stage three, 53, 54, 75–6, 94, 98–9, 115; and institutionalization, 17–19; limiting transformation of art in SFRY, 57; and political economy, 11; rejected in SFRY stage one, 52; three central posts of, 30

Western countries: as "anti-communist," 136; and demise of socialism, 104; and entrepreneurship, 141; Faustian bargain, 54, 66, 72, 136; loans to SFRY, 90, 153n26; and neoliberalism, 106, 141; working class defeat, 112. *See also* market principles

Woodmansee, Martha, 42

Woodward, Susan L., 90, 109–10, 153n26

workers' collectives, 60

working class, 112, 113, 128, 131, 182–3n5

World Bank, 54, 67, 72

writing, 38

youth alliances, 59, 166–7n53

Yugoslav Alliance of Students (SAY), 59, 167n54

Yugoslav People's Army, 177n65

Yugoslavia. *See* Socialist Federative Republic of Yugoslavia (SFRY); *various SFRY entries*

Zavarzadeh, Mas'ud, 44–5

Zemira Alajbegović, 122

Žilnik, Želimir, 166n51

Živadinov, Dragan, 123

Zupančič, Alenka, 124